TRAVELS AND TRANSLATIONS IN THE SIXTEENTH CENTURY

Travels and Translations in the Sixteenth Century

Selected Papers from the Second International Conference of the Tudor Symposium (2000)

Edited by
Mike Pincombe

Studies in European Cultural Transition

Volume Twenty

LONDON AND NEW YORK

First published 2004 by Ashgate Publishing

2 Park Square, Milton Park, Abingdon, Oxon OX14 4RN
711 Third Avenue, New York, NY 10017, USA

Routledge is an imprint of the Taylor & Francis Group, an informa business

First issued in paperback 2017

British Library Cataloguing in Publication Data
Tudor Symposium. International Conference (2nd: 2000). Travels and Translations in the Sixteenth Century: Selected Papers from the Second International Conference of the Tudor Symposium (2000). (Studies in European Cultural Transition: 20).
1. Translators—England—History—16th century—Congresses. 2. Translating and interpreting—Europe—History—16th century—Congresses. 3. English literature—Early modern, 1500–1700—History and criticism—Congresses. 4. Travelers' writings, English—History and criticism—Congresses. 5. Travel writing—England—History—16th century—Congresses. 6. English literature—Translations—History—16th century—Congresses. 7. Travel in literature—Congresses. I. Title.
II. Pincombe, Michael.
820.9'357'09031

Library of Congress Cataloging in Publication Data
Tudor Symposium. International Conference (2nd: 2000). Travels and Translations in the Sixteenth Century: Selected Papers from the Second International Conference of the Tudor Symposium (2000).
p. cm. – (Studies in European Cultural Transition: 20).
Includes bibliographical references and index.
1. English literature—Early modern, 1500–1700—History and criticism—Congresses. 2. Travelers' writings, English—History and criticism—Congresses. 3. Translating and interpreting—Great Britain—History—16th century—Congresses. 4. Great Britain—History—Tudors, 1485–1603—Congresses. I. Pincombe, Michael. II. Title. III. Series.
PR413.T835 2000
820.9'355–dc21 2003056047

ISBN 978-0-7546-0832-5 (hbk)
ISBN 978-1-138-26364-2 (pbk)

Typeset by Express Typesetters.

Contents

Contributors

Amina Alyal is currently senior lecturer in English at Trinity and All Saints College, University of Leeds. She took her first degree at Cambridge and her D.Phil. at York. Her research and teaching interests are in Shakespeare, Shakespeare and film, sixteenth-century literary theory, theories of drama, Renaissance perceptions of gender, and the influence of Italy on Renaissance literature. She is currently writing a book, developing her doctoral thesis, on Shakespeare and *poiesis*, which examines imitation theory in the light of the Petrarchan muse. A future project is partially in draft – a book on Shakespeare and film. She is writing a series of articles on Renaissance subjects. In addition, she is preparing a work of semi-fiction, a collection of essays/stories on perceptions of the artistic from a multicultural perspective. She also teaches drama, and maintains an interest in current theatre productions, including writing programme notes for the RSC and Glyndebourne Touring Opera.

Georgia E. Brown is interested in sixteenth-century literature and she has published articles on Christopher Marlowe, Renaissance historiography, the epyllion, Elizabeth I's translation of Boethius' *Consolation of Philosophy*, and Shakespeare. Her book, *The Generation of Shame*, on literature of the 1590s is in preparation and she is editing a collection of essays on material culture with Juliet Fleming. She is also preparing a book-length study of Renaissance embroidery, entitled 'The Geometry of Words: Reading Renaissance Embroidery'. She is currently working on the interface between Ottoman, Arabic and Western cultures in the sixteenth and seventeenth centuries.

Elizabeth Heale teaches in the English Department at the University of Reading. Dr Heale's teaching covers the literature of most of the early modern period and she is closely involved with an interdisciplinary History and English, early modern MA. Her research interests are in sixteenth-century poetry. Publications include *A Reader's Guide to The Faerie Queene* (2nd edn 1999) and *Wyatt and Surrey & Early Tudor Poetry* (1998). A study of verse from Tottel to Shakespeare called *Chronicles of the Self. Autobiography and Authorship in Sixteenth-Century Verse* appeared in the Early Modern Literature in History series from Palgrave in 2003.

Arthur F. Kinney is Thomas W. Copeland Professor of Literary History and Director of the Massachusetts Center for Renaissance Studies at the University of Massachusetts, Amherst. He is the author, most recently, of *'Lies Like Truth': Shakespeare, Macbeth and the Cultural Moment* (2001) and *Shakespeare by Stages* (2003) among many other books. He is the editor, most recently, of *Renaissance Drama: An Anthology of Plays and Entertainments*; *A Companion to Renaissance Drama; Cambridge Companion to English Literature 1500–1600*;

New Critical Essays on Hamlet; and *The Witch of Edmonton* (for New Mermaids). He is the founding editor of the journal *English Literary Renaissance* and founding editor of the book series Massachusetts Studies in Early Modern Culture as well as editor of the Twayne English Authors Series in the Renaissance. He is the president of the Renaissance English Text Society and a member of the Executive Council of the Renaissance Society of America, and the executive committee of the Folger Library Institute. He is the founder and past president of the MLA Council of Editors of Learned Journals, and was recently a trustee of the Shakespeare Association of America.

Efterpi Mitsi is a lecturer in English literature and culture at the University of Athens, teaching courses on sixteenth- and seventeenth-century poetry, on the culture of the Renaissance, and on literary theory. She has a degree in English literature from the University of Athens and a Ph.D. in comparative literature from New York University. She has taught as a lecturer in English literature at the Department of Foreign Languages and Literatures at the University of Cyprus. She has published articles in Greek and foreign journals on sixteenth-century English literature, comparative literature and travel literature, and has prepared an anthology of women's travel writing on Greece. She is currently working on a book about British travellers to Greece, focusing on the early modern period.

Massimiliano Morini is currently a doctoral student at the University of Florence. He has held a seminar on contemporary British poetry and has taught translation courses at the University of Bologna. He has written books and articles on English fantasy (*Le parole di Tolkien*, 1999) and contemporary British poetry (*Poeti inglesi del secondo Novecento*, 2001). He is also a translator, and has co-edited a handbook of translation from English into Italian (*Manuale di traduzioni dall'inglese*, 2002, with Romana Zacchi).

Melanie Ord teaches English literature at the University of the West of England. She has written articles on 'Narrative Self-Presentation in English Representations of Italy 1570–1611', which she is presently developing as a monograph. She has written articles on Roger Ascham's *Scholemaster*, Thomas Coryat's *Crudities*, and Anthony Munday's *English Roman Life*; and her general research interests include early modern travel narratives, the concept of 'Italianateness', anti-Catholic polemic, pedagogical texts, and courtesy literature.

Mike Pincombe is Reader in Tudor Literature at the University of Newcastle upon Tyne. He has written books on *The Plays of John Lyly: Eros and Eliza* (1996) and *Elizabethan Humanism: Literature and Learning in the Later Sixteenth Century* (2001), as well as numerous essays on mid-Tudor and Elizabethan poetry and drama. Current research projects include an edition and translation of the Oxford neo-Latin tragedy *Philomela* (1607), a book on English literature and theatre in the 1560s, and a mid-Tudor reader (with Cathy Shrank). He is the convenor of the Tudor Symposium.

Mark Robson is Lecturer in English at the University of Nottingham, where he teaches early modern literature and critical theory, having previously worked at the Universities of Manchester and Leeds. His publications include articles on Thomas More, early modern women's writing, biography and critical theory. He is co-editor of *The limits of death: between philosophy and psychoanalysis* (Manchester University Press, 2000). Current projects include an edition of the poetry of Lady Hester Pulter (Leeds Texts and Monographs), a collection of articles on More's *Utopia*, and a monograph tentatively entitled *Rhetorics of the early modern* (both for MUP). Recent papers have included work on Derrida, *Hamlet*, the new aestheticism, ears and promises.

Roy Rosenstein is Professor of Comparative Literature at The American University of Paris, where he has been teaching since 1977. He holds graduate degrees from the Sorbonne and Harvard, and took his doctorate in comparative literature at Columbia University. He has also taught at the University of Rochester, University of Oregon, and City University of New York, as well as in Greece, in Brazil, and at the University of Paris IV. He is co-editor of *Etienne Durand: Poésies complètes* (Geneva: Droz, 1990) and *The Poetry of Cercamon and Jaufre Rudel* (New York: Garland, 1983); and has published many journal articles and book chapters on French, Occitan, Spanish, Luso-Brazilian, Italian, English and American literatures.

Cathy Shrank is a lecturer in Renaissance literature at the University of Aberdeen and is also attached to the Centre for Early Modern Studies at that university. Her research interests cover Tudor and early Stuart literature; the construction of early modern identities (national, regional, civic); humanism; representations of rhetoric and eloquence; and early modern travel writing. Publications include 'Rhetorical constructions of a national community: the use of the king's English in mid-Tudor writing', in Alexandra Shepard and Phil Withington (eds), *Communities in Early Modern England* (Manchester: Manchester University Press, 2000) and 'Andrew Borde and the politics of identity in Reformation England', *Reformation* (2001). She has just finished an edition of Massinger's *The City Madam* for Globe Quartos, and is currently working on a monograph, *Writing the Nation: Humanism, Literature and English Identities, 1530–1580*, and a mid-Tudor reader (with Mike Pincombe).

Benedek Péter Tóta was born in Hungary in 1958. He studied languages and literature at the Benedictine Secondary Boarding School, Pannonhalma. He also studied theology at the College of Theology, Pannonhalma. He went to Loránd Eötvös University, Budapest, where he studied Hungarian language and literature and English language and literature. The title of his Ph.D. dissertation is: '*The Poetry Does Not Matter?* The Process of Creative De-Creation in T.S. Eliot's *Four Quartets*'. He teaches twentieth-century English literature and conducts seminars on Sir Thomas More at Péter Pázmány Catholic University, Piliscsaba, Hungary. As the secretary of the Renaissance research group he takes part in research sponsored by the National Scientific Research Fund, which made available the preliminary works of the present essay. His papers on Eliot and More were published in both Budapest and Zurich. In 2000 he was invited to join the international Board of Supervisors of the 'Thomas More' distance learning project to be launched at the Université Catholique de l'Ouest, Angers, France.

Acknowledgements

The preparation of a collection of essays such as the present volume is always a collaborative effort, and I would like to extend my thanks to all those involved in its production: Greg Walker for his supportive interest in the project, and Erika Gaffney for seeing it through the press; András Péter prepared the index. The contributors have been models of patience and cooperation, and I would like to thank Arthur F. Kinney in particular for agreeing to write the Introduction. Thanks are also due to all those who made possible the conference from which these papers are drawn: to those who came and gave papers, of course, but also (and especially) to Rowena Bryson for providing cakes and ale, and to Linda Anderson, Head of the School of English at Newcastle, for her long-standing and greatly valued support of the activities of the Tudor Symposium.

Mike Pincombe

Note on the text

Primary texts used by each contributor are listed at the end of each chapter. All references to primary texts, including the first, are inserted in the text in parentheses. All secondary texts are listed together in a bibliography at the end of this volume.

Introduction

Arthur F. Kinney

I

In the Tudor period, to translate meant to transport, as Georgia E. Brown notes in Chapter 7 of this volume – that is, to travel from one language (or place) to another. Conceptually, then, translation and travel seem synonymous; what distinguishes them is the degree of abstraction. One emphasizes the abstract, the other the concrete. What both have in common – as idea and in practice – is a concentration on the relational and the referential alongside the self-referential. They both establish and then work by way of patterns, networks, or signifying systems to establish meaning; they rely on analogy, metaphor and simile explicitly or implicitly. In translation theory, Roman Jakobson has identified three major areas of such work: intralingual translation, or the rewording of one sign into another in the same language or system, analogous to aligning life in Tudor London with that in Tudor Norwich; interlingual translation, interpreting the signs of one language by those in another, as in one of the essays here Tudor travellers relate England to Greece; and intersemiotic translation, transferring elements of a verbal sign-system to a non-verbal sign-system such as art or music, as, in this volume (Chapter 8), George Gascoigne will be seen to relate both London and Rome to social and courtly Petrarchan codes of behaviour.[1] The relationship is also chiastic: travel is recorded through language, just as language relies on an external world for its employment. Such connections, however, are never secure nor complete; Edwin Gentzler, for one, notes the suture with its 'gaps, errors, ambiguities, multiple referents and "foreign disorders"'.[2] Thus it seems natural enough that the Tudors, seeing the discrepancies, added to this deep structural relationship a third term to denote a common factor, travail or labour, punning by means of the homonymic *travel* with its commonplace interchangeable spellings of *travel* and *travail*, the connection made both by sound and sight.

All three terms – translation, travel, travail – are conjoined, for instance, at the heart of Thomas More's *Utopia* (1516). It is labour that prevents More from the task of linguistically recording his metaphoric travels to an imaginary land into Latin for the wider humanist community on the Continent, as he writes to Peter Giles, his companion there, in a prefatory letter that stuck like a barnacle to the

1 Roman Jakobson, in Edwin Gentzler, *Contemporary Translation Theories* (London: Routledge, 1993), p. 1.

2 Gentzler, *Contemporary Translation Theories*, p. 4.

paragena, or prefatory matter that accompanied sixteenth-century editions of *Utopia*, both in Latin and later in English and other languages. Amid many occupations and responsibilities, he confesses, how

> can we find time to write? Nor have I spoken a word about sleep, nor even of food, which for many people takes up as much time as sleep – and sleep takes up almost half a man's life! So I get for myself only the time I filch from sleep and food. Slowly, therefore, because this time is but little, yet finally, because this time *is* something, I have finished *Utopia* and sent it to you, my dear Peter, to read – and to remind me of anything that has escaped me.
>
> (p. 41)

The labour is still incomplete until Giles verifies it and corrects it; until then, it has its errors and gaps, its multiple references and ambiguities, many of which will necessarily remain. Nearly a century later, Thomas Nashe's Jack Wilton in *The Unfortunate Traveller* (1594) will visit Rotterdam where he meets 'merry Sir Thomas More, our countryman', still translating his imaginary travels with much effort, 'seeing most commonwealths corrupted by ill custom' in light of Utopia, 'and that principalities were nothing but great piracies which, gotten by violence and murder, were maintained by private undermining and bloodshed' (p. 219). Now the translation is not one of language but of non-linguistic systems, transporting the ideas of Utopian government in an examination of those across Europe, such as Jack Wilton himself is doing. Benedek Péter Tóta's Thomas More (Chapter 5) is doing that too in his *Dialogue of Comfort* – here linguistic travel becomes, in More's mind, not liberty but renewed travail – and the very opposite of the 'comfort' for which his late treatise so ardently, so earnestly, strives. Indeed, it is only when More surpasses both in immobile transcendence, as at Pentecost, a time of linguistic and spiritual wonder, that he manages to redeem linguistic slippage itself.

The author Thomas More and Nashe's persona of Jack Wilton can remain shadowy prototypes behind this collection of essays from the international Tudor Symposium based at Newcastle. Cathy Shrank (Chapter 3) observes that for William Thomas, in his *History of Italie* (1549), Venice seems pertinent and even familiar to English travellers because it too was an island, a trading nation, descended from Brut, while in Naples the fecundity of the land, feeding the luxurious lives of its inhabitants, seems the very opposite of the English nation. Elizabeth Heale (Chapter 1) writes that Robert Baker's account of travel and translation attempts to colonize a wild African off the Guinea coast by dressing him up in European clothes, but the translation does not lead to transformation; he uses their voyage to spy on the English crew and ultimately betray them. Such dangers in travel caused Roger Ascham to make his famous pronouncement against foreign travel, but he can establish the relationship between a native England and foreign soil only through the translating metaphors drawn from Greek epic, alluding to the dangers faced by Odysseus, thus establishing a gap and 'foreign disorder' of his own. Heale argues that such journeys were out of self-interest, but they also resulted in self-knowledge, often at the cost of the wayfaring Englishman. Anthony Munday tried to avoid danger, Melanie Ord (Chapter 4) tells us, by insisting that he bring English civility to his residence at the Jesuit English College in Rome, but this is self-projection again, and for self-interest; it explores new experiences only to reaffirm old ideas, a kind of double translation or a translation that altogether fails. His shortcoming is well known to polysystem theorists who fault those who impose their own parochial and personal meanings rather than open themselves to acknowledge new ones. Gaps disappear and so the potentially instructive analogy becomes instead a reaffirmation of individual, cherished beliefs. Gaps, reversals, differences are all erased, disappear. '[T]he very integrity of the civilized English self', Elizabeth Heale writes, 'could be scattered abroad.' In such situations, Jorge Luis Borges has remarked, 'every writer *creates* his own precursors',[3] such as William Thomas imposes on Venice, or, as Efterpi Mitsi (Chapter 2) observes, William Biddulph yearned of Athens. For Michel Foucault, such discourse, refusing the external evidence, that which might defamiliarize, internalizes everything and so harmonizes it; for Mitsi, it is the sense of a journeying pilgrimage; for Tóta's More, the very idea of comfort.[4] But the Tudors were, on the whole, not so easily persuaded. Perhaps the greatest exemplar for the Tudors of the openly sceptical, ever-revising traveller of the mind was Montaigne, although John Florio, in translating him, colonizes him. It might be expected: Montaigne never left his study; Florio never went to France. In all such instances, as Mitsi recognizes so tellingly, travel, transport, and travail alike eventuate in discourse.

II

In the antique Greek recovered and revered by Tudor humanists, whose ranks constituted the translators, *diapherō* meant 'to carry from one to another, to carry across, to bear through, to transport' – to translate and to travel. But Greek writers added their own metaphorical meanings too, extending the word to mean 'to put the tongue in motion, to speak'. In addition, Heraclitus used *diapherō* to mean 'to toss about, to be disrupted'; Aristotle used it to mean 'to tear asunder, to disjoin', and Plutarch used it for 'to distract'.[5] As the later meanings demonstrate, what the

---

3 Jorge Luis Borges, cit. Michel Foucault, *Language, Counter-Memory, Practice*, trans. Donald F. Bouchard and Sherry Simon (Ithaca, NY: Cornell University Press, 1977), p. 5.

4 Michel Foucault, *The Order of Things*, trans. anonymous (New York: Vintage Books, 1973), p. 292.

5 Henry George Liddell and Robert Scott, eds, *A Greek–English Lexicon* (Oxford: Clarendon Press, 1925), p. 417.

word harboured was not exactitude but slippage. The imperfect fit in transporting meaning through translation or travel permitted, and often resulted in, slightly different meanings that destabilized language and disclosed a fundamental indeterminacy. As Amina Alyal (Chapter 8) argues, the Italy where Gascoigne sets his second edition of 'The pleasant Fable of Ferdinando Jeronimi' (1575) displays an uneven fit between the deceitful and hypocritical Italy of Machiavelli, the Borgias and the papists, and the courtly, literary Italy of Castiglione and Petrarch. Gascoigne's first edition, entitled 'The Adventures of Master F.J.' (1573), makes slippage a structural and thematic point, fracturing his narrative by disjoining the perspectives of the Printer, G.T., and H.W., from F.J. as well as from the author, standing outside such tearing asunder, and the reader who is required to choose, paste and reconstruct the tale. Slippage is used for communication, secrecy and security for Anthony Munday's report on *The English Roman Life* (1582), when he resorts to coded language that both withholds and divulges meaning: he locates Catholic priests 'in Warwickshire, at Master I.T. in Staffordshire, at Master G. of C. and at S.T.F. in the same shire'. As Melanie Ord points out, the work itself 'negotiates [...] between discrete audiences', 'prominent government figures to whom the work is dedicated, and an implicitly Protestant public', but it does so with the seduction of tantalizingly informed secrecy that actually blocks information, for some a translation that does not translate.

Slippage is the structural and thematic principle of Ellis Heywood's Italian dialogue *Il moro* (1556) for Mark Robson (Chapter 6), as the word *More* (for Thomas More, one of the participants in the dialogue) elides into *moro*, *mori*, *moria*. The work plays out Edward Hall's description of More in which his combination of wise folly and foolish wisdom undermines resolute meaning:

> I cannot tell whether I should call him a foolishe wyseman or a wise foolishman, for undoubtedly he beside his learnyng, had a great witte, but it was so myngled with tauntyng and mockyng, that it semed to them that best knew him, that he thought nothing to be wel spoken except he had ministred some mocke in the communicacion.
>
> (fol. 226v)

More recognized the inexactitude of language, as Erasmus did, so that foolish wisdom might be assigned to Christ, wise folly to the sufferings of men. With single words open to multiple interpretation, any translation, even the most literal, could limit or misconstrue meaning and misjudge an author's intention or a text's significance, just as a traveller, judging new sights by old ones, a different culture by his own, reconceives what he sees. For Georgia Brown (Chapter 7), the French language was especially susceptible: 'Some French words like "exemple" have masculine and feminine forms; others change gender depending on whether they are singular or plural! Such slippery terms include "evangille", which is masculine in the singular and feminine in the plural, and "affaire", which is feminine in the singular and masculine in the plural.' For us, there is irony if not parody in translating *semper eadem*, 'always the same', as the motto for both Elizabeth I and her mother, beheaded for treason! We cannot now hope to unravel Elizabeth's intention: respect for her mother? an association with her mother's Protestantism? an attempt to marry France with England? the sheer attraction of the thought? Surely Elizabeth, a translator all her life, and especially adept at French, Italian and Latin, must have sensed the fundamental difficulties of such a motto. It is what More felt, writing to Peter Giles, and doubtless one reason Jack Wilton, seeing and hearing More struggle to give some shared sense of meaning to the term *commonwealth*, quickly scuttled out of Rotterdam to the illusionary security of Luther's Wittenberg, only to find there a scholastic debate.

We can see, as Amina Alyal proposes, that such multiple possibilities for signification in a sign-system such as the words of translation and the sights of travel invite *inventio*, to create out of raw material something that *will* signify. Roy Rosenstein (Chapter 10) lines up various historical sources for Shakespeare's treatment of Richard II: Polydore Vergil, Edward Hall, Richard Grafton, Raphael Holinshed. Shakespeare can create through arbitration. For Rosenstein, Shakespeare's choice is surely Polydore Vergil, but for spectators at the Globe and readers of the quarto and folio texts who know his available resources, there is a constant juggling of adjudication. The same process is apparent, according to Massimiliano Morini (Chapter 9), for John Harington, attempting to turn the courtly and witty epic of Ariosto, the *Orlando Furioso* (1591), into a poem suitable for his godmother, Queen Elizabeth, by making it not a chivalric epic so much as a courtly poem, one he can transform by moral explanations and a text he can shape into allegorical meaning. Verbal and visual slippage is what permits creativity as well as invites it; and in that sense, can be beneficial. Divergence and deconstruction are what allow reconstruction, renewal and rebirth.

Just so: Walter Benjamin, Mark Robson reminds us, wrote that 'no translation would be possible if in its ultimate essence it strove for likeness to the original'. As this collection of essays so vividly and persuasively shows us, translation depends on the travels and the travails of the poetic mind.

Primary texts quoted

Hall, Edward. *The Union of the Two Noble and Illustrate Families of Lancaster and York* (1548; 2nd edn 1550). *STC* 12723.

More, Sir Thomas, *Utopia* (1516), in *The Complete Works of St. Thomas More* (New Haven, CT: Yale University Press, 1965), IV, ed. Edward Surtz, S.J., and J.H. Hexter.

Nashe, Thomas, *The Unfortunate Traveller* (1594), in Stanley Wells, ed., *Thomas Nashe: Selected Works* (London: Edward Arnold, 1964).

PART I

Travels

Chapter 1

Travailing abroad: the poet as adventurer

Elizabeth Heale

In a poem celebrating that epitome of Elizabethan enterprise, Sir Humphrey Gilbert,[1] explorer, speculator, colonial undertaker and mercenary soldier, on the eve of a voyage in 1578, the poet Thomas Churchyard described the heroic toil of the adventurer:

The man that trauels much,
  with mind and body both,
(Whose restlesse lims, & labring thoughtes,
  through heapes of hazards goth).
(sig. H2r)

'Trauels' includes here the senses of 'to make a journey', 'to labour, toil' and 'to weary, tire' (*OED travail v.* and *travel v.*). Gilbert's voyage is not a recreational excursion, but a speculative enterprise, with the straining of 'restlesse lims, & labring thoughtes' a sign of heroic virtue. Although the meanings of the word 'trauel' were becoming separated in the sixteenth century, travel (journeying) and travail (toil, pain) are still interchangeable terms with the meanings closely associated, as Churchyard's poem to Gilbert makes clear. Gilbert's heroic travels testify to his virtuous choice of toilsome but manly adventure rather than slothful, effeminate ease at home.[2] Much of the poem is built on an opposition between 'abroad' and 'home':

Abroade where seruice is,
  much honor may be wonne,
At home our gay vayneglory goes,
  like shadow in the Sunne.
Abroad bare robes are best,
  and Manhoode makes the showe,

1 For a brief biography of Sir Humphrey Gilbert, see the introduction to D.B. Quinn, ed., *The Voyages and Colonising Enterprises of Sir Humphrey Gilbert* (London: The Hakluyt Society, 1940), I.

2 I have benefited from reading David Morrow's analysis of connected ideas of 'travel' in Protestant ideology in his unpublished essay '"Reaping eternall glorie of his restless paines": Edmund Spenser and the ideology of *travell*', given at the Cambridge Spenser Conference in July 2001.

At home yong Maister must be fine,
  or all is lost you know.
(sig. L3r)

As the poem progresses the anaphora mutates from the oppositon 'abroade'/'home' to 'toile'/'rest':

Toyle teacheth men to conquer Fame,
  And flee from foule reproach.
Rest loues to dallie much,
  Like whelp that waues the tayle.
(sig. L4r)

Abroad is synonymous with toil and enterprise, home with sloth. Travel abroad is a sign of manliness while resting at home is to be, in Churchyard's scornful phrase, 'ruld by loue of babes,/[and] womens willes' (sig. K3r).

Churchyard's panegyric to Gilbert, and the spirit of heroic adventuring abroad that he seems to embody, is part of the euphoric discourse of Elizabethan mercantile and colonial expansion. Sir Francis Drake, contributing some prefatory verses to George Peckham's account of Gilbert's last and fatal voyage in 1583, challenged others to join the enterprise of overseas exploration:

Who seeks, by worthy deeds, to gain renown for hire:
Whose heart, whose head, whose purse is pressed, to purchase his desire;
If any such there be, that thirsteth after fame:
Lo, here a mean, to win himself an everlasting name.[3]

For the 'young Gentleman' who speaks in a poem in the 1585 *Paradise of Dainty Devices*, the toil of seeking one's fortune abroad is far more glorious than drudging at home:

To tosse the Seas some thinke a toyle,
Some thinke it straunge abroad to rome,
Some thinke it griefe to leaue their soyle
Their parentes, kinsfolkes, and their home.
Thinke so who list, I like it not,
I must abroad to trye my Lott.

Who lust at home at carte to drudge
And carcke and care for worldly trashe:
with buckled shooe let him goe trudge,
In stead of launce a whip to swash.
A minde that's base himselfe will showe,
A carrion sweete to feede a Crowe.
(pp. 129–30).[4]

3 Quoted in modern spelling from Theodore K. Rabb, *Enterprise and Empire: Merchant and Gentry Investment in the Expansion of England, 1575–1630* (Cambridge, MA: Harvard University Press, 1967), p. 21. The poem prefaces George Peckham, *A true reporte, Of the late discoveries of the Newfound Landes: By Sir Humfrey Gilbert* (1583).

4 The verses are entitled 'A young Gentleman willing to trauell into forreygne partes being intreated to staie in England: Wrote as followeth'.

More cautiously, Sir Henry Sidney, father of Sir Philip, while paying tribute to the noble enterprise of those who travelled abroad, dwells on the terrible dangers that threatened the traveller, and perhaps betrays some relief, as a non-travelling investor, at staying at home himself:

> We shall live and rest at home quietly with our friends, and acquaintance: but hee in the meane time labouring to keepe the ignorant and unruly Mariners in good order and obedience, with howe many cares shall hee trouble and vexe himselfe? ... We shall keepe our owne coastes and countrey: Hee shall seeke strange and unknowen kingdomes. He shall commit his safetie to barbarous and cruell people, and shall hazard his life amongst the monstrous and terrible beastes of the Sea.
>
> (p. 129)[5]

Sir Henry envisages the heroic traveller as one who maintains order and who is so secure in his English integrity and virtue that he seeks out what is strange and willingly braves riot, barbarity and monstrousness. Not everyone uses the euphoric discourse of adventuring abroad, however. Roger Ascham was less certain that English virtue would remain impervious to the dangers and temptations that travel might bring:

> For, he shall not alwayes in his absence out of England, light vpon a ientle *Alcynous*, and walke in his faire gardens full of all harmelesse pleasures: but he shall sometymes, fall, either into the handes of some cruell *Cyclops*, or into the lappe of some wanton and dalying Dame *Calypso* ... If *Scylla* drowne him not, *Carybdis* may fortune swalow hym. Some *Circes* shall make him, of a plaine English man, a right *Italian*.
>
> (p. 225)

Even if the English integrity of the traveller remained untainted by being abroad, the gain to be won in adventuring did not always repay the danger, as George Turberville warned in a poem to his friend P. written before he himself travelled to Moscow in 1568–69:

> In rotten ribbed Barck to passe the Seas
> The foraine landes and straungie sites to see,
> Doth daunger dwell: the passage breedes vnease,
> Not safe the soyle, the men vnfriendly bee.
>
> Admit thou see the straungest things of all:
> When eie is turned the pleasant sight is gone:
> The treasure then of trauaile is but small,
> Wherefor (Friend P.) let all such toyes alone.
>
> (fol. 41v)

5 Rabb, *Enterprise*, p. 22; Sidney's words are quoted in Michael Nerlich, *Ideology of Adventure: Studies in Modern Consciousness, 1100–1750*, trans. Ruth Crowley (Minneapolis, MN: University of Minnesota Press, 1987), I, p. 129.

According to such thinking, the enterprise of travelling abroad could be vain and dangerous, breeding unease, and exposing the English traveller to insubstantial and treacherous pleasures. What was collected and known, the very integrity of the civilized English self, could be scattered abroad. Once embarked, the familiar became strange, stabilities threatened to collapse, and national virtue became susceptible to contamination.

These competing attitudes to travel are clearly visible in the poems I study in this essay. On the one hand travel abroad as a sign of enterprise offered an attractive persona to the poets I study, but such first-person writing all too easily betrays the vulnerability of the virtuous self to 'foreign' contamination. The poems strive on the one hand to promote their writers as men of virtuous enterprise, on the other they betray the disconcerting instability of national differences and moral boundaries. However, for Churchyard and the three writer–travellers with whom I shall be concerned in this essay, the 'travails' of 'travel' were not confined to ordering unruly mariners or overcoming barbarous foreigners and beasts of the sea. Their 'trauels' are not only those of journeying, but also of writing, which is often described as being as painful and laborious as the journey itself.[6]

In Churchyard's view, the travail of writing about adventuring abroad is akin to the heroism of travel itself. As his poem to Gilbert proceeds it becomes clear that his description of the heroic man of enterprise, 'the man who trauels much,/ with mind and body both', refers not only to Gilbert, but also to the poet Churchyard himself, who rouses himself from rest to celebrate Gilbert's expedition in verse:

Where is Churchyard? Doth he sleepe?
  or is he crept in Clowde,
To shunne the vse of penne
  and matter worthy note?

(sig. H3r)

It is the writer's duty and his glory to painfully record and celebrate the heroic adventure of overseas expansion. In a similar vein, in the preface to the 1598 edition of his *Principall Navigations*, Hakluyt described his own travails among manuscripts and books during his Herculean task of gathering the writings of travellers as a labour equal to theirs: 'what restlesse nights, what painefull dayes, what heat, what cold I have indured; how many long & chargeable journeys I have traveiled; how many famous libraries I have searched into; what varietie of ancient and moderne writers I have perused' (1907 edn, I, p. 19).

6 For example, Churchyard uses the term to describe his writing in the preface 'To the Reader' of his *A Discourse of the Queenes Maiesties entertainment in Suffolk and Norfolk* (1578), at sig. B1r, as well as in the 'Verses to Gilbert'. For earlier punning on the 'travel' of reading and writing as well as of adventuring abroad, see Mary B. Campbell, *The Witness and the Other World: Exotic European Travel Writing 400–1600* (Ithaca, NY and London: Cornell University Press, 1988), p. 236.

The prominence in the 'Verses to Gilbert' of Churchyard's own name and experience suggests that his 'trauels' with the pen may have as much to do with self-promotion as with the glorification of English enterprise abroad. This is certainly true of the poetic 'trauels' of the writers with whom I am concerned in this essay. Writing verse is in fact part of the same project of self-advancement that propelled them abroad as adventurers. The early Elizabethan poets I will be discussing – George Turberville who travelled to Moscow in 1568–69, as a 'gentleman desirous to see the world' in the entourage of Thomas Randolph, commissioned by the queen to negotiate trading privileges;[7] Robert Baker, a merchant's factor on a ship trading to the Guinea coast of Africa in 1562 and 1563, and George Gascoigne, impoverished gentleman and mercenary soldier in the Netherlands from 1572 to 1574 – do not write merely in response to the muses. They use verse to make a version of themselves and their achievements known in the world, either in the hope of attracting patrons, or for self-defence, or, in the case of Baker, perhaps to publicize his plight as a prisoner of war. They situate themselves in their poems both as first-person narrators, the adventurers who travel and suffer in the narratives, but also as the poets who write, adopting, at least at the outset of their poems, conventional writerly poses: the urbane, Horatian writer of epistles (Turberville), the epic chronicler (Baker), the voice of the humanist scholar (Gascoigne). As we shall see, the conventionality of the genre within which the poet writes, and the disorder of the narratives that are presented, soon cause conflicts that destroy the coherence and predictability of the verse, producing instead extraordinarily vivid representations of disorientating confrontations between the familiar and the foreign, order and chaos.

George Turberville's three verse epistles from Moscow were probably first printed in 1574 in *Epitaphes and Sonnettes With some other broken pamphlettes and Epistles, sent to certaine his frends in England, at his being in Moscouia. Anno 1569*, appended to *Tragical Tales, translated by Turberville*.[8] As the title-page indicates, it is not just the epistles that refer to Russia. The collection of *Epitaphes and Sonnettes* opens with a poem that bids farewell both to his mother and to his mother country:

> My countrey coast where I
>   my Nurses milke did sucke,
> Would neuer yet in all my life
>   allowe me one good lucke
> …

7 John Erskine Hankins, *The Life and Works of George Turbervile* (Lawrence, KA: University of Kansas, 1940), p. 12 (quoting from a letter of Randolph in the State Papers describing the gentlemen who accompanied him).

8 For the separate title-page, see Turberville, *Epitaphes*, fol. 139r. The earliest extant (joint) edition of *Tragical Tales* and *Epitaphes and Sonnettes* is dated 1587. For evidence that the first edition may date to 1574, see Hankins, *Life*, pp. 36–7.

From thence tis time to trudge
  and hire the hackney post
To shift to ship, to leaue the land
  and seeke a better coast.
                    (fols 145r–147r)

Such enterprise differentiates him from

The slouthfull Groome that sits,
  at home and tels the clocke:
And feares the floud because therein
  lies hidden many a rocke.

But Russia proves a sad disappointment to his hopes of self-advancement. Its icy deserts and the speaker's sense of isolation and of bodily imprisonment recur frequently in the 'sonnettes' both as contrasts to the speaker's now rather warmer thoughts of home, and at the same time as images of his own inner sense of desolation and exile. Russia functions as a shifting signifier deployed both as the other against which the speaker measures his own and his country's civility, and as a figure for himself; mentally and emotionally he feels himself to be like the godforsaken Russian landscape.[9]

The volume contains three verse epistles gathered under the title 'The Author being in Moscouia, wrytes to certaine his frendes in Englande of the state of the place …' (fols 183v–193v). Written to male friends in London, the epistles aspire to a Horatian urbanity and detachment. They declare 'the manners of the men' (fol. 189v), but by now the poet/speaker feels that in leaving his native soil 'ful like a retchlesse man' he has emphatically moved from 'blisse to bale' (fol. 183v). The emphasis throughout is on the outlandishness of the country and the uncouth incivility of the Russians, even when he admires their ingenuity: their buildings of wood and moss, and their windows made of translucent slices of stone sewn together (fol. 188r). Above all he returns again and again to the bodily grossness of the Muscovites: they have fat bellies, drink vast amounts, have greasy wives smoked tawny by the stove fire, and worst of all, the Russian leads a 'bowgards [bugger's] life', preferring 'a boy within his bed' to his greasy wife. In a word, Russia is as bad as Ireland:

Wild Irish are as ciuil as
  the Russies in their kind:
Hard choice which is the best of both,
  each bloodie rude, and blind.
                    (fol. 193r)

As the images of the icy landscapes in the 'sonnettes' served both to define homely Englishness by contrast, as well as to image the poet/speaker's own inner desolation, so the uncouth grossness of the Russians is represented as both deeply

9 See, for example, poems beginning on fols 147r and v; 149r; 151r; 157r; 158r.

alien and at the same time threatening the poet/speaker with contamination. He is forced to join his hosts in drinking, to lie on barbarous bearskins in the same corner as their heathenish idols, and is uncomfortably conscious of and offended by the sexuality of both the men and women. Russia even contaminates the integrity of his speech, as he feels constrained by his part in the trade mission to censure what he writes (fol. 189r). Turberville began his travels by differentiating his manly enterprise abroad from the dull-mindedness of the 'slouthfull Groome that sits,/at home and tels the clocke' (fol. 146r: 'A farewell to a mother Cosin'), but ends up sitting idly by a stinking stove in Moscow through the eight-month winter, presumably being tanned by its smoke to the same tawny colour as his hosts. The poet's concluding advice to his friends flatly contradicts the attitude to travel with which he began:

> If thou be wise, as wise thou art,
>   and wilt be rulde by mee:
> Liue still at home, and couet not,
>   those barbarous coasts to see.
> No good befals a man that seekes,
>   and finds no better place:
> No ciuil customs to be learnd,
>   where God bestowes no grace.
> (fol. 193v)

'Thou were better farre/at home' he tells another friend (Parker) 'And wouldst been loath among such loutes/so long a time to dwel' (fol. 192r). Part of the fascination of the poems is their struggle to maintain the poet/speaker's difference, his gentlemanly English urbanity and superiority, while all the time he feels threatened and contaminated by all that surrounds him: the smoke, sexual appetites, the food and drink, the tyrannical encroachments of an outlandish culture.

The confident association of the travel/travails of English enterprise both by ship and with the pen, found in Churchyard's 'Verses to Gilbert', is here dislocated. Travelling abroad proves a barren experience where nothing can be gained or learned, and much is threatened. Turberville is nevertheless able to make writerly capital out of his apparently barren experiences, presenting himself in print both as a man of bold spirit with news to tell, and as a civil Englishman whose moral difference from the gross Russians is satisfactorily confirmed by his disdainful tone. One hopes this proved a highly sellable combination. The enterprise of travail with the pen is here used to undermine the very travel abroad that enabled the writing in the first place. Nevertheless Russia functions in the volume subtly to disturb Turberville's attempted constructions of a firmly grounded self able to carry a fixed and impermeable mind on his travels. As an anonymous poem in *A Paradise of Dainty Devices* boasted, 'The noble minde eache where can thriue,/And not be drowned in deepe dispayre' (pp. 129–30). Turberville's horrified verse epistles from

Muscovia suggest that such a confident differentiation of self from other may not always be possible.

The differentiation of the civilized English self from the barbaric other proves even more insecure in the narratives of Robert Baker, a merchant's factor trading on ships to the Guinea coast of Africa, whose poems about two voyages in 1562 and 1563 appeared in the first edition of Hakluyt's *The Principall Navigations* in 1589.[10] According to the account in the opening lines of the first poem, the narratives were written during Baker's imprisonment, and that of a fellow sailor, in France. His motive is, possibly, to tell their remarkable story in the hope of raising a ransom in London, or gaining some celebrity by having the poems printed. Practical as may have been the motives for Baker's painful 'trauels' with his pen ('And eke at night I lothe that stile/which I haue writte that day'), he feels his story deserves the full epic machinery of gods and muses. The idea that overseas voyaging was a fit topic for epic verse was later to inspire Luis Camões's epic of Portuguese maritime exloration, *Os Lusiadas* (1572), and Hakluyt's protégé, the Hungarian humanist Stephen Parmenius of Buda. In 1582, Parmenius published a Latin hexameter eulogy of Sir Humphrey Gilbert on the eve of a projected expedition to Newfoundland: *De navigatione Humfredi Gilberti Carmen*. Parmenius's rapturous account of Gilbert's forthcoming voyage invokes the muses and the classical gods, and anticipates the English occupation of America in terms of the scions of one Golden Age (the English) liberating and civilizing the innocent children of another, the native Americans. The contradictions implicit in such a deployment of myth point to only one of the problems of such mythologizing when used of contemporary enterprises. In 1583, Parmenius accompanied Gilbert to the New Found Land himself, intending to write another Latin epic poem on the journey. All that remains is a letter to Hakluyt written in a plain prose that seems more suitable for the matter: 'Now I ought to tell you about the customs, territories and inhabitants: and yet what am I to say, my dear Hakluyt, when I see nothing but desolation?' (p. 171).[11] Parmenius and the epic he had undertaken to write were lost at sea in a storm shortly after the letter was written. Established ways of making sense of the world undergo strange subversions when appropriated for their narratives by poets travelling/travailing abroad. As we shall see, Baker's epic discourse, modelled loosely on Orpheus's journey to the underworld, proves as inappropriate as that of Parmenius and it is soon abandoned.

Baker set out in 1562 with two merchant ships, the *Minion* and the *Primrose*,

---

10 Hakluyt also printed Turberville's epistles from Moscow, albeit in a bowdlerized form (no mention of 'bowgards') in *The Principall Navigations*. See Lloyd E. Berry, 'Richard Hakluyt and Turberville's Poems on Russia', *Papers of the Bibliographical Society of America* LXI (1967), pp. 350–51.

11 Campbell, *Witness*, p. 222, makes a similar comment.

on a trading voyage to the Guinea coast. He describes his first view of Africans in far from flattering terms:

> Their Captaine comes to me
> as naked as my naile,
> Not hauing witte or honestie
> To couer once his taile.
> (p. 132)

To divert themselves, the mariners carry this 'wilde man' to their ship and dress him up in European clothes. But the 'wilde man' proves to have a good deal more wit than the English mariners. He uses his opportunity to spy out the arrangements on the English ship and then returns the next evening with his fellows and steals all their trading goods. Now the Africans are described as 'fiends more fierce' than any of the devils Orpheus met in Hell (p. 134); they are 'blacke burnt men', followers of Vulcan (p. 134). Baker invents a myth in which Jove lets the Englishmen return to England on one condition – that they go no more abroad. Jove tells Vulcan:

> They haue so fruitefull a countrey
> that there is none the like,
> But if they can not be
> therewith content, but still
> Will seeke for golde so couetously,
> worke then with them thy will.
> (p. 135)

Jove voices the contemporary ambivalence about overseas enterprise that we have already noted. However, by the following year, Baker has forgotten Jove's threat, and embarked again on a trading voyage to the Guinea coast. This time the English, as was normal in the period, begin their adventures by ferociously and piratically attacking a French trading vessel. When they eventually arrive off the Guinea coast, a crew of nine leaves the larger ships to row a small trading boat to shore. At this point Vulcan wrecks his revenge by sending down thunderbolts while Aeolus sends 'whirling windes' (p. 137). After two days the small boat is irremediably separated from the larger ships that eventually return to England presuming Baker and his crew have perished. Meanwhile Baker and the other eight sailors are left to row in a small boat along the hostile African coast.

At this point in Baker's narrative the mythological apparatus disappears entirely. At the same time, Baker's descriptions of the Africans change subtly. The Englishmen are now dependent on whatever food Africans on the shore will give them for the small wares they still have. Instead of 'wilde men' and fiends, the Africans are now described as 'Negros' and their food seems wholesome and delicate: 'daintie' dishes of meat and 'wine/much like our whey' (p. 138). However, in spite of such supplies the situation of the English becomes desperate. Confined to their small boat for twenty days, their legs become 'swolne euery ioint' (p. 139), they are scorched by the sun, and are unable to sleep because of the terrible night storms.

By now their boat has strayed into a part of the coast fortified by the Portuguese to protect their trading interests. Although the English are at war with the Portuguese and are bitter commercial rivals, the thought of other Christians nearby offers Baker and his fellows some hope: better to row in a galley and be fed than row up and down hopelessly as at present, or, worst of all, join the 'Negros'. Baker's terminology reverts to the rhetoric of savagery he had used in the first poem:

> But what fauour would ye
> of these men looke to haue:
> Who beastly sauage people be
> farre worse then any slaue?
> If *Cannibals* they be
> in kind, we doe not know,
> But if they be, then welcome we,
> to pot straight way we goe,
> They naked goe likewise,
> for shame we cannot so:
> We cannot liue after their guise,
> thus naked for to go.
> By rootes and leaues they liue,
> as beasts doe in the wood:
> Among these heathen who can thriue,
> with this so wilde a food?
>
> (p. 139)

Surrendering to the Portuguese seems by far the most attractive option, but when they try to do so, they are met by cannons and culverin fire and by stones thrown down from the fort on top of their boat. Hastily, the English row out to sea again and reconsider their options. It is clearly time to try the 'Negros', who may prove less savage than the Christian Portuguese.

This seems to be the case. The Africans on whose mercy they throw themselves seem very different from the cunning 'fiends' of the first poem. Their leader, 'the Kings chiefe sonne', is 'a stout and valiant man/In whom I thinke Nature iwis,/hath wrought all that she can (p. 141). He proves to be noble not only in form but also in sensibility:

> … he perceiuing now the teares,
> which from our eyes did fall,
> Had great pitie on vs,
> and sayd he would haue nought,
> But streight by signes he will'd vs then,
> that we should take no thought.
> As one whom God had sent,
> and kept for vs in store.
>
> (p. 141)

Jove has, in these exigencies, been replaced by the plain Protestant God. The Englishmen who a day earlier had decided they could not live 'after [the] guise' of the Africans now find themselves sitting beside them sharing their food, and lying beside them on the ground to sleep.

However, after a few days, the Africans, concluding that nothing is to be gained by aiding these Englishmen, gradually leave them to fend for themselves:

Some run now in the wood,
 and there for rootes do seeke,
...
Our clothes now rot with sweat,
 and from our backs do fall,
Saue that whom nature wils for shame,
 we couer nought at all.
(p. 141)

Only a ragged loin-cloth seems now to differentiate an Englishman from the naked, root-eating savages who had previously seemed so beast-like and alien. Not only do the Englishmen scrabble with their nails in the ground for roots and lie at night 'as beasts' on the bare earth (p. 142), but Baker anticipates they may lose the last vestiges that differentiate the civilized Christian from the savage cannibal:

Perhaps as weake breake our behest
 which we owe God on high.
And least we liuing here
 among this heathen, might
Perchance for need do that which were
 right hainous in his sight.
(p. 142).

The narrative ends with a final irony. The remnant of three men left alive from the crew of nine are finally rescued, albeit to be then imprisoned, by a French ship, such a one, no doubt, as Baker and his English crew had begun the voyage by assaulting and robbing.

This extraordinary tale of the travails of travelling abroad only appeared in the 1589 edition of Hakluyt's *Principall Navigations*, and indeed its grimly cautionary description of the outcomes of adventuring abroad for gain does not fit well with Hakluyt's enthusiastic project of recording English enterprise.[12] Like the other writers we have been considering, Baker labours on two fronts, not only during the 'great trauels that we/haue past in Heathen lande' (p. 131), where 'trauel' means journeys, trials and labours, but again, on his return, in the pains he takes to write it all down. Cleo, Calliope and the 'muses nine' might get a

12 For a detailed account of Hakluyt's life and intellectual milieu, see George Bruner Parks, *Richard Hakluyt and the English Voyages*, ed. James A. Williamson (New York: American Geographical Society, 1928).

mention, but Baker is keen to claim the narrative as his own: 'the trauell [is] only mine' (p. 131). The culturally prestigious discourse of epic journeying is finally rejected by Baker, not merely because of his own poetic shortcomings, but because it does not permit the first-person narrative of painful and chaotic experience and moral disorder that Baker wishes to present.

My final example of an Elizabethan poem of enterprise abroad is George Gascoigne's 'The fruites of Warre', first printed in his *Posies* (1575). This also proves to be a tale of cultural instability as established generic perspectives and roles give way to a first person narrative of chaotic travails/travel abroad. Gascoigne's artful account of his experience as a mercenary soldier in the Netherlands is written 'uppon this Theame, Dulce *Bellum inexpertis*'.[13] The Erasmian adage (which Gascoigne translates as 'warre seemes sweete to such as know it not' [130. 7]), and the genre, that is, the amplification of a set theme, both appear impeccably humanist. Nevertheless, Gascoigne's self-presentation in the poem shifts ambivalently between the study and the field. In the first half of the poem he poses as a scholar who knows about wars only from books:

> And herewithal I cannot but confesse,
> Howe unexpert I am in feates of warre:
> For more than wryting doth the same expresse,
> I may not boast of any cruell jarre.
>
> (2. 1–4)

The fruit of this scholar's studies is another commonplace, that war is a scourge of God.[14] It is not until stanza 91 in a poem of just over 200 stanzas that the speaker suddenly turns to his own experience of foreign wars to 'prove this true' (91. 1). The speaker (in some sense Gascoigne himself) metamorphoses from scholar to 'Miser', that is, the miserable soldier who goes to the wars to improve his fortunes, 'to advaunce/His staylesse state, by sworde, by speare, by shielde' (73. 5–6).

The sense of scholarly certainty, of carefully ordered truisms and stable moral commonplaces established by the first half of the poem disappears entirely once we embark upon Gascoigne's first-person narrative of service in the Netherlands. If previously he had disclaimed knowledge of wars, it now seems this was because what he has experienced does not come within any bookish definition of wars; it is all too chaotic and unheroic:

---

13 All quotations to Gascoigne are taken from G.W. Pigman's edition of the 1573 volume *A Hundreth Sundrie Flowres* (Oxford: Clarendon Press, 2000), which incorporates material from the revised and expanded volume issued in 1575 as *The Posies*. Pigman's edition (pp. xxviii–xxxviii) provides a very helpful summary of the events in the Netherlands to which the poem refers.

14 Pigman's note on 12. 2 refers the reader to an article on the commonplace by C.A. Patrides, '"The Bloody and Cruell Turke": The Background of a Renaissance Commonplace', *Studies in the Renaissance* XIX (1963), pp. 126–35.

For I have seene full many a *Flushyng* fraye,
And fleest in *Flaunders* eke among the rest,
The bragge of *Bruges*, where was I that daye?
Before the walles good sir as brave as best,
And though I marcht all armde withouten rest,
From *Aerdenburgh* and back againe that night,
Yet madde were he that would have made me knight.
(95)

His travels/travails have not been heroic by any chivalric standards. Absurd and pointless travelling characterizes Gascoigne's account of his experience of the campaign:

I romed have about,
In Zeeland, Holland, Waterland, and all,
By sea, by land, by ayre, and all throughout,
As leaping lottes, and chance did seeme to call.
(99.1–4)

The Netherlands figures as a list of strange place-names located in a confusing geography where normal order is perverted. The taking of Middelburg is described as a chaos of inversions; the 'bravest bragges' prove most cowardly, while the drums beat the attack, those that follow go backwards, and sailors lead the soldiers:

Such triumphs chance where such Lieutenants rule,
Where will commaundes when skill is out of towne,
Where boldest bloudes are forced to recule,
By Simme the boteswayne when he list to frowne,
Where Captaynes crouch, and fishers weare the Crowne.
(108. 1–5)

In this upside-down world, friends prove foes and foes friends. At Leiden, Gascoigne and his English troops find themselves locked out of the city they are meant to be defending:

They neither gave us meate to feede upon,
Nor drinke, nor powder, pickax, toole nor spade,
So might we sterve, like misers woe begone,
And fend our foes with blowes of English blade.
(163. 1–4)[15]

Forced to surrender to the Spanish, Gascoigne and his fellow officers paradoxically find themselves supplied with all they could wish, able

To eate and drinke at Barons borde alwayes,
To lie on downe, to banquet with the best,
To have all things, at every just request,
To borowe coyne, when any seemde to lacke.
(176. 3–6)

---

15 Pigman's edition has 'send our foes', but examination of the 1575 edition confirms that 'fend' is correct.

Not that we should trust the Spanish any more than the Dutch, he hastens to add: 'We might soone sell, all freendship found in Spaine' (178. 7).

Friendship, however, proves as treacherous at home as it is abroad. Gascoigne tells us that having selflessly negotiated the release of his English troops, he finds he is the victim of their slanderous gossip at home: [16]

> we that were their defence,
> With armes, with cost, with deedes, with eloquence:
> We that saved such, as knew not where to flie,
> Were now by them accusde of trecherie.
>
> (188. 4–7)

Travailing abroad in the wars, it seems, can contaminate home as well:

> And who in warre hath caught a fatall clappe,
> Might chaunce at home to have no better happe.
>
> (189. 6–7)

Or was home already contaminated? In the '*Peroratio*' that concludes the poem, Gascoigne faces in two directions at once. On the one hand he makes a firm distinction between England, ruled by its virtuous and foreseeing queen, and the war-torn continent where:

> wicked warres have bredde such cruell care,
> In *Flaunders, Fraunce*, in *Spaine* and many mo,
> Which reape thereby none other worth but wo:
> Whiles you (meane while) enjoy the fruites of peace,
> Still praysing God, whose bounties never cease.
>
> (194. 3–7)

On the other hand, returning to his earlier theme that war is the scourge of God with which he punishes the commonwealth whose prince or whose members cease to be virtuous, he proceeds to review the estates of the English commonwealth, nobility, clergy, lawyers and merchants, finding in each, in spite of the virtue of a few exceptional (named) individuals, evidence of vice and corruption.

The clear differentiations on which Gascoigne's poem seemed to have been built, those between the moralizing scholar and the contaminated soldier, between English peace and continental war, and between native virtue and foreign perfidy, are all collapsed. Gascoigne leaves himself and his readers no safe place of retreat. The seeds of war are already present in the English commonwealth, and for Gascoigne, the secure world of the scholar in his study, even were such a perspective reliable, is neither an option nor apparently desired. In 'L'envoie', the poet/speaker identifies himself again as a 'Miser', one of 'those that in dystresse/Do drive their dayes, till drummes do draw them out (lines

---

16 For a detailed discussion of these events and evidence concerning accusations of treachery against Gascoigne, see Pigman's edition, pp. xxxv–xxxviii.

25–6), but disconcertingly then changes his voice and attitude again to suggest relish for the adventurous life of the soldier: 'If drummes once sounde a lustie martch in deede,/Then farewell bookes, for he will trudge with speede' (lines 29–30). The reader is left, as in the topsy-turvy world of the Netherlands, with no secure perspective from which to judge events: not that of the scholar, nor that of the experienced but disillusioned soldier, nor those of national pride and difference.

Going abroad was important for the poets that we have considered because it offered an opportunity of employment and advancement, in short supply at home. Writing about going abroad could in turn serve their interests as a means of self-promotion, whether for self-justification or in the hope of making themselves known through print. Adventures abroad gave them a hot topic to catch the attention of punters and to represent themselves to potential patrons as men of enterprise and experience, able to deploy the skills of verse, and worthy of protection or further employment. However, the tales that get told are often disconcertingly destabilizing. They undermine the assured generic and moral stances of the gentlemanly traveller, the heroic mythographer, or the humanist expounder of commonplaces, to produce first-person narratives in which the 'I', loosed from home and the familiar, becomes fractured and 'contaminated' by the terrors of the foreign.

Primary texts quoted

Ascham, Roger, *The Scholemaster* (1570), in William Aldis Wright, ed., *English Works of Roger Ascham* (Cambridge: Cambridge University Press, 1904).

Churchyard, Thomas, 'Verses to Gilbert', in *A Discourse of the Queenes Maiesties entertainment in Suffolk and Norfolk* (1578). *STC* 5226.

Gascoigne, George, *A Hundreth Sundrie Flowres*, ed. G.W. Pigman III (Oxford: Clarendon Press, 2000).

Hakluyt, Richard, *Voyages* (London: J.M. Dent & Sons Ltd, 1907).

Hakluyt, Richard, *The Principall Navigations, Voiages and Discoveries of the English Nation, Imprinted at London, 1589*, facs. edn, intro. David Beers Quinn and Raleigh Ashlin Skelton (Cambridge: published for the Hakluyt Society and the Peabody Museum of Salem by the Cambridge University Press, 1965).

The Paradise of Dainty Devices (1576–1606), ed. Hyder Edward Rollins (Cambridge: Cambridge University Press, 1927).

[Parmenius, Steven], ed. and trans. D.B. Quinn and Neil M. Cheshire, *The New Found Land of Stephen Parmenius: The Life and Writings of a Hungarian poet, drowned on a voyage from Newfoundland, 1583* (Toronto: University of Toronto Press, 1972).

Turberville, George, *Epitaphes, Epigrams, Songs and Sonets* (1567) and *Epitaphes and Sonnettes* (1576), facs. edn, intro. Richard J. Panofsky (Delmar, NY: Scholars' Facsimiles & Reprints, 1977).

Chapter 2

Painful pilgrimage: sixteenth-century English travellers to Greece

Efterpi Mitsi

> The voyage is in my view a beneficial experience ... and I know of no better school for the forming of life than its constant exposure to the diversity of form of our nature.
> Michel de Montaigne

> The fruit of travell is travell it selfe.
> Fynes Moryson

The sixteenth-century traveller and the literary outcome of his journey, the travelogue, was the first connection between England and modern Greece. The initial encounters between British travellers and the Greek people, who lived under Ottoman or Venetian subjugation in the same area known since antiquity, resulted from a new economic and political balance between East and West: the naval battle of Lepanto (1571) ensured peace between the Christian West and the Ottoman East, breaking 'the spell of Turkish supremacy'[1] and allowing England to establish the Levant Company, whose goal was not only trading but also enlisting Turkish sympathies against Spain. However, English ships had been sailing to Crete and Chios for malmsey wine since the beginning of the century.[2] In *The Principal Navigations, Voyages, Traffiques and Discoveries of the English Nation* (1589), Hakluyt cites all the English ships which traded in the Aegean, dating the first English factor at Chios in 1533. Hakluyt also includes a 1569 letter by the merchant Jasper Campion, affirming the English presence in the Greek islands, and urging the English to trade in Chios: 'I write not this by hearsay of other men, but of my own experience: for I have traded in this country above this thirty years; and have been married in the town of Scio full twenty four years; so you may assure yourself that I will write but truth' (p. 134).

Although trade in the Aegean expanded in the 1560s and 1570s, it was the

1 Fernard Braudel, *The Mediterranean and the Mediterranean World in the Age of Philip II* (New York: Harper, 1976), II, p. 1088.

2 Terence Spencer, *Fair Greece, Sad Relic: Literary Philhellenism from Shakespeare to Byron* (London: Weidenfeld & Nicolson, 1954), p. 25.

foundation of the Levant Company in 1581 that entitled the English economically to penetrate the East, competing against the Venetians who imposed taxes on the trade of currants,[3] and to travel comparatively safely in the archipelago. The first travellers, who passed through Greece on their way to Constantinople or the Near East, paid little attention to its monuments, focusing instead on their own perilous itineraries. Sailing through the Eastern Mediterranean, merchants (Campion, Sanderson), sailors (Bodenham), adventurers (Sherley), clergymen (Biddulph), travellers (the bona fide Moryson or the 'self-fashioning' Lithgow) visited a land of a (relatively) known ancient past but of an alien and disorienting present.

Although the Greek monuments became known to Europe much later than the Roman ones, the English were aware of the classical past of Greece through its texts. Travellers remarked on the contrast between antiquity and contemporary reality, a dichotomy that soon became a common theme in travel accounts of Greece. The conflict between past and present is emphasized by the notorious Sir Anthony Sherley, 'one of the most arresting personalities in the history of the relations between England and Islam',[4] who visited Cyprus on his way to Persia in 1599. Upon arriving at the island, which had recently fallen to the Ottomans (1571), the Oxford-educated Sherley realized that nothing survived of its ancient splendour, as he records in his *Relations of his Travels into Persia* (1613):

> We found nothing to answer the famous relations given by ancient Histories of the excellency of that island, but the name only (the barbarousness of the Turk, and time having defaced all the Monuments of Antiquity), no shew of splendour, no habitation of men in a fashion, nor possessors of the ground in a Principality; but rather Slaves to Cruel Masters, or prisoners shut up in divers prisons: so grievous is the burthen of that miserable people and so deformed is the state of that Noble Realm.
>
> (pp. 6–7)

A few years later, the Scot William Lithgow uses the same words in his *Travels and Voyages through Europe, Asia and Africa* (1614) to represent the decay of Greece in general, not only of Cyprus: 'In all this country of Greece, I could find nothing to answer the famous relations given by ancient authors of the excellency of that land but the name only' (p. 62). Even Athens disappointed the traveller, as William Biddulph reports in his *Travels of Four Englishmen and a Preacher*

---

3 Kyriakos Simopoulos, *Foreign Travellers to Greece* [Oi xenoi taxidiotes stin Ellada] (Athens: Ekdotiki Athinon, 1981), I, p. 353.

4 Samuel C. Chew, *The Crescent and the Rose: Islam and England during the Renaissance* (New York: Oxford University Press, 1937), p. 239. Anthony Sherley, who was devoted to the Earl of Essex, left England without permission from the queen in 1597 to aid Don Cesare d'Este, claimant to the duchy of Ferrara. After going to Venice to seek employment, without success, he decided to go to Persia, wishing to make head against the Portuguese and open the Red Sea to commerce.

(1609): 'This City was the mother and nurse of all liberall Arts and Sciences: but now there is nothing but Atheism and Barbarisme there: for it is gouerned by Turkes, and inhabited by ignorant Greekes' (p. 10).

Although such disparaging remarks may frustrate the reader's desire to reconstruct sixteenth-century Athens, they denote that Greece was neither the motive nor the object of the early traveller's voyage: it was part of the journey to the Levant, which usually included Constantinople, the mythical city, and the Holy Land. Indeed, the tradition of pilgrimage 'bequeaths to secular travel writing the idea of travel as significant action, and the hope for transformation.'[5] When Sir Walter Ralegh, in his *Discoverie of the Large, Rich, and Bewtiful Empire of Guiana* (1596), calls his journey a 'painful pilgrimage' (p. v), he suggests that his goal, the ultimate object of his desire, is celestial Jerusalem, which will elude him to the end. Although the journey to Greece as a secular pilgrimage, a quest for antiquity, is represented in the eighteenth century, I would like to argue that it originates in the sixteenth, despite the travellers' reticence about the ancient monuments. In Mediterranean travel, the notion of pilgrimage blends with the curiosity not only to witness the legendary Orient but also to rediscover the past. As Fynes Moryson, a graduate of Peterhouse College, writes in his preface to *An Itinerary Containing His Ten Yeeres Travell* (1617): 'From my tender youth I had a great desire to see forraine Countries ... I had an itching desire to see Jerusalem, the fountaine of Religion and Constantinople, of old the seate of Christian Emperours, and now the seate of the Turkish Ottomans' (I, p. xii).

The voyage to the East was such a dangerous, difficult and 'painful travel'[6] for the English that the traveller could hardly focus on the antiquities. Like Ralegh's Eldorado, the famous sites are not seen, their description deferred until the end of the following century. Throughout his journey to Greece, Moryson stresses his misfortunes rather than the monuments he encounters. He admits that 'our guide shewed us not farre out of the high way, the monument famous for the love of the kings daughter Ariadne to Thesius, called the Laberinth of Crete ... but my former adversities had taken from me my wonted desire to see antiquities' (II, p. 80). Also, his Greek journey was not included in the portion of the *Itinerary* which he published. Lithgow, on the other hand, mentions the ancient ruins without trying to identify and describe them:

> In this desert way I beheld many singular monuments, and ruinous castles, whose names I knew not, because I had an ignorant guide: But this I remember, amongst these rocks my belly was pinched, and wearied was my body, with the climbing of steep mountains, which breed no small grief to my breast.
>
> (p. 60)

---

5 Mary B. Campbell, *The Witness and the Other World: Exotic European Travel Writing 400–1600* (Ithaca, NY: Cornell University Press, 1988), p. 120.

6 The phrase is used by both Lavender, the editor of Biddulph's *Travels*, p. 3, and by William Lithgow, *Travels*, p. iii.

Compared to the sixteenth-century French travellers to Greece, Belon, Gilles and Nicolay,[7] Englishmen appear almost indifferent toward the relics of antiquity. The explanation could be that the French interest in antiquities depended on politics, on their closer relations with the Ottoman Porte, archaeology following diplomacy.[8] Also, the English often are more disillusioned in Greece than continental travellers, remarking upon the degenerate condition of its inhabitants and focusing on the contrast between its past splendour and present decay. Finally, English travel accounts, influenced by the genre of adventure, popular after the travels to the New World, fashion a long-suffering yet resilient narrator rather than an erudite antiquarian.

Despite obvious exaggerations, travelling to Greece was arduous, as travellers encountered the strong winds, storms, shipwrecks and pirates of the archipelago and the steep paths and bandits of the mountainous mainland. Their narratives show their desire to speak of their own adventures and misfortunes. For example, Fynes Moryson, after the death of his brother Henry from dysentery in Syria, and still frail after his own illness, sailed aboard a French ship, *John Baptist*, to Crete on 19 October 1596, planning to go from there to Constantinople. During a storm, for which the French sailors held him responsible as a heretic, he was abandoned at a desolate shore, instead of the port of Candia. Moryson's voyage to Constantinople, on 'a little Greeke Barke loaded with Muskedines, and with tunnes of Lemons Juyce (which the Turks drinke like Nectar), and with Onions', was also memorable. The strong winds in the Aegean and the many islands 'made that Channell very dangers, and for my part I was more afraid of the danger because our Candian Merchant growing acquainted with an harlot in the ship, was not ashamed to have the use of her body in the sight of the Mariners that watched, and much blamed him for the same' (II, p. 85).

Hardship and adventure also dominate the journal of Master Thomas Dallam, an organ-builder from Lancashire, who went to Constantinople in 1599 to present Sultan Mahomet III with a marvellous organ, a gift from Queen Elizabeth.[9]

---

7 See Pierre Belon, *Les Observations de plusieurs singularitez et choses memorables trouvées en Grece* (1553), Pierre Gilles, *De Topographia Constantinopoleos et de illius antiquitatibus* (1561), and Nicholas Nicolay [Nicholay], *The Navigations, peregrinations and voyages, made into Turkie* (1551; trans. T. Washington the Younger, 1585).

8 On the French interest in Greece in the sixteenth century, see Olga Augustinos, *French Odysseys: Greece in French Travel Literature from the Renaissance to the Romantic Era* (Baltimore, MD: Johns Hopkins University Press, 1994). On the contrast between French and English travellers, see Chew, *Crescent*, pp. 60–61, and Warner G. Rice, 'Early English Travelers to Greece and the Levant', in *Essays and Studies in English and Comparative Literature* (Ann Arbor, MI: University of Michigan Press, 1933), pp. 205–60, esp. 214–16.

9 The journal kept by Dallam between February 1599 and May 1600, documenting one of the strangest stories of English diplomacy, was written too late to be included in Hakluyt's *Principall Navigations*, and was then neglected by Purchas in

Dallam's story, a rare example of an artisan's impressions of an unknown part of the world, is less about the foreign place than his own ability to survive. Unlike the learned travellers, such as Moryson, Biddulph and Lithgow, Dallam arrived at Greece with neither expectations nor prejudice. Never bored or disillusioned, he was interested in people, in strange foods and even in the prices of things. After visiting Zante, Chios and Rhodes (and having unusual encounters in every place), Dallam reached Constantinople, deciding after four months to return to England against the Sultan's wish. His strange itinerary made him the first English traveller on mainland Greece to leave an account of his journey. Sailing first to Volos, in 'Romalea' (mainland Greece), Dallam crossed Mount Parnassus to get to Lepanto. Pursued by the Turks in the mountains, he was saved by his dragoman who miraculously turned out to be an Englishman from Lancashire converted to Islam. He then walked from Patras to Arcadia to finally get to Zante, where he spent forty days in the Lazaretto. His *Diary* tells us that the difficulty of the journey was unique: 'our waye was so bad as I thinke never did Christians travell the like' (p. 83).

Similarly, endurance and bravery saved the unfortunate Lithgow (who claimed to have travelled to Greece in the first years of the seventeenth century)[10] from a skirmish with a Turkish galley near Cephalonia, from a shipwreck in the Aegean, from starvation in Arcadia, from being robbed, beaten and stripped naked by bandits in Crete, from being forced to drink Malvasie wine (malmsey) 'hourly and oftentimes against my will' and dance with friars at Canea, and above all from temptation, from 'women insatiably inclined to venery' (*Travels*, pp. 74, 78).

The travel account, letter, or journal, containing those exotic, incredible adventures, link past (traveller), present (writer) and future (the reader). Travel becomes discourse; in Lithgow's words the 'toilsome travels [become] now [more than twenty years after his journey] painful labours' (p. iii). Moryson's preface defines travel writing as a self-conscious process of transformation:

> I wrote it swiftly, and yet slowly ... swiftly in that my pen was ready and nothing curious as may appeare by the matter and stile: and I wrote it slowly, in respect of the long time past since I viewed these Dominions, and since I tooke this worke in hand.
>
> (*Itinerary*, I, p. xix)

The book is not only an integral part of the voyage, guiding future travellers who

Purchas His Pilgrimes (1625). Although the manuscipt was purchased by the British Museum in 1848, it remain unnoticed until its publication in 1893. See Stanley Mayes, *An Organ for the Sultan* (London: Putnam, 1956), p. 11.

10 Although studies of travel literature on Greece in the early modern period (Rice, Chew and Spencer) consider Lithgow a genuine traveller to the region, his impressive amount of plagiarism from both English and continental sources, his curious sense of geography and his endless misfortunes, call into question his own claim to authenticity.

might then write their own books, but also a means of imposing a structure on the fluid and alien matter of the foreign place.[11] Travelling abroad attracted Elizabethans, who developed 'a distinct idea of travel as an art', the art of peregrination, 'to be practiced by a properly taught young man in order to complete his education'.[12] The attraction of foreign travel was related to the vast political changes of the century as well as to changes in education, to the study of Latin and Greek authors, to the possibility also to study French. In his preface, Moryson explains that his work is intended as a guide book, useful to future travellers, despite 'continuall change of prices and rates in all kingdoms' (I, p. xix), beginning the book with a 'Table of Small coins' in every country he has visited. He is, therefore, confident of the power of the travelogue to inform and instruct: 'The visiting of forraigne Countries is good and profitable', not just to 'university men [who] are often idiots in wordly affaires', but to all as 'by travel the good become best, the bad prove worst' (I, pp. 357–8).

Yet the opportunity of foreign travel entailed a risk of contamination. In the Orient, the contamination might not relate to the spirit, as in Catholic Italy, but mostly to the body, through the indulgence of the senses, the languorous heat, spicy food, sweet wine and fruit, and unbridled sexuality. Therefore, the repeated recognition of the importance of travelling in sixteenth-century travel accounts of the Levant functions as a defence of travel against attacks such as Roger Ascham's *The Scholemaster* (1570) and Thomas Nashe's *The Unfortunate Traveller* (1594).[13] Moryson refutes the three main objections against travelling: first that it induces vice (by arguing that this false idea is caused by the jealousy of women, who stay at home); second, heresy; and third that the traveller is a malcontent, a tradition starting with Cain, the first traveller. In the 1585 translation of Nicolay's *The Navigations, Peregrinations and Voyages made into Turkie*, John Stell, the author of the book's Epistle, dedicated to both Sir Henry and Sir Philip Sidney, associates travel with knowledge, rhetorically juxtaposing snails (those who stay at home) with birds (travellers to foreign lands):

> For what is more discommendable, what more unseeming a man that is studious especially noble borne, than alwaies to abide at home like a snaile in a shel … [Men should] flie abroade, that they may aspire to the knowledge, and attaine to the sight of great matters. To undertake trauelling … shoulde inuyte all liberall mindes and free natures.
>
> (p. 2)

Moreover, Theophilus Lavender in his preface to *The Travels of Foure Englishmen and a Preacher,* which includes William Biddulph's letters from

11 Augustinos, *French Odysseys*, p. 56.

12 John Stoye, *English Travellers Abroad 1604–67* (New Haven, CT: Yale University Press, 1989), p. x.

13 Andrew Hadfield, *Literature, Travel, and Colonial Writing in the English Renaissance, 1545–1625* (Oxford: Clarendon Press, 1998), pp. 3–5, argues that there was a lively debate in the period over the nature and purpose of representing foreign countries.

Greece, praises contemporary travellers 'who have travelled upon divers respects: Some for pleasure, some for profit, some to see their manners, some to learne their languages, some to get experience, some to get wisdome and knowledge; not sparing any cost, fearing any danger, nor refusing any paines' (p. 5). Fighting insularity, travel is not only educational but also profitable: sight is followed by wonder, and wonder by possession. Considering the role of travel in the early modern period, Stephen Greenblatt argues that 'knowledge depends upon travel ... upon a restless drive toward the margins'.[14] Travel is a source of both knowledge and power; knowledge about the East, the Ottoman Empire, could benefit England's economy as well as consolidate its political role. Elizabethan travellers foreshadowed the importance the region would acquire for England in the eighteenth and nineteenth centuries. When Dallam describes cutting up and stealing a marble from Troy, he unwittingly initiates a convention in English travelogues on Greece. Knowledge about Greece ultimately led to England's appropriation of Greek antiquities, starting with the Earl of Arundel's collection in the early seventeenth century, as well as of the Greek past.[15]

Despite their curiosity, early English travellers display a limited knowledge of modern Greece. Focusing on their personal adventures, their painful pilgrimages, they did not actually 'see' the places and people they visited, or rather saw and recorded only what they already had in mind. Plagiarized, misquoted, mistranslated, transformed and transformable, early travel literature on Greece is fluid, suggesting that most travellers, even when faced with the novelty of Greece, chose 'to speak in other men's voices through translation and quotation'.[16] The travel account is indeed a troubled genre, marked by plagiarism, exaggeration, misrepresentation, and even deception. The intertextual networks of travel accounts imply that the reality of the place is for many travellers irrelevant. Therefore the separation between 'travellers and travel liars'[17] in early accounts of Greece is rather unimportant. Lithgow's description of the region is as legitimate as Sherley's and Biddulph's, accounts which he cannibalizes despite the avowal that his book is 'composed of mine own eyesight, and ocular experience ... excelling far all inventions whatsoever, poetic or

14 Stephen Greenblatt, *Marvelous Possessions: The Wonder of the New World* (Chicago, IL: Chicago University Press, 1992), p. 124.

15 Although Thomas Howard, the Earl of Arundel, did not visit Greece, he used the ambassador to the Porte, Sir Thomas Roe, to purchase Greek antiquities. He also sent his chaplain William Petty to Asia Minor and Greece to enrich his collection, which finally extended to 37 statues, 128 busts, 250 inscriptions, and so on. The first Greek works of art reached England in 1627. See Richard Stoneman, *Land of the Lost Gods: The Search for Classical Greece* (London: Hutchinson, 1987), pp. 43–50.

16 David Constantine, 'The Question of Authenticity in Some Early Accounts of Greece', in Graeme Clarke, ed., *Rediscovering Hellenism: The Hellenic Inheritance and the English Imagination* (Cambridge: Cambridge University Press, 1989), p. 21.

17 Percy Adams introduces the phrase in *Travelers and Travel Liars: 1660–1800* (Berkeley, CA: University of California Press, 1962).

theoric' (*Travels*, p. iii). Since the Middle Ages, the travel writer was bound in a literary culture of set *topoi* and figures, adding a layer to what becomes a palimpsest of writing. Travel accounts on Greece not only cite ancient authors (Homer, Herodotus, Pausanias, Strabo and Pliny), but also rework or repeat earlier or contemporary travel writers, exemplifying Edward Said's definition of the Orient as 'less a place than a topos, a set of references, a congeries of characteristics, that seem to have its origin in a quotation, or a fragment of a text, or a citation from someone's work ...'.[18] Sixteenth-century travellers match (often erroneously) landscape with text, citing its ancient name, myth and history. In the following century, starting with George Sandys who travelled to Greece in 1610,[19] this process becomes almost mechanical, as the numerous quotations and translations from ancient authors require an erudite assembling at home.

Even the merchant John Sanderson, when sailing by Kythera ('Serigo') in 1584, identifies it as the place 'where faire Hellen was borne', and later claims that in Chios he 'went up to a mountayne ... wher the poet Homer lieth buried' (pp. 37–8), saying nothing else about the islands. For more learned travellers, Greece serves as a display of humanist knowledge. In Kythera, Nicolay, who was chamberlain and geographer to the king of France, 'took the pain to seeke out the reliques & antiquities' only after alluding to the myths of Venus, Helen and Menelaus (*Navigations*, p. 41). Biddulph writes that Cephalonia 'was of old called Ithaca, where Ulysses ... was king, who excelled all other Greeks in eloquence and subtlity of wit' (*Travels*, p. 5). This (wrong) identification becomes a point of comparison between past and present, where the modern adventurous spirit excels that of the legendary wanderer: 'He is commended by ancient Writers, for a famous Traveller: but if he were living in these daies, his trauels would be counted nothing, in respect of the trauels of many other now living.' Lithgow quotes from Homer, Virgil and Ovid, occasionally adding his own verse. Rather than described, Mycenae is (erroneously) presented as the place 'from which unhappy Helen was ravished', providing an opportunity to attack not only the Greeks but women as well:

> This cursed custom of base prostitution is become so frequent, that the greater sort of her mercenary sex, following her footsteps, have outgone her in their loathsome journies of libidinous ways. She, being of such an infinite and voluptuous crew, did invite my muse to inveigh against the lascivious immodesty, as the inordinate pattern of all willing and licentious rapes.
>
> (*Travels*, p. 61)

Again, the place becomes a point of departure, an occasion to vent the narrator's own fears and obsessions.

Like Helen, Greeks in general would be condemned by early travellers. In the

18 Edward Said, *Orientalism* (Harmondsworth: Penguin, 1978), p. 177.

19 See George Sandys, *A Relation of a Journey Begun An. Dom. 1610* (1615).

sixteenth century the Greco-Roman world was still mostly understood from the Roman point of view, following Virgil's anti-Greek bias: Greeks were not to be trusted since they had taken Troy by a dishonest device.[20] Ironically, the Greek people were accused of being deceitful like their ancestors, and at the same time 'so far degenerated from [them] that they were not worth troubling about', fully deserving the Turkish conquest.[21] Rather than denoting a nationality, the term Greek identified all Christians of the East (considered schismatic), differentiating them from ancient Greeks.[22] By examining the use of the word *Greek* in sixteenth-century literature, Terence Spencer has shown its derogatory meaning, signifying either 'merry', 'mad' and 'gay', or 'twister', 'cheat' or 'crook'.[23] When the first Englishmen visited Greece they found those meanings true indeed: Greeks were dark, degenerated, deceiving, superstitious and barbarous. Greece, like any foreign place, is a mirror, and the travel account can only describe its reflection as it appears in the mirror, a fragmentary and distorted vision. Captain Roger Bodenham, in his 'Voyage to Scio' (1551), writes that Cretans 'would drink wine out of all measure' (I, p. 5);[24] and Sherley confirms that Greeks 'may well be called merry, for in the evening ... they will dance up and down the streets, both men and women'.[25] Biddulph finds them 'very superstitious, subtle and deceitfull people, insomuch that it is growen to a prouerbe amongst the Italians: Chi fida in Grego, sara intrego. That is: He that trusteth to a Greeke,/Shall be intreaged, and still to seeke' (*Travels*, p. 79). Prejudices defining Greeks as 'silly', 'base and beggarly', 'rascals', 'barbarous and uncivil' are validated, leading accounts to contradictions since travellers (Dallam, Moryson, Lithgow) often receive the hospitality of the people.

Similarly, early travellers issued warnings against the deceit of Greek women, though theirs was not a case of subtle deceit. Biddulph cautions readers that Greek women are 'light as water' and 'exceeding proud and sumptuous in apparell' (p. 89). They are represented by 'a Greeke whore called Charatza Sophia' who had many lovers 'to provide her with the apparell she wanted', finally divorcing her husband 'because he kept her not fine enough'. The author

20 Spencer, *Fair Greece*, pp. 30–31; see also Robert Eisner, *Travelers to an Antique Land: The History and Literature of Travel to Greece* (Ann Arbor, MI: The University of Michigan Press, 1991), p. 51.

21 Spencer, *Fair Greece*, p. 12.

22 Iole Vigopoulou, 'The First Approaches', in 'Travellers: Images of Greece', *Kathimerini* (2 April, 2000), pp. 14–15.

23 Spencer, *Fair Greece*, pp. 35–40.

24 Bodenham reports: 'There are in that island of Candia many banished men, that live continually in the mountains. They come down to serve to the number of 4,000 or 5,000. Every one was armed with his bow and arrows, a sword and a dagger; and had long hair, boots that reached up to the groin, and a shirt of mail hanging, the one half before, and the other behind' (p. 5).

25 Sherley's opinion as stated in *A true Report of Sir A Sherlies Journey* (1600), cit. Spencer, *Fair Greece*, p. 41.

accuses the Englishmen who marry Greeks while in the East, and 'maintain them gallantly, to the consuming of the wealth, diminishing of their health, and endangering of their owne soules' (p. 81). Travellers implicitly identify the region with its women, their descriptions and assumptions suggesting that the representation of the Orient in European texts is 'a fantasy built upon sexual difference'.[26] Starting with Nicolay's *Navigations*, the portrait of the women of Chios signifies the erotic and dangerous Orient as well as the allure of the past:

> As for the women and maidens, I doe not thinke (without offence too any other) that in all the East partes are any more accomplished in beautie and good grace & amorous courtesie: for aboue the singular beautie, wherewith nature hath so well indued them, they do attyre themselves so finely, & have so modest countenance & grace, that men would indye them rather to be Nymphs or Goddesses, then women or mortal maidens.
>
> (p. 37)[27]

However, their 'modest countenance' contrasts with the licence of their sexual customs, which are then described by Nicolay: 'if a mayden doth lose her maydenhead before she is marryed ... she is bound to giue a ducat unto the Captayne of the night, and after may use it at her pleasure without feare or danger' (p. 42). Lithgow summarizes the previous travellers' impressions, adding his own misogynist exaggerations:

> The women of the city Sio are the most beautiful dames (or rather angelical creatures) of all the Greeks upon the face of the earth, and greatly given to venery ... Their husbands are their panders ... they make whores of their own wives and are contented, for a little gain ['a zechin of gold, nine shillings English'] to wear horns.
>
> (*Travels*, pp. 86–7)

Although Dallam's view of the women of Chios is centred on their revealing costume, unlike other travellers, he does not emphasize the bawdy or immoral: 'they stoode in such order as we myghte se theire facis and bristes nakede, yeat weare they verrie richly appareled ... I thinke that no parte of the worlde can compare with the wemen in that countrie for beautie' (*Diary*, p. 46). Dallam is probably the only traveller of the era to have dinner with eight Greek women, whom he met at a church, in Zante; his effort to communicate with the Greeks is prompted by interest rather than prejudice. However, in all accounts, the women of Greece are constructed by the travel writer, transformed by his gaze, supported and distorted by desire. In the East the viewer–writer constructs himself as the male Western subject, in opposition to the erotic, feminine Orient. The Protestant

26 Meyda Yegenoglou, *Colonial Fantasies: Towards a Feminist Reading of Orientalism* (Cambridge: Cambridge University Press, 1998), p. 11.

27 The French traveller's interest in women may account for the popularity of his book. Within twenty years of its publication, there were two more editions in French, two in Italian, one in Dutch, one in German and one in English.

masculinity of the English traveller to the Levant is constantly threatened by corruption and emasculation, lurking behind feminine beauty.

Despite its geography, the traveller placed contemporary Greece in the Orient rather than Europe. Although Greece was part of the political and social order of the Ottoman Empire, it was at the same time distinguished from it by its language, religion and legacy, and this was indeed noted by travellers. It formed a paradox or even an irony, as according to Said the demarcation between East and West and the construction of Asia as the 'other world' originated in ancient Greece through texts like Aeschylus' *The Persians*. The irony is recognized by early travellers: 'Formerly, in derision, they termed all other nations *Barbarians*; a name now most fit for themselves, being the greatest dissembling liars, inconstant and uncivil people, of all other Christians in the world' (Biddulph *Travels*, p. 98). Such pronouncements attest to an early modern Orientalism, a discourse used in Greece to separate the past from the present, resulting in the political construction of Greek antiquity as an ideal ultimately embodied by England.

The sixteenth-century travel account not only documents a cultural exploration related to British economic and imperial expansion but also initiates an interest in Greece, leading to the ensuing quest for antiquities and to their systematic removal. In Italo Calvino's *Invisible Cities*, Marco Polo tells the Great Khan that 'Elsewhere is a negative mirror. The traveller recognizes the little that is his, discovering the much he has not had and will never have.' In the negative mirror of Greece, the traveller saw that the (absent) past could be reinvented and repossessed.

Primary texts quoted

Biddulph, W., *The Travels of Foure Englishmen and a preacher into Africa, Asia, Troy, Bythinia, Thracia, and the Blacke Sea*, ed. Theophilus Lavender, (1609). *STC* 3052.

Bodenham, Roger, 'Voyage to Scio in 1551', in Richard Hakluyt, ed., *Principal Voyages and Navigations* (1599–1600), repr. in Raymond, Beazley, ed., *An English Garner: Voyages and Travels Mainly during the 16th and 17th Centuries* (Westminster: Archibald Constable, 1903), I, pp. 1–5.

Campion, Jasper, 'The English Trade to Scio, 1539–70', in Hakluyt (1599–1600), repr. in Beazley, I, pp. 132–8.

Dallam, Thomas, *The Diary of Master Thomas Dallam* (1599–1600), in J.T. Bent, ed., *Early Voyages and Travels in the Levant* (London: The Hakluyt Society, 1893).

Hakluyt, Richard, 'The Antiquity of the Trade with English Ships into the Levant' in *The Principall Navigations, Voyages, Traffiques and Discoveries of the English Nation* (1598–1600; Glasgow: James MacLehose, 1903–1905), V, pp. 61–3.

Lavender, Theophilus, ed. W. Biddulph, *The Travels of Foure Englishmen* (1609). *STC* 3052.

Lithgow, William, *The Totall Discourse: Travels and Voyages through Europe, Asia, and Africa for Nineteen Years* (1614; Leith: William Reid, 1814).

Moryson, Fynes, *An Itinerary Containing His Ten Yeeres Travel* (1617; Glasgow: James MacLehose, 1907).

Nicolay [Nicholay], Nicholas, *The Navigations, peregrinations and voyages, made into Turkie,* trans. T. Washington the Younger (1585). *STC* 18574.

Ralegh, Walter, *The Discoverie of the Large, Rich, and Bewtiful Empire of Guiana* (1596; rpr. New York: Lenox Hill, 1970).

Sanderson, John, *The Travel of John Sanderson in the Levant* (1584–1602), ed. William Foster (London: The Hakluyt Society, 1931).

Sherley, Anthony, *His Relation of his Travels* (1613). *STC* 22424.

Stell, John, 'Epistle', in Nicholas Nicolay, *The Navigations*, trans. T. Washington the Younger (1585). *STC* 18574.

Chapter 3

Foreign bodies: politics, polemic and the continental landscape

Cathy Shrank

In their 1990 article, '"Studied for action": How Gabriel Harvey read his Livy', Anthony Grafton and Lisa Jardine decisively demonstrate the 'goal-directed' nature of reading history in early modern Europe.[1] Whilst the 'goal-directed' nature of reading and writing history has received much critical attention, however, the related art of topography – the description of land- and cityscape – has received rather less coverage. This essay seeks to redress some of the imbalance by looking at the use made of topography by Tudor writers as a part of their general strategy of employing history as a means of warning, and advising, their monarchs, ministers and compatriots. It argues that these topographical accounts are more than passages of redundant prose, or the sixteenth-century equivalents of *The Rough Guide* or *The Lonely Planet*. Rather, they help explain the histories they accompany. The essay uses early modern medical theory to highlight the importance of place in determining national character, suggesting that – if we are to understand early modern writings touching on the potentially corrupting nature of foreign travel as anything other than empty (and now faintly amusing) rhetoric – then it is vital to restore this physiological context.

English, Welsh and Scottish writers seem to have been particularly attached to topography as a method of elucidating their political and historical message. Unlike their continental equivalents, such as Machiavelli's *Istorie fiorentine* (1525) or Domenico Buoninsegni's *Istoria fiorentina* (1580), Francesco Guiccardini's *Storia d'Italia* (1561), Marco Antonio Sabellico's *Historie vinitiane* (1544), or De la Noue's *Politicke and Militarie Discourses*, all the major histories written by sixteenth-century English, Scottish and Welsh writers are prefaced with topographical descriptions. This is as true of their accounts of continental history, such as William Thomas's *Historie of Italie* (1549) or Robert Dallington's *View of Fraunce* (1604), as of their own: Raphael Holinshed's multi-volume *Chronicles*, first published in 1577, John Major's *Historia Maioris Britanniae* (1521) and Hector Boece's *Scotorum Historiae* (1527) all begin with

1 Anthony Grafton and Lisa Jardine, '"Studied for action": How Gabriel Harvey read his Livy', *Past and Present* CXXIX (1990), pp. 30–78, at p. 30.

a description of the land and peoples in question. From the thirteenth century and Geraldus Cambrensis's *Topographiae Hiberniae* onwards, there is a tradition within English, Welsh and Scottish historical writing of including topographical sections; William Caxton even felt the need to supply topography where it was lacking, appending his *Descrypcyon of Englonde* (which, with typical English acquisitiveness, appropriates Wales, Ireland and Scotland under the label 'Englande') to John Trevisa's translation of the *Polychronicon* in 1498. These topographical sections, moreover, are used to help explain the history that follows, as Thomas notes in his *Historie of Italie*, stating that he has added 'this little discourse' – 'the descripcion of Italie' – 'to the entent the wise maie the better vnderstande the cause of those things, that to my purpose I must hereafter treate vpon' (fol. 1v).

This is not to say that continental writers ignored topography: the Frenchman Jean Bodin – whose treatise on history Philip Sidney recommended to his younger brother Robert in 1580 – even draws attention to the debt owed by historians to geographers in his *Methodus ad facilem historiarum cognitionem* in 1565, pointing out that 'we [historians] have plucked and wrested from the geographers alone the accounts of the Scythians, Indians, Ethiopians, and Americans' and that 'historians use geographical data' to such an extent 'that if any art is essential to them … geography must seem so in the highest degree' (p. 25).[2] The recognized role of topography within the political domain, meanwhile, is demonstrated by the practice of Venetian ambassadors during this period of delivering reports (*relazioni*) to the Senate at the end of their tenure. These records consist mainly of descriptions of place and people and were used to build a picture of the land and governments being dealt with, and hence inform diplomatic policy. Nevertheless, topography features less prominently within histories by sixteenth-century continental authors: it is dispersed through the book, rather than appearing as a distinct unit of its own, at or towards the beginning of the work, as they do in works by English, Scottish and Welsh writers. Owing to the significance of topography to the work, More's *Utopia* consequently belongs to this 'British' tradition. Unlike Plato's *Republic*, More's imagined commonwealth is given a geographical setting, and topography plays a key role in the search for the 'best' common weal, as it is used to help convey how, and why, this unfamiliar society works. The seeming equality of the Utopian lifestyle is reflected in, and explained by, the uniformity of their housing. Similarly, the protective isolation of this self-contained island is a crucial feature, enabling its social structures and practices. Cut off from the world, Utopians need not engage in continual warfare with neighbouring countries, and can be protected from the 'polluting' aspects of more mercantile societies.

More's *Utopia* also reveals the potency of topography as medium, combining

---

2 See Katherine Duncan-Jones, *Sir Philip Sidney, Courtier Poet* (London: Hamish Hamilton, 1991), p. 171.

as it does the history that is inscribed in the landscape, and the landscape that shapes history. On the one hand, Utopia's name and island status are permanent memorials of its foundation, when King Utopus renamed the former peninsula of Abraxa 'Utopia' and ordered its separation from the mainland: an extreme example of what the antiquarian John Leland calls the 'footprints [*vestigia*]' of history, which are imprinted in walls and ditches and changes to the landscape.[3] On the other hand, as we have seen, this physical insularity has subsequently enabled the ideological insularity of the Utopians, divorced from the money-oriented societies of the mainland.

The connection between topography and the workings of the body politic – latent in More's *Utopia* – underlies much travel writing of the period, as in Dallington's *View of Fraunce*, where the physical geography of France is continually explained by recourse to bodily metaphors. The rivers of France, for instance, are compared to 'veines and arteries', enabling the healthy circulation of 'commodities to her seuerall Prouinces', just as the body benefits from 'their apt conueyaunce of the blood or spirit, from the liuer and heart, to each part thereof' (sigs B3r–v).[4] Continuing the use of corporeal motifs, an analogy drawn from the physiognomy of animals is later used to inveigh against the abundance of *châteaux* in the French interior and illustrate how countries should best be defended. 'It is judged by the wisest', Dallington states:

> that in great kingdomes, such as France, no places should be fortified but the frontiers; after the example of Nature, how armeth the heads and heeles of Beasts, but never the Bowels nor middle parts.
>
> (sig. D3v)

Corporeal imagery provided sixteenth-century writers with a vital resource, linking as it did the land – anatomized as a body – with the institutions of government that comprised the 'body politic' and which were again described and explained through bodily discourse. Further to that, early modern medicine – with its belief in humoral theory – provided a useful explanation for the formation of different national characters.

The theory of the four bodily humours (or complexions), inherited from the ancient Greeks, dominated medical practice in early modern Europe. Under this scheme, everything was formed from four elements, each of which was linked to one climatic quality: fire (hot), air (cold), earth (dry), water (moist). Within the

---

3 John Leland, *Syllabus et interpretatio antiquorum dictionarum*, in his *Genethliacos* (1543), sig. F4r.

4 The passage on these Gallic waterways also shows the interplay between 'literary' and 'non-literary' topographies, as, bringing together in matrimony the Rhine and Seine (the 'Savoy Prince and Princess of Burgandy' [sig. B4r]), Dallington imitates and acknowledges the marriage of Thames and Medway in Book IV of Spenser's *Faerie Queene*, the second three books of which had been published a few years earlier, in 1596 (IV. xi. 8–53).

human body, these elements paired up to form the four humours, the proportions of which determined an individual's temperament, as well as their physical constitution. The sanguine person was therefore naturally hot and moist; the phlegmatic, cold and moist; the choleric, hot and dry; the melancholic, cold and dry.[5] This balance was also influenced by various factors, including age, sex, diet and place of birth, which might dry out, moisten, heat up, or cool down the body, thus altering the relative strengths of the different humours. As Vivian Nutton explains, from Hippocrates' *De dieta* in 400 BCE onwards, it was believed that:

> health depends not simply on nourishment, but on the quantitive balance between the intake of nourishment and physical activity; and that it was further affected by such factors as the age and constitution of the individual, the seasons, changes in wind direction, place of residence, the weather in a particular year, and the rising and the setting of the planets.[6]

Early modern medical handbooks consequently advise their readers on how to ensure they achieve the humoral balance necessary for mental and physical well-being. What interests us here, however, is the widespread belief that temperament was affected by the area in which you grew up, as 'soyle' and 'ayre' combine with socio-economic factors to create the nature of persons and races. Castigating a criminal from northern England, for example, the rhetorician Thomas Wilson declares in his *Arte of Rhetorique* (1553) that 'the soyle (where he was borne) giueth him to bee an euill man: considering he was bredde and brought vp ... among the men on Tinsdale and Riddesdale' (fol. 50r). Similarly:

> The Shire or Towne helpeth somewhat, towardes the encrease of honor. As it is much better to bee borne in Paris, then in Picardie: in London then in Lincolne. For that both the ayre is better, the people more ciuill, and the wealth much greater, and the men for the most part more wise.
> (fol. 7v)

Within this schema, climate, like diet, exacerbates certain humours. According to Bodin, 'the southerners', who, as a result of the heat, 'abound in black bile', are therefore 'plainly implacable' and 'especially given to all carnal pleasures and lust', in contrast to the northerly Scythians, deemed by 'Hippocrates ... not fitted for love, on account of the excessive coldness and dampness of their bellies' (*Method*, pp. 102–3).

There is thus a ready equation between a hot climate and the irascibility and carnality of its inhabitants, and although women (and children) possessed different physiological compositions from men (and were thus affected by external factors in different ways), it should be understood that, for these

5 See W.S. Copeman, *Doctors and Diseases in Tudor Times* (London: Dawson's, 1960), pp. 87–8.

6 See Vivian Nutton, *Medicine at the Courts of Europe, 1500–1837* (London: Routledge, 1990), p. 16.

sixteenth-century writers, it was the male character that constituted the national character that in turn affected national history. 'Vndoubtedly the fleshly appetite with vnnaturall heate and other thynges in them that be vicious ... passe all the terms of reason or honestie,' Thomas writes of the Italians in his *Historie of Italie* (fol. 4v). This fevered temperament is consequently manifested in the sexual mores of the country, the abundance of whores, and the volatile political climate. The Neopolitans, for example, are accused of great 'inconstancie', so that:

> It seemeth, that the realme of Naples is predestinate to haue in it, continuall tyrannies, sedicions, falshead, rebellions, warres, destruction of citees, rauishmenes, and flambe, with all the other calamitees that of auarice and ambicion (the true mothers of such plages) maie grow.
> (fols. 113v-14r)

The passage connects historical events ('tyrannies, sedicions' and so forth) with manifestations of character (avarice and ambition). It is also immediately preceded by a passage that connects character with climate and landscape, as Thomas describes the volcanic terrain, noting the 'heate' of the sulphur, which causes the ground to shake and occasionally results in an outbreak of 'flambe', the same word used of civil upheaval a paragraph later, in the quotation above. A connection is drawn semantically between the heat that disturbs the earth and the hotheadedness that disturbs the state. The sulphurous soil has a further link to the political unrest, moreover. Its excessive fecundity is said to feed the appetites of those who live there, so that (according to Thomas, following the Neopolitan historian Pandolfo Collenuccio), 'the wonderfull mutacions that haue happened [there] procede of the desire that men had vnto the pleasers and commoditees of the countrey' (fol. 113v). The ground is so rich, that is, that the inhabitants become habituated to abundance, and through habit, become opulent and greedy for more: a devotion to luxury that is apparently characteristic of those 'who dwell in fertile valleys' (Bodin, *Method*, p. 141).

'History', as Bodin defines it, is 'primarily accounts of human affairs', and is consequently dependent on 'human agency' and 'human activity' (*Method*, pp. 28–9). This humoral theory of national or regional character consequently fits neatly with models of history being developed by humanists such as More and Ascham, where – in More's *History of Richard III* (*c*. 1513–18) and Ascham's *Report of the Affaires and State of Germany* (1552) – character sketches of monarchs and statesmen are used to help explain history.[7] National character is merely character writ large. Both are affected by place, and, in turn, both affect history. In the light of this medical connection between place and character, it is also intriguing that one of the earlier sixteenth-century travel books, *The Fyrst Boke of the Introduction to Knowledge* (1547), written by the physician

7 See Lawrence V. Ryan, *Roger Ascham* (Stanford, CA: Stanford University Press, 1963), p. 158.

Andrew Borde, in which he records the 'naturall diposicion' of the peoples of Europe and the near East, was initially designed to include a section on anatomy (p. 17).

These topographies, however, are not only used to explain history and national character; they also perform a more symbolic function, and here the 'creative' aspects of the genre come to the fore. Divorced from the need to depict the terrain as accurately as possible on the page, topography allows a degree of artistic licence. Within the early modern period, for example, there is a recurrent tendency to call England an island, which it is not. Wales might well have been amalgamated with England by the Acts of Union of 1536 and 1543, but Scotland most certainly had not. Even after the accession of James I and VI in 1603, Scotland and England were two separate kingdoms, and would continue to be so until the Act of Union in 1707. Yet it suited English writers to call England an island: it suited their habit of subsuming Scotland under the label England, and it suited the defensively insular mood which, according to Venetian accounts *c.* 1500, was apparently endemic to the English people.[8] This xenophobic trait was only exacerbated by the series of parliamentary acts that effected England's break from the Roman Church in the 1530s. Published by the king's printer Thomas Berthelet, these did much to propagate a vocabulary of historically justified imperial sovereignty and vaunted isolation. England was promoted as an island kingdom, entire and complete within itself, sentiments found echoing throughout the sixteenth- and seventeenth-century literature, in speeches such as John of Gaunt's 'This England' in Shakespeare's *Richard II* (II. i. 31–68), or in Marvell's evocation of 'that dear and happy isle,/The garden of the world' in his distinctly anti-papal poem, 'Upon Appleton House' (lines 321–2).

The ability to model England into something it was not (an island) holds obvious iconic advantages, as the physically contained nature of this island jewel, recurrently personified as female, also acquired connotations of chastity, an image strengthened by its repeated description as a garden, a zone which, in medieval literature such as the *Roman de la Rose* (itself derived from the biblical Song of Solomon), had been associated with virginity. In this way, she (or it) could be contrasted usefully with the rest of that sprawling, interconnected mass of continental Europe, most of which was also Catholic and, within Protestant idiom, consequently open to accusations of lewdness and excess. Thomas is just one of those many Tudor writers subscribing to this image of England as an island, 'environned with the ocean sea', as he habitually expresses it. When, at the beginning of the *Historie of Italie*, Thomas describes Italy as 'almost an ilande' (fol. 1r), therefore, he is drawing an explicit comparison with England (signalled by that key word, island). Allegedly at least, England shares Italy's

8 Charlotte Augusta Sneyd, ed. and trans., *A Relation or Rather a True Account of the Island of England ... about the Year 1500* (London: John Bowyer Nichols and Son, 1847), p. 21.

island-ish status. It is also, like Italy, a trading nation, and it too is agriculturally well endowed. This glowing image of Italy, however, is quickly undermined by the distinctly sexualized vocabulary that sets the tone for the rest of the volume. Italy, Thomas continues, is an 'open lappe to receiue the trade of all countreys: and as it were to offre all men helpe it seemeth willingly to put it selfe into the sea' (fol. 1v). The land assumes the sexual laxity of which its inhabitants stand accused, and the topographical description becomes emblematic, underscoring the ideological message of Thomas's text. As Thomas's jibe ('the open lappe') is counterpoised against praise for Italy's economically strategic, and welcoming, position (with the land jutting into the sea 'to offre all men helpe'), Thomas's work displays the characteristically divided attitude of the English towards Italy, as found in Ascham's vituperative outburst in *The Scholemaster*, written in the late 1560s, and melodramatic depictions of dastardly Italians on the Jacobean stage.[9] On the one hand, Italy's culture and civility, its agricultural and mercantile riches are to be emulated; on the other, its 'popery', perceived lasciviousness and habits of deceit are to be renounced.

The duality of English attitudes to Italy – as both an example to imitate and a warning to avoid – owes much to the legacy of Rome, home of the classical culture Tudor schoolboys were brought up to imitate and admire, but also the site and origin of the ecclesiastical depravity they were increasingly being taught to abhor. As Ascham observes in *The Scholemaster*:

> Time was, when Italy and Rome have been to the great good of us that now live, the best breeders and bringers up of the worthiest men, not only for wise speaking, but also for well doing, in all civil affairs, that ever was in the world. But now that time is gone; and though the place remain, yet the old and present manners do differs as far as black from white, as virtue and vice.
>
> (pp. 148–9)

The negative example set by Rome was commonplace from the 1540s onwards, found in works by writers as diverse as the antiquarian Leland, and the physician and ex-Carthusian monk Borde, both of whom repeatedly deplore the corrupted morals of the formerly learned city. Within these increasingly polemical descriptions of the papal seat, moral and political decay are recurrently epitomized by the imperial ruins that dominate the city, which are, as Thomas puts it, 'a witnesse to the worldes ende of their tyranny' (fol. 22v): a parallel between history and cityscape that was no less apparent to Thomas than to the rather more famous French poet, Joachim du Bellay, who arrived in Rome five

9 See Ascham, *Scholemaster* (1570), ed. J.A. Giles, *The Works of Roger Ascham* (London: John Russell Smith, 1864), III, 148–9. For examples of stage Italians, see Thomas Dekker, *Honest Whore* (1604–05), Anon., *The Revenger's Tragedy* (1607), John Webster, *The Duchess of Malfi* (1612).

years after Thomas's departure, and who published his meditation on the city nine years after Thomas's *Historie of Italie*.[10]

Despite Felix Raab's comment that Thomas 'had nothing but good to report of the Italians', the *Historie of Italie* is double-edged throughout, mingling approbation of architectural splendour and the productive soil with disapproval of sexual and political behaviour in particular.[11] Thomas's *Historie of Italie* is presented 'as being exceedyng profitable to be redde' precisely 'because it intreateth of the astates of many and divers common weales, how thei ben, & now be governed' (sig. A1r). The political message is clear, and, as Andrew Hadfield has pointed out, Thomas's text proceeds to lay out a range of constitutional alternatives, from the near-exemplary (Venice) to the downright disastrous (Naples).[12] The anticipated audience of these histories, moreover, extended beyond the aristocratic patron to include a general readership, the 'indifferent and not curious', who may need encouragement to peruse the pages further, encouragement provided by impressing upon them the necessity of these historical lessons to the health and stability of the common weal, since as citizen–subjects, they too had a part to play, and a stake, in national history.

Rome, Venice, Naples and Florence dominate Thomas's text, and all provide pertinent examples of how land or cityscapes can be used to reflect, or endorse, the political message that Thomas draws from each. These topographical descriptions veer from the symbolic – the ready message spelt out by the ruins of Rome – to the explanatory, where the opulence of certain houses in Florence that 'seeme rather the buildynges of princes than of priuate men' (fol. 138r), like Dallington's French châteaux, pre-empt the history that follows, in which we see the city repeatedly torn by the civil strife caused by over-mighty rival dynasties. Yet the primary function of both forms of topography is to proffer positive and negative examples to their English readership. Within Thomas's history (Rome apart), Naples is offered as the strongest example of misrule. The unstable and fractious politics of the region act as more than an example of the naturally febrile and inconstant inclinations of the southern temperament, troubled with Bodin's black bile. As a monarchy, Naples provides a direct warning to English rulers, and to English subjects, of how not to behave if they want to preserve the integrity of their state: Neopolitan monarchs are consequently used to illustrate the dangers of over-reliance on foreign powers; their subjects are used to show the crippling effects on the polity of the discontent arising among the well-fed peoples of a land that is, like England, notably fertile.

---

10 See Joachim Du Bellay's *Le premier livre des Antiquitez de Rome* (1558) and *Les Regrets et autres oeuvres poetiques* (1558).

11 Felix Raab, *The English Face of Machiavelli: A Changing Intepretation, 1500–1700* (Toronto: Toronto University Press, 1964), p. 20.

12 Andrew Hadfield, *Literature, Travel, and Colonial Writing in the English Renaissance, 1545–1625* (Oxford: Clarendon Press, 1998), p. 26.

Where Naples is an exemplum of the 'ambicion' born of an easy life, Venice, on the other hand, is a held up by Thomas as a symbol of what men can achieve through industry and application. Its description even acquires some Utopian echoes. Like Utopia, Venice is an artificial island and has a similarly admirable, easily defensible harbour, with the passages of entry known only to local seamen, and 'so daungerous ... that whan any shippe cometh in, she taketh furst pilottes to sounde the waie: whiche in effect is reputed to be one of the greatest sureties' (fol. 74r), just as, in Utopia, 'hardly any strangers enter the bay without one of their pilots' (p. 42). The site of the city itself is said to be 'meruailouse': the miracle of metropolis built out of a swamp by skill and endeavour. The Venetians are even credited with countering the disadvantages of the marshy location, which – according to contemporary medical theory – risked inducing slothfulness and 'a generall torpidity of minde and body', owing to the dampness operating on the humours and fostering melancholic and phlegmatic types.[13] As the sixteenth-century verse comments:

> The Sanguine, Choller, Flegme and Melancholy,
> The latter two are heavie, dull of sense,
> Th'other two are more joviall, quick and jolly.[14]

The Venetians, however, have managed to make the spot 'holesome' by drying out the air 'throughe the muche haunte of people and the great noumbre of continuall fyres' (fol. 73r). The Venetian constitution proves a similarly marvellous and complex construction. For Thomas, it has ensured the enviable stability, and economic and military successes, of the Venetian polity and consequently merits a description five times as long as any of the other constitutions noted by Thomas. The example of Venice is all the more pertinent because of its perceived similarities, and connections, with England: it is a trading nation; it is an island; and both draw their mythical origins from Trojan stock (Brutus, in the case of England/Britain; the Heneti, in the case of Venice, who 'after the destruction of Troie came with Athenor into Italie' [fol. 85v]). Yet even Venice, this shining exemplum of good government, holds a warning: namely, the 'corrupcion ... so crept in amongest the judges' (fol. 81v). The channels of justice, in other words, are becoming clogged, just like the channels of water which surround the city, 'where the mud encreaseth daiely' (fol. 73v). An ideal constitution is, like Venice's ideal island status, only preserved by continual vigilance.

As the example of Venice shows, the health or state of a body and mind is not just given; it is maintained. The balance of humours is not stable, but is affected by diet, climate, exercise, even a change in the wind. The Scythians'

13 Quotation from Tobias Venner, *Via recta ad vitam longam* (1628), sig. B2r. Although written a century later, Venner's opinions are representative of sixteenth-century medics.

14 Cit. Copeman, *Doctors and Diseases*, p. 88.

cold bellies, for example, are exacerbated by their habitual riding. Borde, meanwhile, in his *Dyetary of Health* (1542), warns the 'Fleumatyke man' not 'to liue neare waterysshe or morysshe ground', lest he aggravate his 'colde and moyste' condition, and advises the 'Melancoly man' (who is 'colde & drye') against consuming desiccating foodstuffs, such as 'all meate the whiche is burnet and drye', and 'hote wynes' (pp. 288–9). As Tudor Englishmen and women travelled abroad, they witnessed their bodies reacting to the unaccustomed climate. In the heat of the Italian summer, Thomas, 'that before time could in maner brooke no fruite', 'after [he] had been a while in Italie ... fell so in loue withall, that as longe as [he] was there, [he] desyred no meate more' (fol. 2v). These bodily changes, witnessed daily, are converted, in polemical passages like those found in Ascham's *Scholemaster*, into images of metamorphosis, where Italy appears as 'Circes court', transforming Englishmen into 'very swine and asses ...: very foxes with subtle and busy heads, and where they may, very wolves, with cruel malicious hearts' (p. 68). It is important to remember that – despite their apparent subscription to humoral theory – sixteenth-century writers do not display a consistent attitude towards the connection between place and temperament. Dallington, for example, imagines transplanting the English to France, an operation which would create 'the right idea of *Platos* happy state' (sig. B4r). No mention is made of the potentially transformative nature of this shift on the English national character. Nevertheless, this rhetoric of monstrous and diabolic transformation, whereby the Italianate Englishman figures as a devil incarnate, cannot be dismissed as hysteria: at its core, this concept of translation is based on contemporary medical theory, and surfaces as a very real fear in tracts such as Edmund Spenser's *Present View of the State of Ireland* (ms. 1598, pr. 1633), where 'such English, as were planted above towards the west' are 'degenerate' and 'almost now grown like the Irish' (p. 68). This 'dangerous infection', described in medical terms, is also attributed, in part, to the habits of fostering, whereby the infant sucks in Irishness at the wet nurse's breast (p. 71). Un-Englishness is consequently something the traveller can catch, as John Lyly puts it in *Euphues and his England* (1580), so that 'most of our trauailers, which pretend to get a smacke of strange language to sharpen their wits, are infected with vanity by following their wils' (p. 13). Thomas Dekker mocks this outlook in his *Patient Grissel* (1603). 'How *Italy*?' comes the rant:

> Away you ideot: *Italy* infects you not, but your own diseased spirits: *Italy*? Out you froth, you scumme, because your soule is mud, and that you haue breathed in *Italy*, you'll say *Italy* hath defyled you.
>
> (III. i. 92–5)

Nevertheless, even as Dekker ridicules this attitude, his satire, and the medical language used, demonstrates the existence of the very target he satirizes.

Finally, let us turn to Robert Dallington's *Method for Trauell*, published with his *Viewe of Fraunce*, and the means by which Dallington's tourist is instructed to ward off the pollutants encountered abroad. From the outset, Dallington's *Methode* is offered as a wholesome foodstuff, a dietary supplement to help guard against foreignness. The analogy is drawn from humoral theory, as Dallington laments the 'multiplicitie' of foreign books, that 'weaken' 'our vnderstandings ... with unseasonal commodities, (like stomacks with raw fruites) that we are not able to digest them into any good blood either of knowledge or virtue' (sig. A2r). In contrast to this continental diet of fruit, Dallington provides a dish that is 'true English bred, though an alian borne'. Within the subsequent treatise, the author draws attention to the dangers of travel, and in particular, the dissolution of identity necessarily incurred by journeying abroad, as the tourist is required to lose a sense both of self and nation: 'He ... that intends to *Trauell* out of his own country, must likewise resolue to Trauell out of their country fashion, and indeed out of himselfe,' Dallington notes (sig. B1r). In particular, the traveller is advised to guard against losing his religion, since 'it is to be feared, that he which is of one religion in his youth, and of another in his manhod, will in his age be neither' (sig. B1v). It is the state of flux that is regarded as dangerous, leading as it does to atheism, which is in effect a dangerous non-identity in an age of increasing confessionalization, when national identity was being drawn ever more strongly along doctrinal lines. The description of Rome, meanwhile, as 'the seminarie and Nurserie of English fugitives (& yet a place most worthie to be seene)' (sig. B2r), both recognizes the dangerous allure of Rome (and its dual identity, as a source of intellectual inspiration and moral corruption) and exposes the potential corruption of the experience abroad. The choice of diction – 'seminarie' and 'Nurserie' – taps into horticultural vocabulary, transforming Rome into a hot-house, perverting English allegiances, a warped version of nature reflected in the metaphors of familial alienation that pepper the Protestant-fuelled diatribes of Wilson's *Art of Rhetorique* against those ambiguously gendered 'pouder[ed]' talkers that 'seeke so far for outlandish English, that they forget altogether their mothers language', so that, 'if some of their mothers were aliue, thei were not able to tell what they say' (fol. 86r).

To guard against the disintegration of identity and loss of faith, Dallington's reader is advised to follow a strict regimen of exercise for both the mind and body, fending off ill thoughts as you would ill health through watchfulness and the careful intake of well-regulated nutrition. The *Method for Trauell* consequently includes a chart setting out a programme of mainly mental activity. Throughout the period abroad, the reader is enjoined to keep his mind occupied with two activities, 'preservation' and 'observation', pursuing the latter by scrupulously taking notes in order, at the end of the journey, to compile topographies of the countries traversed, and Dallington's *View of Fraunce* which accompanies the *Methode* is here offered as an example of the type of work he recommends, and the sort of chorographical and constitutional material the reader is encouraged to record. 'Preservation', meanwhile, breaks down into the two main categories of 'minde' and 'bodie', with the traveller urged to protect the latter through diet and exercise; and the former through 'keeping his religion' and 'bettering his knowledge'. Sloth, in other words, is the gateway to disease and foreignness and must be kept at bay with judicious activity.

In contrast, experiences that threaten to weaken the integrity of body and mind are to be shunned: tennis 'if vsed with too much violence' (sig. B4v) and conversations with Jesuits pose particular risks here. The body abroad is presented as being in a continual state of siege, subject to physical attack. Infection is as much a mental as a corporeal phenomenon, early modern meanings of the verb *infect* encompassing both 'to affect with disease' and 'to imbue with an opinion or belief, esp. a pernicious one' (*OED*, *infect*, vb, 4, 7). As the Jesuits feature as 'inueiglers of greene wits', deploying the 'smooth incantations of an insinuating seducer' (sig. B2r), the vocabulary chosen relates closely to the body: 'inveigle' is drawn from the Old French *avegle*, 'to blind'; 'insinuate' had, by 1598, already acquired a sense of penetration (*OED*, *s.v. insinuate*, vb, 1 b). Dallington therefore recommends sealing off the body, cutting down on contact with potentially corrupting others, the tongue 'tyed' and the 'eares' 'stop[ped]', and discouraging the tourist from 'shew[ing] his mind or money' or from 'hear[ing] anything repugnant to his religion'.

Preaching this message of self-containment, Dallington's advice is here very much in tune with that prescribed by Ascham in his *Scholemaster*, where those who wish to journey abroad are pressed to follow the example of Ulysses, that wise and witty traveller. According to Ascham, the Ithacan king was 'not ... commended so much, nor so oft in Homer, because he was ... "skilful in many men's manners and fashions;" as because he was ... "wise in all purposes, and wary in all places"' (p. 150). Unlike the sixteenth-century Englishman, that is, he was not tempted to ape the fashions and ideas encountered on his travels. As Ulysses enables his men to resist the Sirens by blocking their ears with wax, and parries Circe's enchantments with the sour–sweet herb *moly* (glossed by Ascham as 'the study of virtue, hard and irksome in the beginning, but in the end easy and pleasant'), the Greek hero becomes emblematic of the body abroad, hermetically sealed and in continual meditation on safe and wholesome topics.[15] In recommending keeping a journal of travel, Dallington thus ensures his reader fills his mind with diligent thoughts, proof against foreign infection. Communing with the text of the diary, the traveller is also locked off from foreign interaction, and it is notable that Sir Politic Wouldbe's comedown in Jonson's *Volpone* (1605) is not only caused by the fact that he is a manic and inept note-taker of the most trivial of his experiences abroad (parodying the exact type of activity suggested

---

15 Ascham's version, in which Ulysess 'stop[s] his ears with wax' (*Scholemaster*, p. 151), conflates Ulysses with his men; the legend usually relates that Ulysses did not block his ears, but lashed himself to the mast so that he could hear the Siren song in safety, without throwing himself overboard.

by Dallington), but that he also elicits the help of others in the pursuit of knowledge, and fails to remain self-contained.[16]

To conclude, when describing and discussing Bodin's 'affairs of men', Tudor writers used two separate, but connected, discourses, both inherited from ancient Greece: the one, the vocabulary of political theory, of the state as body; the other, the language of medicine, as practised by Galen and Hippocrates. Both provided them with analytical tools: the means of unravelling and explaining historical cause and effect, of communicating the wheres, the hows and the whys. Furthermore, both provided them with rhetorical resources, enabling the emotive impact of depicting the bowels and members of the common weal, or polemical portrayals of hot-blooded and bilious foreigners. Tudor writers used topography to enforce the political advice they hoped to distribute through their histories. More subtly, though, we can also see a blurring between the use of landscape as an explanation for behaviour, and as a metaphor for it.

Primary texts quoted

Aggas, Edward, trans. François De la Noue, *Politicke and Militarie Discourses* (1587). *STC* 15215.

Ascham, Roger, *The Scholemaster* (1570), ed. J.A. Giles, *The Works of Roger Ascham* (London: John Russell Smith, 1864), III.

Borde, Andrew, *A Compendyous Regyment or A Dyetary of Helth* (1542), in *The fyrst boke of the introduction of knowledge made by Andrew Borde* ..., ed. F.J. Furnivall (London: N.T. Trübner [Early English Text Society], 1870).

Borde, Andrew, *The Fyrst Boke of the Introduction to Knowledge* (1547), in *The fyrst boke*, ed. Furnivall (as above).

Bodin, Jean, *Method for the Easy Comprehension of History*, ed. and trans. Beatrice Reynolds (New York: Octagon Books, 1966).

Dallington, Robert, *A Methode for Trauell, shewed by taking the viewe of Fraunce* (1604). *STC* 6203.

Dekker, Thomas, *Patient Grissil* (1603), in *The Dramatic Works of Thomas Dekker*, ed. Fredson Bowers (Cambridge: Cambridge University Press, 1953–61), I.

Leland, John, *Genethliacos illustrissimi Eaduerdo Principis Cambriae, Ducis Coriniae, et Comitis Palatini* (1543). *STC* 15443.

Lyly, John, *Euphues and his England*, in *The Complete Works of John Lyly*, ed. R. Warwick Bond (Oxford: Clarendon Press, 1902), II.

---

16 Jonson further subverts the stereotype of the Englishman abroad by having Sir Pol brought down by a fellow Englishman (Peregrine), not – as might be expected – by an Italian.

Marvell, Andrew, *Poems and Letters*, ed. H. M. Margoliouth and Pierre Legouis (Oxford: Clarendon Press).

More, Thomas, *Utopia* (1516), ed. and trans. George M. Logan and Robert M. Adams (Cambridge: Cambridge University Press, 1989).

Shakespeare, William, *Richard II*, in *The Norton Shakespeare*, ed. Stephen Greenblatt, Walter Cohen, Jean E. Howard and Katharine Eisamann Maus (New York: W.W. Norton, 1997).

Sneyd, Charlotte Augusta. ed. and trans., *A Relation or Rather a True Account of the Island of England ... about the Year 1500* (London: John Bowyer Nichols and Son, 1847).

Spenser, Edmund, *A View of the State of Ireland*, ed. Andrew Hadfield and Willy Maley (Oxford: Blackwell, 1997).

Thomas, William, *The Historie of Italie* (1549). *STC* 24018.

Venner, Tobias, *Via recta ad vitam longam* (1628). *STC* 24645.

Wilson, Thomas, *The Arte of Rhetorique* (1553). *STC* 25799.

Chapter 4

Representing Rome and the self in Anthony Munday's *The English Roman Life*

Melanie Ord

Anthony Munday's *The English Roman Life* (1582) recounts Munday's infiltration of the English College at Rome in 1579 and identifies foreign seminaries with subversive activities. It is a work which is not only anti-Catholic, but also self-defensive, for in residing in the English College, in participating in Roman educational and religious practices, and in lending ear to treasonous speeches against Queen Elizabeth and the Privy Council, Munday himself occupies an uneasy position between fidelity to Protestant England and vulnerability to the seductions of Catholic Rome. This essay looks both at Munday's representation of Catholics, and at his strategies of self-representation within a Catholic milieu. The first section rehearses various social and literary contexts of *The English Roman Life*, and considers ways in which government attempts to identify the activities of Jesuits with subversive practices impact upon Munday's own self-presentation. It is principally concerned to trace conflicts in *The English Roman Life* between Munday's narrative strategy of authorizing his account by a first-hand engagement in the scenes he witnesses, and his polemical purpose of exposing the subversive activities of Jesuits and English scholars at Rome. The second section provides a close textual analysis of the tensions demonstrated by Munday as an English Protestant traveller to Rome. It analyses Munday's self-conscious representations of the reasons motivating his travel to, and residence in, what the Protestant divine Joseph Hall in *Quo vadis?* (1617) calls 'the very pommell of the chaire of pestilence' that is Italy (p. 94). It explores his distinction between secular and religious travel as a means of discriminating between loyal (or Protestant) and disloyal (or Catholic) English subjects. It examines Munday's related insistence that he has successfully resisted the challenge presented by Rome to his Anglo-Protestant identity (which reads as an implicit standard against which to judge those whose residence in Italy results in a loss of religious allegiance to England). And it ends with his attempts to challenge Catholic depictions of the holy influence and uninterrupted genealogy of Rome.

I

In *The English Roman Life* Munday is predominantly concerned to indict 'unnatural' Englishmen who steal from England to take up residence under the pope's jurisdiction, where they nourish treasonous thoughts against their own country before returning home to subvert the queen's subjects.[1] He can therefore be said to align his account of his experiences at Rome with government apologies, state proclamations, and controversial works of the early 1580s, which express two distinct, but related, concerns. The first consists of anxieties surrounding not only travel to, but also return from, Rome, a city possessing threatening associations in this period as the symbolic centre of Catholic resistance. 'You have visited that Romish Babylo[n]', Meredith Hanmer writes in his *Great Bragge and Challenge of M. Champion* (1581) of the renowned Jesuit missionary, Edmund Campion, 'that great city which beareth rule over the kings of the earth', and in so doing 'yee have found ... a platforme for government which you thinke expedient to bee established in this Realme in matters Civill and Temporal' (fols 12r and 18r).[2] The second theme is a concern to associate foreign seminaries with subversive, and potentially treasonable, activities. England, Munday warns in *The English Roman Life*, will be vulnerable to invasion when the people are 'secretly persuaded, as I doubt not but there is a good number, and more and more still shall be, by the priests are sent over daily, and they must war within, while others hold them play without' (p. 19). A marginal note to this sentence reads: 'The Pope seeketh to accomplish his desire by the subject that must betray his own country.' Such comments recall government depictions of foreign seminaries as institutions set, in the words of William Cecil's *Execution of Justice in England* (1583), to 'nourish and bring up persons disposed naturally to sedition, to continue their race and trade and to become seedmen in their tillage of sedition' (p. 6), places which provide a subversive alternative education to a reformed grammar-school practice. Compelled to return to England to convert its inhabitants, to spy on English affairs for the benefit of Spain, and to support a Spanish claim to the throne, seminarians weaken subjects' allegiance to Queen Elizabeth by reconciling them

1 Catholic apologists, of course, maintained that Catholics were 'banished' from their native country by vigorous penal statutes, the fear of imprisonment, the requirement to attend Protestant church services, and the necessity of forcing their consciences by taking the Oath of Allegiance, which required the subject to renounce all foreign jurisdictions.

2 From 1579, the students of the English College at Rome were required to swear an oath promising to return to England on a proselytizing mission. Edmund Campion, a former student and fellow of St John's College, Oxford, who defected to Rome and returned with Robert Parsons on the first English Mission, departed for England on 18 April 1580, arrived at Dover on 24 June 1580, and was captured at Lyford Grange in Berkshire on 16 July 1581.

to the authority of the pope, 'a foreign potentate and open enemy' (p. 37).[3] They thus 'bring the realm not only into a dangerous war against the forces of strangers ..., but into a war domestical and civil, wherein ... neither the vanqueror nor the vanquished [can] have [just] cause of triumph' (p. 9), a challenge indeed to the kind of clear-cut religious and national distinctions available in Protestant polemic. Returning English Catholics, corrupted by exposure to religious and political relativity, and equipped with a superior Jesuit education, were set to undermine their native country and take it over 'from within'.

In reporting treasonable speeches against Queen Elizabeth and the Privy Council, in commenting on the channels of Jesuit communication, and in mentioning preparations for the first English Mission, *The English Roman Life* recalls the kind of information contained in intelligentiary reports to Sir William Cecil and Sir Francis Walsingham on the activities of English Catholics abroad.[4] Yet it fails to supply specific details enabling the government to monitor the arrival of Jesuits and seminary priests in England. There is no estimate of the numbers of English papists at Rome, no physical descriptions of those intending to return to England, and only the slightest information regarding the identity of those affording them hospitality, albeit delivered in cipher, in a possible attempt to approximate to the format of government reports. Catholic priests, for example, reside 'in Warwickshire, at Master I.T. in Staffordshire, at Master G. of C. and at S.T.F. in the same shire' and one might hear mass at 'Master S. his house on the backside of P.' (p. 31). Such abbreviations witness Munday's attempt to negotiate between information pertinent to two discrete audiences: the Privy Council (to whom the work is dedicated), with its inside knowledge of those to whom Munday refers, and a public audience presumably unable to decipher the code, but impressed by the appearance of confidential material. This relative lack of specific political details points to *The English Roman Life* as a popularized version of the kind of information contained in government reports. On his travels, Munday poses as the son of an English Catholic gentleman 'whom I refuse here to name' (p. 20); he 'omit[s] for divers causes' (p. 15) the names of Englishmen at Rome prepared to support the pope in an armed invasion of England; and he describes a letter from the English priest Master Woodward at Amiens to William Allen at Rheims, as containing 'things which I am not to speak of here, because they are not to be read of everyone' (p. 11).

The English Roman Life, then, reveals Munday's attempt to recommend

---

3 All of the seminaries were established in countries under Spanish rule: the College at Rome was governed by the pope and the Jesuits, and those at Rheims and Douai in Spanish Flanders were under the protection of the Duke of Guise, and Philip I, respectively. (The seminary at Douai, which was founded by William Allen in 1568, moved to Rheims in 1578 and returned to Douai in 1593.)

4 Many such reports can be easily accessed in the *Calendar of State Papers, Domestic Series, of the Reigns of Edward VI, Mary, Elizabeth*, ed. Robert Lemon and Mary Anne Everett Green (London: Longmans, 1856–71).

himself to the government by demonstrating editorial, personal and polemical skills in documents participating in official anxiety over Counter-Reformation Catholicism. It also reveals his effort to exploit a profitable literary market for his anti-Catholic material. The title-page to the 1582 edition attempts to whet the reader's appetite by its eclectic range of contents: a voyeuristic description of the manner in which Englishmen live at Rome; a controversial account of the 'dissention betweene the Englishmen and the Welshmen [with] the banishing of the Englishmen out of Roome [and] the Popes sending for them againe'; a condemnation of the 'paltrie Reliques' of Rome; and 'a number other matters, worthy to be read and regarded of every one', an inclusivity which stands in marked contrast to Munday's obtrusive editorial policy elsewhere in the text of vetting that material '*not* to be read of everyone' (my emphasis). The mixture in *The English Roman Life* of the esoteric and the popular negotiates, as does Munday's coded information, between discrete audiences, which include prominent government figures to whom the work is dedicated, and an implicitly Protestant public who yet retain an interest in Catholic ritual.

Munday's frequent practice of cutting short his rehearsal of treasonous speeches with the comment that there was more matter 'not here to be rehearsed' (p. 19) is a rhetorical strategy to increase the impression of Roman corruption, and to strengthen the sense of Munday's possession of politically sensitive information. It also, however, reflects his precarious position as a Protestant reporting Catholic slanders against Queen Elizabeth and the Privy Council. Whilst to quote fully such outrageous insults threatens to compromise the impression of his own loyalty to the state, to omit such speeches altogether would make him unable to authorize this work's principal claim that English Catholics at Rome freely engage in seditious and potentially treasonable speeches against queen and country.

Munday signals his aptitude for state service by demonstrating not only his capacity for compiling authoritative reports (and for controlling and censoring the printed dissemination of his 'evidence'), but also his facility for the role-playing talents required of the spy. Mistaken at Paris for the recalcitrant son of an English Catholic gentleman, Munday adopts and successfully maintains this persona at Rome, in an act of improvisation which recalls objections in anti-travel writings of the period to the uncertain issue of 'experience'. Munday's attempt to maintain this identity while conversing with a priest at the College acquainted with the family to which he pretends to belong, although implausible, is a strategy which allows him to testify to the extent to which he inspired confidences of a treasonable nature by conduct indistinguishable from that of the College's Catholic residents. It also provides a source of dramatic interest, for it introduces the possibility of discovery, challenges his skill in improvisation, and exploits a gap in awareness between the Catholic priest and the implicitly Protestant reader. As the English College staff have a duty to reclaim Munday for the Church, and as this priest in particular is 'glad to see me at Rome, and well hoping in short time to make me a new man' (p. 33), Munday's adoption of this disguise points towards the threat of conversion represented by Catholic Italy, while also supporting a claim for God's providential care for him as an English Protestant.

Munday's disguise as the disobedient son of an English Catholic presents an interesting inversion of Protestant representations of Jesuits as men who cloak seditious purposes under professions of religious sanctity. Yet Munday's persona as a Catholic youth given to 'many delightful pastimes' (p. 31) is strangely analogous to Munday's account of his own seduction by the secular attractions of Europe. Munday had helped to create his own narrative persona as one who had 'always addicted my mind to so many youthful devices' (p. 24) by beginning *The English Roman Life* with the kind of prodigal motif popularized by such works of imaginative fiction as John Lyly's *Euphues: The Anatomy of Wit* (1578) and *Euphues and his England* (1580). Munday accompanies his description of his journey from Boulogne to Amiens (where he was robbed by a disbanded group of soldiers) with a reflection on 'our former quiet being in England, carefully tended by our parents and lovingly esteemed among our friends, all which we undutifully regarding, rewarded us with the rod of our own negligence' (p. 7). Perhaps Munday's attempt to recall in his own addiction to 'youthful devices' the filial ingratitude of those defecting to Rome is a strategy to signal his aptitude for employment by a government that used prodigal Englishmen (in the shape of former Catholics) to discover Jesuit plots against England. Thomas Christopher (alias Dingley), for example, requests William Cecil, Lord Burghley's 'pardon for the errors of young men led amiss by the wrong counsel of others' and 'promises as amends to give up some of the parties' presently engaged in attempts against England.[5] Munday's acknowledged complicity in certain non-specific Catholic practices, the lack of a satisfactory explanation of the reasons motivating his trip, and the absence of certain defining aspects such as the length of his stay in Rome and his involvement in the religious aspects of college life, lead one to think that he may have encouraged a certain degree of speculation about his religious identity in the hope of capitalizing upon the governmental use of Catholics and former Catholics in discovering Jesuit plots against England.

Munday's adoption of a fashionable literary motif of prodigality in *The English Roman Life* does, however, sit uneasily with the warnings developed in other of his pamphlets against Jesuit attempts to encourage young Englishmen to travel without parental authorization. In his *Discoverie of Edmund Campion* (1582), for example, Munday had advertised how 'perswaders' in England offer young gentlemen keen to travel 'such sufficiencie of money, as shall bring him to their Seminarie at Rheimes, beside Letters for his entertainement there, shall be given him' (sig. C2v), a comment which recalls Munday's own dependence

5 See the entry for 24 August 1592 in *CSPD, 1591–1594*, no. 116.

upon Catholic hospitality while travelling in Europe. This characterization reads as a subversive equivalent to letters of advice to sons preparing to travel to Italy, which prescribe a plan of study for the young traveller as an inoculation against a possible attraction to Catholicism. Indeed, this kind of characterization seems also to have helped influence anti-travel pronouncements such as those by Joseph Hall, who objects that sending abroad 'our sonnes to learne to be chaste in the midst of *Sodome*' puts us in league with 'factors of *Rome*, whose trade is the transporting and placing of our popish novices beyond the seas' (*Quo Vadis?*, p. 12).

Munday was present at the College at a time of escalating racial tension between the English scholars and their Welsh rector, Maurice Clenocke (whom Munday calls Doctor Morris), a situation which occasions a further instance of Munday's conflicted self-presentation in *The English Roman Life*.[6] Although Munday describes Jesuits as sowers of sedition, in siding with the scholars against Clenocke (who had conceived a strong dislike for Munday), Munday is led to support demands for Jesuit rule. Indeed, by fomenting the dissension, Munday involved himself in the attempt to facilitate the transfer of the government of the English College from Clenocke to the Jesuits. Jesuits 'labour for the profit of our studies' (p. 85), Munday writes, in a comment which acknowledges the high reputation of Jesuit discipline; they promise to show impartiality 'being none of our nation or country' (p. 85); and it was only through their entreaty that Clenocke had allowed Munday to continue at the College beyond the standard eight-day period of hospitality.[7]

As the resolution of this intra-college dispute guarantees Munday's admission to the seminary, the emphasis placed on this incident in *The English Roman Life* is a possible attempt to validate the claim made in the title-page that Munday was 'sometime the Popes Scholler in the Seminarie among them [the English scholars]'.[8] Whilst referring specifically to Munday's position in the English College at Rome, this resonant phrase also suggests his participation in a Jesuit education on a pan-European scale, which included bases at Rheims, Douai and

---

6 For an account of the genesis of this quarrel, see Anthony Kenny, 'From Hospice to College 1559–1579', in *The English Hospice in Rome* (Exeter: Catholic Records Press, 1962), pp. 218–73.

7 See Richard Haddock's letter of 9 March 1579 to William Allen, printed as Appendix One to Ayres's edition of *The English Roman Life*, for the care taken by the Jesuits for the scholars at the time of the dissension in the English College.

8 Although Robert Parsons notes in a letter to William Goode, printed as Appendix Two to Ayres's edition of *The English Roman Life*, that Munday and Nowell 'by no means could be admitted into the seminary, but had their answer from the cardinal twice to depart again' (p. 108), Anthony Kenny authenticates Munday's claim to have been registered among the students of the English College by identifying him as the 'Antonius Auleus' listed in the papers of Cardinal Morone, Protector of England ('Antony Munday in Rome', *Recusant History* VI [1961–62], pp. 158–62).

Valladolid; certainly, Munday's account in chapter one of *The English Roman Life* of receiving letters recommending him to Doctor Allen at Rheims seems designed to increase the impression of his knowledge of a broad-based Jesuit educational movement. Only by convincing the reader that his name was registered in the Table of Scholars, and that he 'observ[ed] all orders that the Schollers dyd, bothe in going to the Schooles, in walking for our recreation, & all other thinges', can Munday authorize his exposé of the activities of English Catholics at the College in his 1582 *Breefe Aunswer* (sig. D4v), a refutation of two recently published defences of Edmund Campion.

The English Roman Life was written not only to 'content those desirous how I attained to Rome' (p. 21), but also to satisfy those 'doubtful whether I have been there or no, albeit the proofs thereof sufficiently are extant to be seen' (p. 5). Munday's concern with the printed dissemination of his 'evidence' (his care to 'note down nothing ... that might impeach me either with error or untruth, malice or affection to any' [p. 1]), might be read not only as an attempt to distinguish *The English Roman Life* from the false narratives of Catholic Europe, but also as a response to contemporary accusations that his anti-Jesuit writings lack veracity and credibility. George Elyot's *A Very True Report of the Apprehension and Taking of that Arche Papist Edmond Campion* (1581), for example, described Munday's account of Campion's arrest in *A Breefe Discourse of the Taking of Edmund Campion* (1581) as an over-hasty, and hence inaccurate, version of Campion's capture, which reflects Munday's commitment to commercial imperatives rather than to the truth.[9]

Munday's attempts to defend his Protestant integrity from hostile reports may also be read as an implicit challenge to Edmund Campion and his associates' attempt to indict him as an unsatisfactory witness at their trial in 1581, on the basis that 'beyond the seas he goeth on pilgrimage, and receiveth the sacrament, making himself a Catholic, and here he taketh a new face, and playeth the Protestant'.[10] Munday defends himself from this charge of 'atheis[m]' by claiming that, while abroad, he was a true Protestant who only '*seemed* to favour their religion, because he might thereby undermine them and sift out their purposes' (my emphasis) – a justification which differs from his insistence in *The English Roman Life* that he travelled to Rome simply for pleasure. This instance points to the vulnerability of the traveller and informer to charges of complicity in the scenes he witnesses and describes. Although we do not know for certain Munday's motives for travel, Celeste Turner, Munday's biographer, supports Campion's charge of religious inconstancy by describing him as travelling to

9 The title-page to George Elyot's *Apprehension and Taking of that Arche Papist Edmond Campion* (1581) advertises Elyot as the 'chiefest cause of the finding of the sayd lewde and seditious people'.

10 Cit. Richard Simpson, *Edmund Campion: A Biography* (London: John Hodges, 1896), p. 430.

Rome 'as a convert, not a spy'.[11] Only when the activities in England of his former colleagues at the English College 'revived an old uneasiness' at the 'awe experienced before their altars, in the smoke of their incense, in the partaking of their wafers', did Munday invent the theory that he travelled to Rome to 'undermine them [the English scholars at Rome] and sift out their purposes'.[12] (More recently, Tracey Hill's useful materialist analysis of Munday describes him as one given to 'switching sides and betraying sometime associates', a comment which may also be taken to suggest that Munday resided in the English College at Rome as a Catholic, rather than as a Protestant who adopted a Catholic guise in order to acquire politically valuable information, or as a means to obtain material for a possible future publication.[13]) Turner's account, which lends weight to Campion's charge that Munday freely changed religious affiliation according to location, leads us to a consideration of Munday's attempts to defend his Protestant integrity from the implications attending his acknowledged complicity in Catholic practices at Rome.

II

In answer to those who seek to damage his reputation by insisting on his complicity in the scenes he reports, Munday claims that it is the condition of travel which necessitates outward conformity to Catholic practices:

> And because my adversaries object against me, that I went to mass, and helped the priest myself to say mass: so that (say they) who is worst, I am as evil as he. I answer, I did so indeed, for he that is in Rome, especially in the College among the scholars, must live as he may, not as he will; favour comes by conformity, and death by obstinancy.
>
> (p. 66)

Fynes Moryson, an English Protestant traveller to Rome in 1594, refers to a barely less compromising position when he writes in his *Itinerary* (1617) that he 'must either seeme to consent [to mass] by silence, or maintaine arguments ful of danger in that place' (I, p. 260). Munday further justifies his participation in Catholic practices by asserting that, although 'rash heads being in England would do many goodly matters at Rome', such as accusing the pope and cardinals of immorality and exposing as counterfeit the tenets of the Catholic faith, 'if they

---

11 Celeste Turner Wright, 'Young Anthony Mundy Again', *Studies in Philology* LVI (1959), pp. 150–68, at 155.

12 Celeste Turner, *Anthony Mundy, An Elizabethan Man of Letters* (Berkeley, CA: University of California Press; London: Cambridge University Press, 1928), p. 52.

13 Tracey E. Hill, '"By All Privy Means": History, Power and Representation, the Case of Anthony Munday, 1581–93' (unpublished doctoral dissertation, University of Essex, 1995), p. 22.

were at Rome, and beheld the merciless tyranny executed on the members of Christ, … they would be as ready to do anything for the safeguard of their lives as I was' (pp. 66–7). Munday insists that to apply to his behaviour in the midst of the college critical standards formulated and maintained in England is to show (at worst) hypocrisy, or (at best) naivety, to the compromises involved in travel.

Munday justifies his participation in Catholic practices not only by referring to the threat of religious persecution, but also by insisting that, as an impecunious traveller, he is dependent upon Catholic hospitality while abroad. This is an aspect of his self-presentation with rather troubling implications for his expressed allegiances. The prospect of being 'entertained to our high contentment' (p. 15) at the English College leads him to proceed to Rome on the suggestion of factors for the pope, in flagrant disregard of the advice of the English ambassador to Paris to return instead to England. His willingness to deliver letters to Owen Lewis and Maurice Clenocke, in order to gain assistance 'toward the bearing of our charges' (p. 16) towards Rome, sees him facilitating a potentially treasonable Jesuit correspondence. And his repeated acknowledgement of Catholic generosity aligns him with Catholic attempts to claim hospitality as a central defining feature of Rome, in order to recall 'reuoulted children' to the Mother Church.[14]

Munday is more interested in the treasonable implications of residence *in* Rome than in travel *to* or *from* it. Yet the first chapter of *The English Roman Life* is of strategic importance in describing how he journeys to Rome via Amiens, Paris, Lyon, Milan, Bologna, Florence and Siena, discovering *en route* a 'general agreement of treason' (p. 21) against Queen Elizabeth and her government.[15] Through the cumulative effect of reporting those treasonable speeches discovered at every stop on his journey towards Rome, Munday dramatically heightens the image of Rome as the centre of European vice and intrigue, the place 'from whence … treason should chiefly proceed' (p. 21). Witnessing 'such devilish devices to be talked on by the way, we might well judge Rome to be Hell itself, in that all things should go forward as it was there determined' (p. 21). To imagine an increased exposure to treasonable enterprises the nearer one approaches to Rome is of course to reverse Catholic depictions of the holy influence exerted by this city. In Gregory Martin's *Roma Sancta* (1581), for example, religious truth spreads 'from the very head … through out the whole body of the world' as Jesuits venture forth from Rome 'for the reclayming of infected countries' (p. 172).

---

14 The quotation is from *A Discoverie of J. Nicols Minister, Misreported a Jesuite, Latelye Recanted in the Tower of London* (1581), sig. A2v.

15 John Bossy, 'Rome and the Elizabethan Catholics: A Question of Geography', *Historical Journal* VII (1964), pp. 135–42, provides a historical and geographical account of the routes by which students travelled to the Continent, and priests returned on the English missions.

Chapter one of *The English Roman Life* also allows Munday to precede his account of Rome with a structurally significant description of the reasons dissuading travel to the seminary at Rheims. Although provided at Amiens with a letter of recommendation to William Allen at Rheims, Munday recalls the 'true and undoubted religion used in our own country' and entreats his wavering travelling companion, Thomas Nowell, to travel instead to Paris, endeavouring to 'try all means that might be ere I would forsake my faith' (p. 13). Yet, at Paris, Munday and Nowell were persuaded by factors for the pope to proceed to Rome, and supplied with letters 'that we might there be preferred among the English students' (p. 16). Whilst in the dedication to an earlier pamphlet entitled *The Mirrour of Mutabilitie* (1579) Munday had expressed anxiety about travel to *Rome*, in *The English Roman Life* this becomes an anxiety about travel to *Rheims*. If Munday dissuades Nowell from travel to Rheims because entrance to the seminary there represents a 'yielding' (p. 13) to Catholic doctrine, why does not travel to Rome also represent a forsaking of the faith? Munday's wish to deflect attention from the moral and religious compromises involved in travel to Rome by attributing such compromises to Rheims is a possible attempt to defend his Protestant identity from the implications involved in the attempt to authorize his narrative by an intimate acquaintance with specifically Roman forms of corruption.

Munday defends himself against possible challenges to his own motivations as a Protestant traveller to Rome by using his travelling companion, Thomas Nowell, as an irresolute foil to his own response to Italy. Aware perhaps of the possible objection that by participating in conversations with the scholars at the English College, he gave Catholics abroad as much information of events in England as he gave the Privy Council of Catholic activity in Europe, Munday distracts the reader from considering his own participation in such conversations by establishing Nowell as one deep in Catholic confidence.[16] When encouraged to visit the vault of St Priscilla by the joint praise of Nowell and the Jesuits, Munday again shifts attention away from his own complicity in Catholic ritual by claiming that Nowell 'was even all one with them, his company was required of everyone, and he as lewd in speeches against his country as the best: so that I was esteemed I cannot tell how' (p. 65). Munday notes how difficult it is to gain intelligence of the speeches that passed between Nowell and the Jesuits, 'for either they had fully persuaded him, or he joined into consent with them, so that he would never report anything that had passed between them, he liked so well

16 Philip Ayres, in the introduction to his edition of Munday's *The English Roman Life*, notes that 'in 1583 Nowell was dismissed from the College as unsuitable for the priesthood and that he subsequently became a spy against Catholics in England .... By a cruel irony, his "Catholicism" was to be perpetuated in the 1590 edition, in which not one of Munday's aspersions on the unfortunate Nowell's religious inclinations was deleted' (p. xv).

of everything' (p. 35). This ambiguous statement expresses Munday's unwillingness fully to acknowledge his own vulnerability to Jesuit proselytizing. The conceit that because Nowell 'liked so well of everything' he refused to report his conversations with the other members of the college supports the equation Munday frequently makes in *The English Roman Life* between fidelity to the truth and the maintenance of a critical distance from the scenes he describes. Whilst *Munday's* disguise tokens a split between his outward conformity to, and inner dissent from, his Catholic hosts, and advertises his loyalty to England by facilitating his discovery of treasonous enterprises, *Nowell's* disguise is made to signify his new-found conformity to Catholicism.

Munday concludes *The English Roman Life* with a brief description, and an accompanying wood-block illustration, of 'the Christian suffering and merciless maryrdom [*sic*]' of Richard Atkins (p. 100), an English Protestant who travelled to Rome openly to rebuke Catholic idolatry.[17] This illustration shows four episodes in Atkins's career in Rome: (1) upsetting the sacrament; (2) disturbing a mass at St Peter's; (3) riding to execution; and (4) being burned at the stake. Munday's account of the bravery shown by Atkins at his death is placed in self-conscious opposition to Munday's description in chapter five of *The English Roman Life* of the cowardly manner of Edmund Campion, Luke Kirby and others at their execution ('as the eyewitnesses can bear me record' [p. 68]) and is intended to recall Munday's own *Discoverie of Edmund Campion* and his *Breefe and True Reporte, of the Execution of Certaine Traytors at Tiborne* (1582). Despite the prominence given to this dramatic episode in the title-page to *The English Roman Life*, the account of Atkins's execution occupies a marginal position in the text, for Munday is concerned to structure his own apparent conformity to Catholic practices in implicit opposition to the strategy adopted by Atkins in his travels to Rome. This is an aspect of Munday's self-presentation which signals to the reader that, although Atkins is the right kind of Protestant *martyr*, he is the wrong kind of Protestant *traveller*. Fynes Moryson's experience of the necessity of maintaining an outward conformity to Catholic practices while travelling in Italy leads him specifically to advise those to 'stay at home who are so zealous, as they will pull the Hostia or Sacrament out of the Priests hand' (III, p. 415). Thomas Coryat's later attempts, described in *Coryats Crudities* (1611), to convert to Christianity a Jewish rabbi in the heart of the Venetian ghetto in 1608 by 'sharpely tax[ing] their superstitious ceremonies' (I, p. 375) points up the wisdom of such advice, for Coryat's procedure quickly descends into a potentially life-threatening situation from which he is rescued on the command of Sir Henry Wotton, English ambassador to Venice, who witnessed the scene

---

17 A Catholic version of the execution was published as *The Copie of a Double Letter Sent by an Englishe Gentilman from beyond the seas, to his frende in London, Containing the True Advises of the Cause, and Maner of the Death, of one Richard Atkins* (1581?).

from a passing gondola. Munday, in contrast, sees himself as one equal to the task, if not of rhetorical (even theatrical) disputation with Jesuits, then to resisting and exposing Catholic practices whilst testifying to the superiority of the Protestant faith.

Catholic claims, such as that made by William Allen in *An Apologie and True Declaration of the Institution and Endevours of the Two English Colleges* (1581), that many travellers 'intending not precisely any matter of religio[n], have yet by Gods careful providence, that over-reacheth mans purposes to his salvation, been happily by them [the English Colleges] converted to Christian faith and life' (fol. 25r) legitimize Munday's depiction of Nowell as one Catholicized through travel to Europe. Many Englishmen at the colleges at Rome and Douai, Allen says, began their travels 'either wholy doubtful, or plaine Protestants' (fol. 69v). Even Robert Parsons travelled to Italy with the intention of studying medicine at Padua, and claimed to have first visited Rome 'more to see the profane monuments of Caesar, Cicero and other such like, than ... places of devotion', a comment which exploits an opposition available to the period between Italy as the home of humanist retrieval and Italy as the home of the papacy.[18] A possible awareness of this potential slippage between travel and Catholic conformity leads Munday to confirm his Protestant identity by repeatedly distinguishing Protestant and Catholic motives for travel to Europe. The priest at the English College who first engages Munday in conversation regards the proper purpose of travel as pilgrimage, noting that 'there ought none to come hither, the place being so holy, ancient, and famous, but only such as with earnest endeavour seek and thirst after the Catholic faith': an attempt to claim Rome squarely for Roman Catholics. Munday, however, describes his visit to Rome as a kind of mock- or anti-pilgrimage, undertaken 'only for the desire I had to see it, that when I came home again, I might say, once in my life I have been at Rome' (*English Roman Life*, p. 24). Such attempts by Munday to assert a fundamental opposition in Protestant and Catholic motivations for travel, point to his concern to maintain a clear ideological distance from the 'other' residents at the English College, even at the expense of representing his trip as a pleasure-seeking, rather than intelligence-gathering, exercise. Indeed, Munday is able to assert his national and religious loyalties in this context only by confounding those prescriptions for 'profitable', as opposed to 'pleasurable', forms of travel expounded by moralists such as Roger Ascham and Joseph Hall.

William Allen indicts such secular motives for travel by attributing slanders against Rome to 'unhonest Pilgrimes' (*Apologie*, fol. 98v). Like the priest at the English College who describes Munday as one 'come more upon pleasure than any devotion, more desirous to see the city than to learn the virtues contained in it' (p. 24), Allen holds that such men

18 Cit. Bernard Basset, *The English Jesuits from Campion to Martindale* (London: Burns & Oates, 1967), p. 21.

> seeke not after any things of excellent fame for vertue, learning, regiment, religion, devotion: but according to their owne tast, hunt after nothing, aske for nothing, but where the Stewes be ...: and so partly of that they find, partly of that they feyne, partly of that they borow of wanton Poetes, ... they make up a fardel of malicious slaunders and detractions of Popes and Princes.
>
> (fols 98v-99r)

Gregory Martin's *Roma Sancta* contains similar objections to travellers who,

> for curiositie, or gayne, or whatsoever other vanitie, take great paines to abuse their travel and tyme in paltrie. They will tell perhappes goodly tales of the Capitol, the Amphitheatre, of Trajans pillar, Neroes palace, Diocletians bathes, the seven hilles, & so foorth. but the Christian pilgrime & religious Reader whom I would instruct, in these thinges taketh only this delight, to se the ruines therof, and how they are neglected, al Christian monumentes comming in their places; to se the victorie of Christ over the Divel, ... of Rome the spouse of Christ over Rome the whoore of Babylon.
>
> (p. 10)

As a eulogy to the piety and charity of post-Tridentine Rome, Martin's text provides a useful comparative focus to Munday's Protestant construction of Rome. By privileging contemporary Catholic Rome over ancient profane Rome, Martin inverts a Protestant insistence that travellers to Italy are to avoid the seductions of Catholicism while pursuing the aesthetic pleasures of antiquity. Martin is specifically concerned to re-deploy terminology employed by Protestants against religious Rome to secular Rome. Having associated Rome's classical past with the Whore of Babylon in the above quotation, Martin poses the following rhetorical questions:

> Where ar the palaces of Octavius, of Nero, of Nerva, of Adrian, of Gallienus? the monstrous bathes of Antoninus and Diocletian? Here is left an old wall, and there stand certayne broken pillers, and therfore some say, this was such a thing, and some doubt therof: The *Amphitheatre* yet sheweth what it was in those daies, but it hath fallen ever since as much as time could weare it, and falleth continually, and would make thee afrayd to passe within the danger therof.
>
> (p. 54)

Whilst Protestant commentators identify contemporary, Catholic Rome with the biblical Antichrist in pointing to the fall of Babylon, Martin attributes these objections to a classical Rome which 'falleth continually'.

Although Martin enforces a distinction between classical and Catholic Rome by redirecting attention away from profane monuments towards what he calls 'antiquities of godlines' (p. 10), he is also concerned to establish a continuity in devotion between ancient and contemporary Rome. Rome, Martin observes, is 'alwayes like it self' (p. 9), and confirms all one might read of the city in the scriptures. Jesuits, for example, are engaged in 'renewing and reviving some

Primitive graces and Apostolical spirits, to shew that his hand is not abridged or weakened' (p. 160); indeed, they not only maintain but also surpass 'the old Romane stampe' (p. 182). Munday's attempts in *The English Roman Life* to reveal the city's relics as inauthentic – the remains of saints are merely broken bones; Christ's manger, an old crib; and a piece of the cross, rotten wood – strike at Catholic attempts to ground the authority of their Church on the antiquity of its foundation. For Martin, a visible continuity in practices of belief means that Rome 'is old many wayes, old fayth, old charitie, old devotion, old Churches, old Relikes, old Sainctes' (p. 9). But for the Protestant divine Meredith Hanmer; 'It is longe sithence the grace of God is departed from the Church of Rome' (*Great Bragge*, fol. 12r); the Society of Jesus is 'a new order, [with] new maysters newe men, new lawes, [and] new leaders' instituted as 'the last refuge & onely shift to upholde the ... ruinous walles' of Catholicism (fol. 3v). Munday attests to his role as an English Protestant traveller by demonstrating subversive Romish practices to 'every good subject' in terms which recall those deployed by Hanmer and others. In Rome, a stone venerated as that on which the cock crowed when Peter denied Christ 'seem[s] to be but lately made' (p. 48); a door purported to be that through which Christ went to judgement has 'painting on [it] that is not very old' (p. 51); and one of the nails whereby Christ was nailed to the cross has 'the blood yet fresh upon it' (p. 54). These read as jokes on Catholic attempts to make the ancient devotion of the Catholic Church 'present' to its believers.

Although scripture affirms that Christ was nailed to the cross by only three nails, Munday has counted over a dozen in Rome. This multiplicity supports objections to the 'merchandise of Rome' (p. 78), to Catholicism as a marketable and therefore cheapened commodity, and to the Church of Rome as an institution capitalizing dishonestly upon the faith of its members. In claiming that effective merchandising is the only basis upon which is 'increase[d] the genealogy of the holy relics in Rome' (p. 61), Munday also seeks to subvert the significance attached by Catholic writers to their Church's unbroken spiritual tradition. Munday's frequent comments that relics are 'marvellous precious' (p. 53) play on the money commanded by Catholic fables of authenticity, or intrinsic worth. The religious blindness of Rome, which is expressed most forcibly in the worshipping of worthless goods, is invoked by Munday as a moral spectacle capable of confirming English subjects in loyalty to the Crown. 'O my dear countrymen,' Munday writes,

> think how God hath given over these men, that repose credit in such abominable untruths, whereby he is robbed of his glory, and the worship which we ought of duty to give to him is bestowed on a rabble of rascal relics, a dunghill of most irksome and noisome smell, and they themselves become spectacles to the world, following the Whore of Rome as her puddle of accursed filthiness.
>
> (pp. 63–4)

Munday describes *The English Roman Life* as an antidote to the false narratives of the Catholic faith. Presenting those persuaded to Catholicism by 'our secret seducing priests' with 'the bare and naked truth, which craveth neither shadow nor any coloured device', Munday hopes that 'they may vomit up that Antichrist and his abominable inventions, and cleave only to that which God himself hath commanded' (p. 59).

Munday's account of the Catholic belief in 'every feigned invention' (p. 74) bears self-conscious relation to his own attempt to authorize his work by providing satisfactory proof to those 'doubtful whether I have been there [to Rome] or no' (p. 5).[19] In attempting to assert his own credibility by representing Catholicism as a false narrative, Munday recalls comments made by Jack Wilton, the witty narrator of Thomas Nashe's *The Unfortunate Traveller* (1594), who refuses to report those Catholic 'miracles' he heard on his travels lest he be 'counted the most monstrous lyer that ever came in print' (p. 280). Munday, of course, differs from Wilton in devoting so much narrative space (almost one-third of the entire work) to 'such frivolous and foolish stuff' (p. 64) as Catholic relics, miracles and other 'fables'. This comment points to the tensions involved in being an avowedly non-Catholic writer representing relics for what is perceived as a non-Catholic audience. On the one hand, Munday's detailed itemization of Catholic relics, which repeatedly draws attention to the limits of his own memory, allows him to testify to the veracity of his account, and strengthens his claim for *The English Roman Life* as a personal record independent of any written description of Rome. (By omitting to describe relics he has not personally witnessed, Munday both asserts his actual experience of Rome and supports a claim that he 'will not be found in an untruth' [p. 48].) On the other hand, Munday's detailed account of relics focuses critical attention on the extent of his participation in Catholic forms of worship. Fynes Moryson, in *his* travels to Rome, refused to dwell long on those things 'into which none but Papists may safely inquire', preferring to 'returne to the monuments which lie open to every mans view' and to 'set downe the chiefe [relics] by heare-say' (I, pp. 275–7).

In a similar conflict, Munday calls the scholars at the English College to witness that he visited relics 'in their company, as it is a custom and an order among them, to go from church to church all the Lent time, to the stations as they call them' (p. 54), an implicit claim that by engaging in such structured exercises he has travelled profitably. But he also describes 'trudging to the seven churches' (p. 41) as a penance enjoined for breaking the orders instituted by the rector and Jesuits, a strategic claim that, despite his Catholic disguise, he is fundamentally incompatible as a Protestant with Catholic educational, religious and social

---

19 In 1581, Munday had attempted to refute accusations that he had not attended the seminary at Rome by deriving confirmation from Luke Kirby (a Catholic against whom he had testified, and whose execution he would subsequently describe) in the Tower.

practices. Such opposing assessments betray a tension in *The English Roman Life* between Munday's attempt to authorize his account by attesting to his personal participation in Catholic practices, and his endeavour to distinguish himself from those 'other' Englishmen who 'zealous[ly]' (p. 57) resort to relics, and who are named or otherwise implicated in his other anti-Catholic pamphlets detailing the capture of 'seditious' Englishmen returned from Rome. Such tensions are further evidenced in Munday's failure to describe his return to England at the end of the text. This is a possible attempt to distinguish his own motivations and allegiances from those returning Catholics identified in *The English Roman Life*, as in other of his anti-Catholic material. But it is a decision which denies him an opportunity to equate his own departure from Rome with a symbolic rejection of Catholicism (conventionally presented as a fleeing from Babylon); which leaves his textual persona in a kind of perpetually suspended conformity with his Catholic hosts; and which gestures further to conflicts present in the text between Munday's narrative and polemical strategies.

Primary texts cited

Allen, William, *An Apologie and True Declaration of the Institution and Endevours of the Two English Colleges* (1581). *STC* 369.

Calendar of State Papers, Domestic Series, of the Reigns of Edward VI, Mary, Elizabeth, ed. Robert Lemon and Mary Anne Everett Green (London: Longmans, 1856–71).

Cecil, William, *The Execution of Justice in England* (1583), in Robert M. Kingdon, ed., *The Execution of Justice in England by William Cecil and A True, Sincere, and Modest Defense of English Catholics by William Allen* (Ithaca, NY: Cornell University Press, 1965).

Coryat, Thomas, *Coryat's Crudities: Hastily Gobled up in Five Moneths Travells* (1611; Glasgow: James MacLehose, 1905).

Elyot, George, *A Very True Report of the Apprehension and Taking of that Arche Papist Edmond Campion the Pope his Right Hand, with Three other Lewd Jesuite Priests* (1581). *STC* 7629.

Hall, Joseph, *Quo Vadis? A Just Censure of Travell As It Is Commonly Undertaken by the Gentlemen of Our Nation* (1617). *STC* 12705.

Hanmer, Meredith, *The Great Bragge and Challenge of M. Champion a Jesuite, Commonlye Called Edmunde Campion* (1581). *STC* 12745.

Martin, Gregory, *Roma Sancta* (1581), ed. George Bruner Parks (Rome: Edizioni di Storia e Letteratura, 1969).

Moryson, Fynes, *An Itinerary* (1617; Glasgow: James MacLehose, 1907–8).

Munday, Anthony, *A Breefe Aunswer made unto Two Seditious Pamphlets … Contayning a Defence of Edmund Campion and his Complices* (1582). *STC* 18262.

Munday, Anthony, *A Discoverie of Edmund Campion, and his Confederates* (1582). *STC* 18270.

Munday, Anthony, *The English Roman Life* (1582), ed. Philip J. Ayres (Oxford: Clarendon Press; New York: Oxford University Press, 1980).

Nashe, Thomas, *The Unfortunate Traveller* (1594), in Ronald B. McKerrow, ed., *The Works of Thomas Nashe*, rev. F.P. Wilson (Oxford: Basil Blackwell, 1966), II.

[Nicols, J.], *A Discoverie of J. Nicols Minister, Misreported a Jesuite, Latelye Recanted in the Tower of London* (1581). *STC* 19402.

PART II

Translations

Chapter 5

The European transmission of *caritas* in More's *Dialogue of Comfort*

Benedek Péter Tóta

Ruminating on the eve of his death in 1534, Sir Thomas More, the former Lord Chancellor of England, ascribes his *Dialogue of Comfort* (1534) to a Hungarian meditating on the eve of a nation's disaster in 1527 or 1528. Casting his eyes from the West to the East, More examines his own individual fate in the light of the future of a nation – and vice versa. This allegorical and metaphorical setting can also be seen to reflect the existential scope of the historical situation both in Hungary and England. The oscillation between the imprisoned More's understanding of his individual case and his view of the current events in the nation of Hungary speaks to a yearning on his part to establish a self-defensive distance between himself and his text, since attacking Henry VIII from the king's own prison would have been too dangerous. This may be the reason for the authorial anonymity claimed in the title, which says that the *Dialogue* was 'made by an hungaryen in laten' (p. 3).

Still a general means of communication in the Renaissance, Latin also renders this work universal; and the universality of the *Dialogue* is also emphasized by the other languages mentioned in the title informing us that it was 'translatyd out of laten into french, & out of french into Englysh'. The universality is further accentuated by one of the speakers' wish, at the end of the *Dialogue,* that it be put in remembrance 'not in our own langage onely, but in the Almayne tong to' (p. 320), that is, in Hungarian and German. However, the introduction of these vernaculars turns the universal issue local and national again through the act of *translatio*, an intellectual transfer from the East to the West. This is how Sir Thomas More brings his ideas home to his readers.

The central concept of the *Dialogue* is 'comfort' itself, as interpreted in the personification of the 'comforter, the holy spryt' (p. 5). This rendering endows the public–political components with private–personal aspects. In addition, the various languages mentioned at the very beginning and very end of the *Dialogue* offer the possibility of a paraphrase of the cardinal motif as it is concluded in the final dedication: 'I besech our lord to breth of his holy spirite into the readers brest, which inwardly may tech hym in hart, without whome litle availeth all that all the mowthes of the world were able to tech in mens eares' (p. 320). With this movement the decision to compose in a multilingual context can be taken as a devotional attitude.

We know More read, wrote and spoke in English, Latin and French and translated from Greek into Latin and from both Greek and Latin into English. On the other hand, he seemed to have been illiterate in German and Hungarian. However, the overflow of languages in the *Dialogue* calls for vigilant attention. This abundance speaks of *glossolalia*, the gift of tongues (cf. Acts 2. 4) and the ability to interpret them for the good of other people, thus serving their improvement, encouragement and consolation, that is – comfort (cf. 1 Cor. 14: 3).[1] In this way Sir Thomas More's experimental fiction, geographically located in the East, has become a supranational and supraterritorial Pentecostal experience.

More's informal *Dialogue* is arranged as a formal spiritual exercise. It consists of three books concentrating on comfort from the points of view of the theological virtues of faith, hope and love, respectively, culminating in the commemorative recollection of the Eastern – and Easter-time – events of Christ's passion, death and resurrection. As a spiritual exercise, it is worthy to be enfolded by the Holy Spirit, the Paraclete, in the multilingual frame outlined above. This Pentecostal event, however, does not remain a marginal phenomenon, but percolates the whole *Dialogue*; and the multilingual paraphernalia play a special role in an interim chapter 'Of flatery'.

This chapter articulates the role of language-use in a spirited way. Vincent and Antony, the two Hungarian interlocutors, exchange tales to interpret the theme. Vincent tells us two stories about a great prelate 'in Almayne' who was never 'saciate of heryng his own prayse' and was 'longyng sore to be praysid' (p. 213). Antony rehearses the custom of 'Kyng Ladislaus' who would let his servants' praise pass by uncontrolled if they said the truth, but would correct them otherwise. The paratactically related anecdotes give way to some of the languages that can be heard in the framework of the *Dialogue*, such as 'the Almayne tonge' and 'laten' (p. 214), and they may also sound languages that can be audible inclusively through the persons in question: Hungarian through Vincent and Antony, together with Polish and Czech through Vladislav II, King of Bohemia, who was elected to the Hungarian throne in 1490. With this excess of languages we have come round to the Pentecostal adventure.

The cell where Sir Thomas More was imprisoned in the Tower was filled with inspiration to find the appropriate means of articulating the message of comfort. The Christian humanist discovered his medium in foreign languages which gave him the gift of speech (cf. Acts 2: 1–11) known as *glossolalia*. In St Paul's first letter to the Corinthians it is listed among the spritual gifts (1 Cor. 12–14).

Paul instructs the readers that 'there are all sorts of service [*ministratio*] to be

1 English quotations from the Bible (except John's Gospel) are from A. Jones et al., eds, *The Jerusalem Bible* (London: Darton, Longman & Todd, 1966).

done, but always to the same Lord' (12: 5): 'The particular way in which the Spirit is given to each person is for a good purpose [*ad utilitatem*]' (12: 7). In Paul's enumeration, the following spiritual gifts may be found: one may have 'the gift of preaching with wisdom [*sermo sapientiae*] given him by the Spirit' (12: 8); another may have 'the gift of recognizing spirits [*discretio spirituum*]' (12: 10); 'another the gift of tongues [*genera linguarum*] and another the ability to interpret them [*interpretatio sermonum*]' (12: 10). However, because not all speak languages or interpret them, Paul enunciates the greatest gift that surpasses all the 'eloquence of men or of angels [*linguae hominum et angelorum*]' (13: 1) – which is *caritas* or 'love'. This love is never boastful or conceited, never rude or selfish, and does not take offence (cf. 13: 4–5). Paul points out that love 'delights in the truth [*veritas*]' (13: 6), and that love does not come to an end because it endures whatever comes. In contrast to this true love and loving truth, however, the gift of languages will not continue for ever. Although love is the supreme gift, Paul also acknowledges other spiritual gifts, especially prophecy as a gift of talking for the benefit of other people (14: 1–4). For the sake of edification, even the gift of tongues and the gift of interpretation can be complementary (14: 5); and, what is more, 'anybody who has the gift of tongues must pray for the power of interpreting them [*qui loquitur lingua, oret ut interpretetur*]' (14: 13). Thus Paul draws to his conclusion, saying that anyone's gift of tongues or interpretation must always be for the common good (14: 26). Paul's words echo in Vincent's 'propre experience' (p. 213) and in Antony's apophthegm in More's *Dialogue*. In the mirror of Vincent's tales, two varieties of the same caricature appear; while Antony's story reflects a graceful example. Let us examine each in turn.

When Vincent 'was first in Almayne', he met a great prelate: '[G]loriouse was he very far above all measure & that was greate pitie for it did harm, and made hym abuse many greate giftes that god had givyn hym. Neuer was he saciate of heryng his own prayse' (p. 213). One day he 'made an oracion in a certeyne maner wherin he likyd hymself so well' that he wanted to hear how his audience 'wold commend it'. Having been asked, everybody was fallen into a deep study 'for the findyng of some exquisite prayse'. Then they gave their verdicts 'in good ordre as it had bene a greate mater of the comen well in a right solempne counsayle'. As for his own contribution, Vincent says:

> for my part I quyt my selfe metely well & I likyd my selfe the bettre because my thought my wordes beyng but a stranger, went yet with some grace in the Almayne tonge, wherin lettyng my laten alone, me listid to shew my connyng And I hopid to be likyd the bettre, because I saw that he that sat next me & shuld say his sentence after me was an vnlernid preest for he cold speke no laten at all But whan he came forth for his part with my lordes commendacion, the wily fox had be so well accustumyd in court with the crafte of flatery, that he went beyond me to to far.
>
> (p. 214)

In the light of St Paul's first letter to the Corinthians, we can make out what happens to conceited people if they miss the point of language-use or the gift of tongues. The prelate violated the verbal act of *oratio*, the gift of preaching given him by the Spirit. He did not use it for a good purpose as he did not serve the common good, but was conceited and interested in his very self only, thus offending the supreme gift of love. Due to his abuse of the gift given him by God, his oration was not for the benefit of the community, he did not promote their improvement, but caused their deterioration. This mock-Pentecost is effective enough and influences those present. Vincent, though apologetic – 'I will not say it vncle for no bost' (p. 214) – actually *is* boastful, and thus hurts perfect love; and being proud of his own skills in languages, his grace and eloquence, he despises the spiritual gift of languages and ends as what Paul calls 'a gong booming [*aes sonans*] or a cymbal clashing' (13: 1). As a punishment, he was beaten in this lip-service or commendation-competition by a priest whom the standards of humanism would have declared illiterate. But Vincent does not give up, and clashes with his contender. He made 'a solempne vowe' that next he 'wold flater in laten … for though [he] could be content to be out runne of an horse yet wold [he] no more abide it to be outrunne of an Asse' (p. 214/13–18). Vincent's animated yet asinine – because 'dis-inspirited' – metaphor might even resonate the *aes sonans*, or booming gong of the Vulgate, as the vulgar hee-haw of 'an Asse'. So much for eloquence as the gift of tongues; but there is more.

The language-game of the gift of languages goes on. The last speaker

> not a doctour onely but also somewhat lernid in dede in the lawes of the church … markid euery mans word … to study out a bettre to passe it The man evyn swet with the labour … How be it in conclusion whan it came to his course, we that had spoken before hym, had so taken vpp all among vs before, that we had not left hym one wise word to speke after.
> (p. 214)

So he said 'not one word':

> for whan he saw that he could find no wordes of prayse that wold passe all that had bene spoken before all redy the wily fox wold speke neuer a word, but as he that were ravishid vnto havyn ward, with the wonder of the wisedome & eloquence that my lordes grace had vttrid in that oracion, he fet a long sigh with an oh fro the bottom of his brest, & held vpp both his handes, & lyft vpp his hed, & cast vpp his yien into welkyn, and wept.
> (p. 215)

The act of the doctor in question seems to complete the mockery and serves the parody-like paraphrase of the life of the spirit.

The Christian's spiritual life is detailed in St Paul's letter to the Romans. Paul teaches his readers that '[t]he Spirit himself and our spirit bear united witness' (8: 16). 'From the beginning till now the entire creation, as we know, has been groaning in one great act of giving birth; and not only creation, but all of us who possess the first-fruits of the Spirit, we too groan inwardly as we wait for our bodies to be set free' (8: 22–3). He continues: 'The Spirit too comes to help us in our weakness. For when we cannot choose words in order to pray properly, the Spirit himself expresses our plea in a way that could never be put into words' (8: 26–7). Antony is right when he says that the doctor 'playd his part very properly' (p. 216), because useless abuse does not really need words. In addition, though the doctor's act brings the gift of languages to an end, because it is a hypocritical act, it cannot contain love, and thus turns love inside out (cf. 1 Cor. 13: 8). Such behaviour questions the integrity of human words and thoughts. This attitude negates truth, love's delight. The highest gift of the Spirit is debased.

No wonder, then, that at this point Antony guides their discourse into the direction of veracity concerning the value of 'that great prelates oracion' (p. 216). Vincent is ready 'to say the truth', in other words, that 'it was not to disprayse howbeit surely somwhat lesse prayse might haue seruid it by more a greate deale than the halfe. But … had it bene the worst that euer was made the prayse had not bene the lesse of one here'. With this shift, Vincent prepares his second tale, relating how 'they that vsid to prayse him to his face neuer considerid how mich the thing deseruid but how gret a lawd and prayse them selfe could give his good grace'. And going on in a more general way, Vincent adjusts his scope:

> those that are of such vayngloriouse mynd (be they lordes or be they meaner men) can be mich bettre contentid to haue their devices commendid than amendid and require they their seruauntes & their frend, neuer so specially to tell them the very trewth, yet shall they bettre please them yf he speke them fayre than yf he tellith them truth.
>
> (p. 217)

In the second tale, 'the selfe same prelate'

> had on a tyme made of his own drawyng a certeyne tretice, that shuld serue for a leige betwene that countrey & a greate prince In which treatice hym selfe thought that he had devisid his articles so wisely, & enditid them so well, that all the world wold alow them wherypon longyng sore to be praysid, he callid vnto hym a frend of his a man well lernid & of good worship, & very well expert in those maters, as he that had be diuers tymes Embassiatour for that countrey, & had made many such treatices hym selfe. Whan he toke him the treatice, & that he had redd it he askyd hym how he likyd it and said But I pray you hartely tell me the very trouth and that he spake so hartely that the tother had went he wold fayn haue herd the trowthe And in trust therof, he told hym a fawte therin at the heryng wherof, he sware in greate angre By the masse thow art a very fole. The tother afterward told me, that he wold neuer tell hym trowth agayne.
>
> (p. 217)

According to this second tale, truth, love's delight, that of the highest gift of the Spirit, is at stake. In this second Pentecostal adventure the prelate's use of language puts truth at risk. This hazardous way of speaking on the prelate's part

– swearing in great anger (p. 218) – hurts love, as such speech takes offence (cf. 1 Cor. 13: 5). The 'frend' in question is of interest, too. He is no better than the prelate, either. He is also involved in the same businesses as the prelate and he is also in need of some gifts of the Spirit, namely, the gift of recognizing spirits and that of interpretation. Our friend takes the prelate's words at face value. Due to his mistake on the basis of his lack of understanding, he can be punished by losing the courage to tell the truth again. This kind of corruption of our spiritual gifts does not serve any good: neither improvement, nor encouragement; neither consolation – nor comfort. At this desperate juncture, Antony speaks.

Antony keeps his words on flattery within the bounds of truth. He is not against commendation, but he distinguishes it from 'false flatery' (p. 218). He agrees that people who need it are of 'vaynegloriouse mynd' and exhorts them: 'yf they be content to here the truth, let them than make mich of them that tell them the trouth, & withdraw their eare from them that falsely flater them & they shalbe more trewly seruid than with xxte requestes praying men to tell them trew'. Those who are able to make such a distinction are the ones who are gifted with *discretio*, which is one of the gifts of the Spirit. This gift is demostrated by Antony's *jeu d'esprit*.

Antony reveals that 'Kyng Ladislaus' typically used *discretio* 'among his seruauntes' (p. 218) supported by his interpretation of their *glossolalia*:

> Whan one of them praysid any dede of his or any condicion in him yf he perceyvid that they said but the truth he wold let it passe by, vncontrollid But whan he saw that they set a *glose* vppon it for his prayse of their own makyng beside than wold he shortly say vnto them: I pray the good fellow whan thow say grace at my bord, neuer bring in gloria patry without a Sicut erat. Eny act that euer I did, yf thow report it agayne to myn honour with a gloria patry neuer report it, but with a sicut erat that is to wit, evyn as it was & none otherwise And lift me not vpp with no lies for I love yt not.
>
> (p. 218)

Antony's *bon mot* about truth in Kyng Ladislaus's translation is transferred to its proper place in the discourse of love, as it is love's true delight. Language-use accompanied with such gifts of the Spirit nourishes other spiritual gifts, such as 'the greater corage to thencrease' of praiseworthy things in other people (p. 218).

When this dialogue – one of Sir Thomas More's last discourses – culminates in truth as a spiritual value, we have to recall the fact that according to St John's first letter 'the Spirit is truth' (1 John 5. 6), and that Jesus's last discourse in John's Gospel[2] communicates the 'Paraclete' who is the 'Spirit of Truth [*Spiritus veritatis*]' (14: 17). It is the Paraclete who grants interpretation, encouragement and comfort.[3] It is through loving Jesus who is the Truth – and 'the King of kings'

---

2 Quotations from John's Gospel are from R.E. Brown, ed. and trans., *The Gospel according to John* (London: Geoffrey Chapman, 1966).

3 See ibid., pp. 1136–7.

(Revelation 17: 14) and 'the Ruler of the kings of the earth' (Revelation 1: 5) though his 'kingdom does not belong to this world' (John 18: 36) – that we can enjoy the performance of the Paraclete. Due to this principle, the Paraclete cannot be accepted through mundane customs and the attitudes of this world (cf. John 14: 17). Acting according to Christ's love, however, the Spirit of Truth will bear witness on our behalf in case of persecution, and will guide us along the way of all truth concerning our own life and other people's lives.

In More's discourse, then, the role of languages and translation can be interpreted – on the one hand – as the means of transforming the 'crafte' (p. 214) of a false flatterer into the art of an ideal orator–courtier, and – on the other hand – as the means of reflecting the essence of an idealized king – an *exemplum gratiae* – in the manner of a *speculum principis*, both human roles being rooted in the supreme idea of truth. This conclusion could well comfort More, the imprisoned Tudor orator–courtier. More gives voice to it towards the end of the last chapter in the third book of the *Dialogue*, the title of which says that 'The consideracion of the paynefull deth of Chryst, is sufficient to make vs content to suffre paynefull deth for his sake' (p. 312). There he says:

> let vs fence vs with fayth, & comfort vs with hope, & smyte the devill in the face with a firebrond of charitie For surely yf we be of that tendre lovyng mynd, that our master was & not hate them that kill vs, but pytie them & pray for them, with sorow for the perell that they worke vnto them selfe that fire of charitie throwne in his face, stryketh the devill sodaynly so blynd, that he can not see where to fasten a stroke on vs.
> (p. 318)

These words are a spirited paraphrase of 1 Cor. 13, and they also paraphrase Jesus' words on the cross asking for forgiveness for his persecutors (Luke 23: 34), words also paraphrased by St. Stephen, the first Christian martyr (Acts 7. 60). This allusive and interpretative *translatio* can really comfort More and provide him *cum forte Christi*. That is how More conforms himself to the idea of the Christian humanist as the orator–courtier of comfort.

Beyond this Renaissance, Christian and humanistic end, there is another siginificant concern. The richness of languages in the context of this *Dialogue* does not follow the simple paradigmatic series of translation. German does not belong to the sequence of Latin, French and English. Vincent's remark that he will put his uncle's 'good counsayle in remembrauns, not in our own langage onely, but in the Almayne tong to' (p. 320) urges the reader to pay special attention to Germany in this parallelism. As we have seen, Germany appears as a country of true distinction in the course of the *Dialogue*. The country immediately left an indelible print on Vincent's memory when he 'was first in Almayne' (p. 212). Germany does not escape Antony's attention, either. He notes with approval

> that all germanye for all their diuers opinions yet as they agre together in profession of christes name so agre they now together in preparacion

> of a comen power in defence of cristendome ageinst our comen ennymy the Turke And I trust in god that this shall not onely help vs here to strength vs in this warr but also that as god hath causid them to agre together in the defence of his name so shall he graciously bryng them to agree together in the truth of his fayth.
>
> (p. 38)

This seemingly far-fetched utterance comes into focus at once through the guidance of the keyword 'truth'. It can be taken as the presence of the Johannine Spirit. When Jesus promises the coming of the Paraclete, the Spirit of Truth (John 15: 26), he goes on to say that he said this to prevent our faith from being shaken, literally speaking: to prevent us from being scandalized ('lest you be scandalised [*ut non scandalizemini*]': 16: 1). As R.E. Brown notes:[4]

> For Johannine thought (6:61; 1 Jn 2:10) 'scandal' is what trips up a disciple and takes him from Jesus' company; or if we *transfer* the scene from Jesus' ministry to the lifetime of the Johannine church, 'scandal' is what causes one to give up the true Christian faith and withdraw from the community.

This thought might even be *transferred* to More's Europe. In this *translatio* this hidden language-reference can disclose the theme of the German Reformation. In this way More's flattering attention to the German language not only stresses the universality of this *Dialogue*, nor only disseminates the Christian ideas of humanism, but also tries to recollect the dismembered parts of Europe and Christianity. With this ecumenical attitude, the humanist philologist – surpassing his acts of religious controversy – realizes catholicity: 'till god bryng vs together agayne, eyther here or in hevyn' (*Dialogue*, p. 320). This is what transforms More into a reconciled Christian humanist of ultimate tolerance *cum translatione fidei Christi in omnes gentes mundi universi*.[5]

Primary works referred to

Bible – *Novum Testamentum Graece et Latine*, ed. A. Merk (Rome: Sumptibus Pontificii Instituti Biblici, 1933).

Bible – *The Gospel according to John*, ed. and trans. R.E. Brown (London: Geoffrey Chapman, 1966).

Bible – *The Jerusalem Bible*, ed. A. Jones et al. (London: Darton, Longman & Todd, 1966).

More, Sir Thomas, *A Dialogue of Comfort against Tribulation* (1534), in *The Complete Works of St. Thomas More* (New Haven, CT: Yale University Press, 1976), XII, ed. Louis L. Martz and Frank Manley.

4 See ibid., p. 690.

5 Cf. Matthew 28. 19; Luke 24: 47; Mark 16: 15–17.

Chapter 6

Translatio Mori: Ellis Heywood's 'Thomas More'*

Mark Robson

> No translation would be possible if in its ultimate essence it strove for likeness to the original.
>
> *Walter Benjamin*

Let us begin with a nose. In Ellis Heywood's Italian dialogue, *Il Moro*, a fictionalized disputation on the nature of true value set in Thomas More's garden and first printed in 1556, there is a key moment in which Moro, Heywood's figure for Thomas More, tells his guests an anecdote about a gathering which is supposed to have occurred the previous day (Ellis was the son of the dramatist John Heywood and his mother was Joan Rastell, More's niece).[1] The occasion for the anecdote in Heywood's dialogue is the end of a discussion of wealth and its value in determining the best route to happiness. In rejecting the views put forward by Lorenzo, who has spoken in favour of wealth, Moro speaks of Lorenzo's incremental errors in argumentation and compares him with Pattensono, his Fool. Pattensono, in the anecdote offered by Moro, makes an initial error which leads him into a series of further and greater errors in his attempts to compensate for his initial indiscretion. The incremental series begins when the Fool comments upon a guest of Moro's who, we are told, possesses an unusually large nose:

---

*A version of the material presented here first appeared in my unpublished doctoral thesis, 'Posthumous Representations of Thomas More: Critical Readings' (University of Leeds, 1996). I am grateful to my supervisor, David Lindley, and to my examiners, Paul Hammond and Thomas Healy, for their comments on this work at that stage. A short version was presented at *The Second International Conference of the Tudor Symposium*, 'Anglo-Continental Literary Relations in the Sixteenth Century', at the University of Newcastle, 7–9 September 2000. My thanks go to the organizer, Mike Pincombe, for the opportunity to speak, and to the participants for their comments.

1 References to *Il Moro* cite the English (E) and then the Italian (I) page references, that is, the page numbers of the Italian edition given in facsimile. In order to make more apparent the difference between the 'real' Thomas More, Patenson, and others, and those who appear in *Il Moro*, I have retained the Italian versions of names in my discussion when referring to Heywood's characters.

> After staring in the man's face for a while, he said, 'By my blood – this gentleman has one whale of a nose!' We [Moro and his guests] all pretended not to hear lest we embarrass the good gentleman. Realizing that he had erred, Patenson tried to put himself in the right again by saying, 'I lied in my throat when I said that this gentleman's nose was so large. On my word as a gentleman, it is quite a small nose.' When they heard this, everybody wanted to laugh out loud, and they ordered that the fool be chased away. But Patenson, who wanted to preserve his honor, would not let the affair end this way because, of all his virtues, the one he most often bragged of was that whatever he set out to do always came out right. To arrange the matter more to his own advantage, he went to the head of the table and said, 'Well I just want to say one thing: this gentleman has no nose at all.'
>
> (E 20/I 52–3)[2]

Lest the comic character of this episode escape us (as it easily might), Moro concludes that, 'Everybody laughed so hard at this tale that they almost dislocated their jaws' (E 20/I 53).

It is worth spending a little time considering the nature of the Fool's errors here. Pattensono's opening remark is an error not because he gives a false description, but because his comment causes embarrassment. Pattensono next accuses himself of lying, attempting to reground his speech through his social position, offering his word 'as a gentleman'. Even if we put aside the question of whether Pattensono is a gentleman, his original comment was not a lie, and thus Pattensono's attempt to ground his discourse in a hierarchical social structure serves only to call that structure itself into doubt, since the other guests are asked to prefer his word over the evidence of their own eyes. The appeal that he makes is thus not to a hierarchy which might be said to structure the world, but to one which would force the hearers to ignore the world. Pattensono's action in performatively 'giving his word' calls on his audience to posit an alternative world in which his discourse would be true.[3] The limits of the social structure

---

2 More seems to have had few qualms about mocking those who possessed large noses. Among his Latin epigrams are two humorous pieces on those thus afflicted. See More's Latin poems 'On a man with a huge nose from the Greek' and 'To a man with an extremely long nose from the Greek' in *The Complete Works*, III, 2, pp. 158–9 (no. 102) and 250–51 (no. 228).

3 In using the term 'performative' here I am alluding to a body of work too extensive for summary at this time. The starting-points for a consideration of performative language remain J.L. Austin's *How to Do Things with Words* (Oxford: Oxford University Press, 1962; 1976) and 'Performative Utterances', in *Philosophical Papers*, 3rd edn (Oxford: Oxford University Press, 1979), pp. 233–52. My own interests lie in the development and critique of this work, however, particularly within deconstruction. See, for example, Jacques Derrida's *Limited Inc*., ed. Gerald Graff (Evanston, IL: Northwestern University Press, 1988); and Paul De Man's *Allegories of Reading: Figural Language in Rousseau, Nietzsche, Rilke, and Proust* (New Haven, CT: Yale University Press, 1979), among many other pieces which might be cited here.

appealed to are revealed by his inability to make his discourse match the 'reality' of the objective world of perception. Unable to enforce the power of his performative utterance, Pattensono's concluding declaration, prompted by pride, denies the referent altogether: 'this gentleman has no nose at all'. He has moved from a mimetic if ludicrous description, through a disjuncture between discourse and referent which calls into question the grounding of that discourse and attempts to be its own ground, to a denial of the existence of the referent itself. Pattensono's pride is activated by an attempt to make the 'real' situation accord with a former speech (not given in the dialogue) in which he has bragged that anything he attempts will have a favourable conclusion (another failed fiction which offers itself as foundational), but his discourse can only be rendered valid by a denial of the validity of the world to which it claims to refer.

Pattensono's ridiculous attempts to preserve his social standing and honour are demonstrably futile – they end in mocking laughter. What prompts this descent into the ludicrous, this slippage into a discursive estrangement from the material realm of the referent, is precisely Pattensono's failure to take sufficient account of the context into which his discourse was projected. The inappropriateness of his initial comment leads him into a groundless relativism in which his only hope is to deny the significance of the objective realm that he has ignored. Another way of putting this would be to say that the ground of interpretation for his discourse lies in a fictional realm that is itself posited by that discourse, and it is the purpose of that discourse to carry out the phenomenalization of this realm. Expressed in more formulaic terms as a chiasmus, we might suggest that the ground for the discourse is the discourse which phenomenalizes that ground. It is the appearance of this chiasmic figure that makes this anecdote so emblematic for my reading of the dialogue.

Yet to leave the reading here is to run the risk of repeating Pattensono's error. For Pattensono is, of course, a Fool. It is his purpose to provoke laughter, it is part of a characteristic discourse of fooling to indulge in linguistic chicanery, to push the connection of signifier to signified up to and beyond breaking point. The Fool's exploitation of linguistic instability is thus the mark of a stable relationship between the signifier 'Fool' and the signified of fooling as a practice. The laughter of the characters in *Il Moro* symbolically restabilizes this relationship, but this actually places the relation of linguistic sign to material referent further in question, for the opposition of stability and instability runs the risk of collapse. Pattensono's words are effective in that they produce laughter, they act upon those who hear them, but they do so by progressively abandoning their referential function. As their constative dimension is hollowed out, with the comments bearing less and less relation to the guests' perception, the performative success of the Fool's statements increases, with his comments becoming funnier. What is revealed is thus not simply the figure of chiasmus that I identified above, but also its potential for failure. Pattensono's performative utterance thus succeeds as it simultaneously fails. It succeeds as a performative *because* it fails as a constative.

However, there is something here that may offer a way out of this potential collapse, for that which is constituted as the stable element is the *material* world. We must remember that this text is part of a series of representations of Thomas More which, following his execution, begin the movement towards his canonization. More only became a saint in 1935, but the fact that this campaign took four hundred years to achieve its aim should not lessen our sense of *Il Moro* as a text written for a purpose. It is characteristic of such texts that they focus on iconic and allegorical features of their subject's life, inheriting this strategy from hagiographical and martyrological works. The temporal realm is inevitably diminished in favour of an emphasis on both the cause for which the putative martyr has died, and the glories of eternal life which he or she has attained in leaving this, fallen, one. Thus we find an allegorical moment of textual self-cognition, in which the text reveals its own framework and its own position within the debate on value that structures the dialogue. Moro's use of this anecdote as a way of discrediting both Pattensono and Lorenzo points to a grounding for value that lies beyond the material, in the spiritual realm, and this movement of transcendence is indicative of a mode of meaning-production pursued elsewhere in the text.

Another version of this tale helps to bring some of these ideas into focus. An anecdote very similar to this one was printed in John Heywood's 'First Hundred of Epigrams', and John Heywood's version has a number of differences from that published by his son. Entitled 'Of the foole and the gentlemans nose', Heywood *père*'s anecdote makes no mention of More, neither does it name Patenson, and the reactions of the guests are markedly dissimilar:

> One gentleman havyng on other at meate,
> That guest havyng a nose deformd foule and great.
> The foole of that house, at this tyme standyng by,
> Fell thus in hand with that nose sodeinly.
> Nose *autem*, a great nose as ever I sawe.
> His master was wroth, & cride hense with that dawe.
> One saide: talke no more of great noses ye foole,
> Lest ye be talkt withall in the whippyng schoolle.
> The foole warnd of great noses no more to speake,
> To mend that faut, this way these woords did breake.
> Saide I, this is a foule great spittell nose?
> Byr lady I lyed, it is a fayre littell nose.
> Will not that foole be had hence (quoth the master?)
> Thou wilt foole (quoth one) by walkt with a waster,
> If thou speake of any nose great or small.
> The foole at thyrd warning, mindyng to mend all,
> Stept to he boord againe criyng as he gose,
> Before god and man, that man hath no nose.
> The foole was feakt for this: but what of that?

> The great faute here to note, he amended nat:
> Whiche is this: not the wise, but the foole ye see,
> In clokyng of one faute, makth fautes two or three.[4]

There is little hilarity here. The Fool is repeatedly warned to speak no more of noses, and his comments provoke anger, not a stifled laughter. The moralizing ending of the elder Heywood's poem fails to respond to the Fool's function, but so too does his master. The Fool is 'feakt', meaning beaten, thrashed or whipped, and the poet is indifferent even to the punishment, eager that the reader arrive at the proper conclusion.

Presented in this way, rather than as an example of convivial tolerance, the story seems an odd one for Ellis Heywood to have chosen. More is not named in the earlier piece, as I have already noted, and the decision to use this poem in the dialogue requires that it be framed carefully for it to fit in with the vision of More that Heywood seems to wish to create, as we shall see. This offers more than one possibility in reading its significance. First, it might be assumed that the potential readers of an Italian dialogue, printed in Italy, might not be aware of John Heywood's text.[5] The darker aspects of the poetic version then simply do not come into consideration for these supposed 'intended' readers. Or, second, it could be taken as an indication that there is a kind of whitewashing here of More, that his reputation is being cleansed of troubling concerns about violence and intolerance.[6] Certainly, Heywood's version of More is, on the surface, entirely positive. Perhaps, then, Heywood is using this anecdote to point up the difference between Moro and the figure of the Fool's master in the poem, to Moro's (and More's) advantage. There is a third possibility, however. It might be that Heywood chose this poem precisely *because* it provokes a sense of unease. Behind the laughter of Moro and his guests there lies something more disturbing, and this resonates with other currents in Ellis Heywood's text. Here, as in so many works of this period, as the noisy laughter provoked by folly dies away, it is replaced by disquiet.

4 This is labelled as epigram 87 in this copy, but is actually number 86.

5 Clearly there have been some English readers of the text. See, for example, three copies of *Il Moro* held by the British Library.

6 For modern assessments which have chosen neither to ignore nor to attempt to explain away these troubling aspects of More's character, see Richard Marius, *Thomas More* (London: Weidenfeld, 1993), Jasper Ridley, *The Statesman and the Fanatic: Thomas Wolsey & Thomas More* (London: Constable, 1982), and Anthony Kenny, *Thomas More* (Oxford: Oxford University Press, 1983). These stand in marked opposition to works such as Louis L. Martz's *Thomas More: The Search for the Inner Man* (New Haven, CT and London: Yale University Press, 1990), and to the popular humanistic figure of More as the 'man for all seasons'.

I

What I want to focus on from this point forward is the explicit thematization of what I would like to call 'translation' in *Il Moro*, since there appear to be several levels of translation in play here. The first form of translation is straightforward. The text was first printed, in Italian, in Florence in 1556; a proposed English version has either been lost or was never published. In the absence of an English text there is little to be said about this movement from one language to another, although it is possible to examine the transformations of some of the source texts, such as the John Heywood poem that I cited above.

What I want to propose is that this is a translation in several senses. First, there is the representation of More, and its relationship to what we (in modern terms) would think of as historical accuracy. Second, there is the role played by the works of others in the construction of the content of this text, most obviously More's own work.[7] At the level of content, *Il Moro* is a dialogue which portrays an encounter between Thomas More and six fictional disputants, in which they debate questions of value, and the third mode of translation is that of the concepts brought to bear upon the content of the dialogue, such as happiness, riches, love (*amore*) and death, and how they are accorded different values according to the contexts in which they appear in the text. Finally (for this discussion, at least), there is a 'litteral' translation which may be discerned within the structure of the dialogue: from Thomas More to S. Tomaso Moro, to Death, to the Fool.[8] Of particular interest is the way in which these elements, particularly death and folly, interact to set up links between the image of More that the text presents and the discussion of value that forms its content. *Il Moro* is structured around these intersecting moments of translation, and this text is characteristic of attempts to represent More after his death in its obliqueness and its creation of a likeness of More (as MEMENTO MORI, always given in capitals in the Italian text), using the word 'likeness' to denote a More-like figure rather than an attempt at historical record. This, I suggest, is one of the strategies used to reveal More's *translation* through martyrdom.

These different modes of translation do not always sit comfortably with each other. A version of translation which works on the basis of a transmissive or mimetic model cannot easily be reconciled with one that works at the level of the signifier, or with another that emphasizes the importance of the transcendence of the material realm altogether. These varying conceptions of translation oscillate

---

7 On More and translation, see my 'Writing limits in William Roper's *Life of Thomas More*', in Warwick Gould and Thomas F. Staley, eds, *Writing the Lives of Writers* (Basingstoke and New York: Macmillan/St Martin's Press, 1998), pp. 79–89.

8 The obvious reference here is to Erasmus. Also pertinent is *Moor*, which is used in More's family seal. This is reproduced in Gordon Rupp, *Thomas More: The King's Good Servant* (London: Collins, 1978), fig. 26. The original is held at Stonyhurst College, Lancashire.

between immanence and transcendence, between ideal content and ideal form. Historiographical representation traditionally seems to assume a communicable content (or truth) which can be separated from the mode in which that truth is communicated; martyrological texts similarly work upon an ideal content, which may be manipulated in order to fit a form which is itself the guarantor of truth.[9] Yet the kind of litteral translation that *Il Moro* also contains, based primarily upon the syllable 'mor', works according to a principle of similitude which is (at least at first glance) based upon a contentless form. The connections between love, death, folly and Thomas More appear beguilingly contingent. Yet we must not, in noting this contingency, neglect the performative dimension of this linguistic connection. This performativity contains, and communicates, a necessity that the signifiers taken in isolation cover as much as they reveal. However much one might suspect that this is 'just' wordplay, the exploitation of the 'mor' syllable in the creation of this kind of connection between concepts is pervasive enough within European culture in this period for Patricia Parker to suggest that it is a 'commonplace'.[10]

II

Il Moro begins with and as a translation of a name: *More* to *Moro*. This name manages to be both proper and improper: proper in that it refers, it 'belongs', to an individual, to 'Thomas More'. Here properness or propriety would familiarly be associated with referentiality, connected to life and presence. Yet this form of translation is also improper in that it gestures towards a jest, towards a play which begins not in life but in death: *Moro* to *Mori*. There is a suspicion here of a movement away from reference as a function towards death and absence. From here it is not far to a further play, the 'mor-' root clearly linked through Latin etymology to foolishness (*morio*, *morus*, *moror* – all leading to 'fool'), and to More's use of 'morosophi', transliterated from Greek, to name his wise fools in *Utopia*.[11] This linguistic playing acts as a memento of Erasmus's pun,[12] and also

9 Work by historians such as Hayden White and Dominick La Capra have done much to complicate this model of historiography, but the distinctions that I am making here between form and content have a strategic pertinence for this discussion.

10 Patricia Parker is also working on this nexus around the syllable 'mor', and has extended this work far further than it is possible to do here. I am grateful to Professor Parker for the opportunity to read an unpublished paper, 'Mulberries, Moors, and More', presented to the London Renaissance Seminar, 9 October 1999, which has helped to crystallize some of the ideas contained here.

11 See Thomas More, *Utopia*, p. 18. This is the root of the modern word 'sophomore'.

12 See Erasmus, *Praise of Folly*, p. 3, in which Erasmus plays upon the Latin title of his work, *Encomium Moriae*, as he dedicates it to More in the prefatory letter.

of Edward Hall's description of More, in his *Union of the two noble and illustrate families of Lancastre and Yorke* (1548), in which he seems uncomfortable with the proximity of wisdom and folly that More's behaviour at his death evidences:

> I cannot tell whether I should call him a foolishe wyseman or a wise foolishman, for undoubtedly he beside his learnyng had a great witte, but it was so myngled with tauntyng and mocking, that it semed to them that best knew him, that he thought nothing to be wel spoken except he had ministred some mocke in the communicacion.
>
> (fol. 226v)

Erasmus's pun, and the unease with More that Hall expresses, take us to the final transformation: *Mori* to *Moriae*. Hall's account of More comes in his chronicle of the year 1535, the year of More's execution, and Hall uses More's scaffold humour as justification for his ambivalence towards More's character. Thus even the humour which marks More's foolishness is related back to death through its context. Folly does not replace death as a signified, then, but each exists as the future anterior of the other: it will always have been there. In this, we may see an indication of the relationship to folly which the text is to establish.

From Thomas More to S. Tomaso Moro to Death to the Fool: *More, Moro, Mori, Moriae*. The permutations of More's name allow for the possibility of multiple readings, and Heywood's invocation of Moro sustains not a single meaning but several simultaneously. The name outlives the person to whom it refers, it acts as a memorial, a reminder, a memento – but of what? If the signification of the name itself is unstable, drawing us in several directions, then what of the one to whom it refers?

III

From More to Moro. This 'impressive but now nearly forgotten dialogue' takes the form of a 'disputation' between S. Tomaso Moro and six fictional characters – Lorenzo, Lionardo, Carlo, Paulo, Alessandro and Piero – but it is Moro who dominates the proceedings.[13] Although the debates themselves consist almost entirely of speeches by characters other than Moro, his is always the final word, and this word is decisive, even if that decision is deferred.

At the opening of the dialogue, the purpose of the text is described. In his dedication to Cardinal Pole, Heywood makes a self-effacing reference to More,

13 This phrase is Arthur Kinney's assessment of the text, which includes a discussion of its place in relation to models of humanist rhetoric. See Arthur F. Kinney, *Humanist Poetics: Thought, Rhetoric, and Fiction in Sixteenth-Century England* (Amherst, MA: University of Massachusetts Press, 1986), pp. 151–3. My use of the term 'disputation' accords with the definition provided by Peter Burke in his essay, 'The Renaissance Dialogue', *Renaissance Studies* III (1989), pp. 1–12, at p. 4.

proposing that his representation speaks in a manner 'so cold that it does not even correspond to More dead [*che ne ancho al Moro morto corrisponderebbe*]' (E 2/I 7). The presence of this reminder of '*Moro morto*' before the text proper starts poses a number of questions about the status of the vision of More that Heywood has created. Heywood is suggesting that this representation is not 'life-like', that is mimetic, and this is an impression reinforced by the fact that we have no evidence that it is based upon any specific event that could correspond with Heywood's dialogue. It is not only an inadequate version of a living More, however, for Heywood claims that Moro is not even as vivid as More after death. Heywood would seem to be attempting to create a figure not so much of More, then, as of 'More-ness', constructing an approximation rather than a representation. No doubt this is a piece of rhetorical (dis)ingenuity on Heywood's part, but the dedication alerts the reader to the fact that *Il Moro* does not correspond neatly to the genres of biography or 'straight' historical representation.

Certainly Heywood's concern in *Il Moro* is not to produce a documentary testament to More's life. This is made evident in the opening section of the dialogue, in which Heywood introduces those who are to take part in the debate. Heywood offers the reader only the Christian names of the six men, claiming that their surnames would not translate well into Italian (E 4/I 13). More's name is translated into Moro, and Heywood's emphasis on the question of translation makes clear the difference that such a process interposes between *More* and *Moro*. We are told that the dialogue took place in the period following More's resignation from the Chancellorship, which would place it between May 1532 and April 1534, when More was committed to the Tower. *Il Moro*'s lack of historical specificity is also marked by the presence of the Fool, since Patenson was no longer a member of More's household at this time, having been gifted to the Lord Mayor of London; More felt unable to look after him following his resignation. Equally, the invitation to the six friends to stay the night at Moro's Chelsea home at short notice implies a level of financial comfort at odds with the picture of pecuniary restraint in the More household at this time given in the biographies of Roper and Harpsfield.[14] Again, Heywood's purpose would appear not to be representation.

Within the text, there are several passages which reflect upon the task of creating a work such as *Il Moro*. These gesture towards allegories of reading, in which the text offers a moment of self-cognition. For example, Lionardo gives us another angle from which to view Heywood's project in the writing of *Il Moro*, sketching a theory of the relationship of representation to its referent:

---

14 See William Roper, *The Lyfe of Sir Thomas Moore* (ms. c. 1557), pp. 52–3; Nicholas Harpsfield, *The life and death of Sir Thomas Moore* (ms. c. 1557), pp. 143–5.

> A deed continues to exist in an unchanged state only while it is being performed. Books, on the other hand, remain forever in that very form set by their authors. And since these divine geniuses continue to speak, they live on inside us far more vividly [*in una piu fresca memoria*] than do those about whom they speak.
>
> (E 36/I 92)

For Lionardo, any representation reveals the absence of the deed, not its presence. Asserting the primacy of the text, Lionardo's closing comment prompts a question about Heywood's project. Heywood's purpose in *Il Moro* is not conventionally representational, as I have already suggested, and whilst Heywood may not recognize himself as a 'divine genius', the implication that the voice of the writer has more 'life' than the subject of the discourse emphasizes Heywood's subjectivity in the creation of a vision of More.[15]

Similarly, Carlo responds to Lionardo's argument in the immediately following passages by recognizing that the fact of being remembered is not in itself a guarantee of worth – an extrinsic evaluative code is needed to gift honour, and it is honour that Carlo values. This offers an alternative explanation for the non-mimetic nature of Heywood's text. Accurate representation in the sense of adequation to the object being represented is of no value *per se*, since being remembered falls (as have riches and intellect earlier in the dialogue) into the realm of the indifferent, and what is required to create a reputation for virtue is a representation that is qualitatively appropriate. Heywood's image of 'More-ness' (*Moro*), then, is just such a presentation.

Moro further questions the value of a reputation that goes beyond the grave:

> what that life might be that the dead live here from the fame of their names, I have never been able to understand. A name is not a substantial part of the soul or body of anyone ... beyond these two there is nothing.
>
> (E 41/I 104)

In his play on More's name, Heywood contradicts Moro's speech. Dissociated from the body and soul the name remains, and the use of that name belies the insubstantiality that Moro claims for it; even if its use cannot be known by Moro himself, a name may take on a phenomenality that allows it to act in the world, even beyond the death or absence of that which it names.

This offers a further recontextualization of Heywood's project in relation to honour. If posthumous reputation or representation can have no meaning for the subject of that representation, then the meaning must be created by the representor and within the specificity of the historical moment of representation. The production of a 'genuine' image of More cannot be privileged over a vision

15 I have approached the question of voice in 'Swansongs: Reading voice in the poetry of Lady Hester Pulter', *English Manuscript Studies, 1100–1700* IX (2000), pp. 238–56.

of More-ness by appeal to More 'himself' – such an appeal would be meaningless. Equally, any attempt on the part of the writer to achieve immortality through writing would, by the same token, be pointless. Thus it is the effect of the representation in the world that is of significance. Such a view of the text as active, even substantial, lies within any attempt to produce a 'monumental' text. This is a far from uncommon view of the role of the literary text in the early modern period, and one that must be borne in mind in any modern interpretation. As Virginia Cox states:

> One of the principal discrepancies between modern and pre-modern perceptions of literary discourse is that literature is no longer conceived of today, as it was within the classical, rhetorical tradition, as something 'continuous with reality', as 'action in the world'. Like a classical oration, a Renaissance literary work was often addressed to a specific, closely studied audience and intended to persuade its listeners to a particular line of action.[16]

Cox is making reference to an Italian tradition of Renaissance dialogue, but the view expressed here extends beyond that specific generic case. The model of textual performativity that I am arguing for here again makes clear that such texts cannot be read as simply representational, even if the genres in which they participate are now commonly read as such.

IV

From *Moro* to *mori*. The discussion of riches draws to a close with a consideration of the deaths of misers. Concluding earlier discussions in the text, Moro has rejected the proffered values by denying the worth of any reputation or honour after death, as we have seen. The debate on 'love' is cut short, and any judgement on 'knowledge' is deferred. The idea of a multifarious pleasure in all things is also rejected. All of these negative moments in the argument are part of the dialectical structure of the dialogue, and we are meant to read this discussion as progressing towards an ending which is also a logical conclusion. The final speeches are those of Paulo and of Moro himself, and both are explicit in their invocation of death.

Paulo offers three reasons for his belief that no happiness can be found in this life. First, human desire is infinite, but the means available to satisfy that desire are finite, thus any attempted satisfaction is futile. Second, it is God's will that man be unhappy on earth, and Paulo cites original sin as corroboration for this view. Finally, there is the ineluctable movement towards death. The central image

---

16 Virginia Cox, *The Renaissance Dialogue: Literary Dialogue in its social and political contexts, Castiglione to Galileo* (Cambridge: Cambridge University Press, 1992), p. 34.

of Paulo's sermon on death is taken from More's uncompleted work of 1522, *The Last Things*. This *eidolopoeia* by quotation, allowing the dead More to speak through the repetition of his writings, is far from flattering in the form expressed through Paulo. The human condition is figured as a movement towards death, but Paulo's humourless quotation of More's vivid metaphor of humanity placed in a cart on the road to execution is allowed to float free from the anchoring discussion of virtue and sin that constitutes the rest of More's text. The decontextualization of these words brings Paulo to the point of misinterpretation, for Paulo's response to his reading of More is desperation and misery. Again laughter, or the lack of it, is the mark of a necessary contextualization, but of a context that is not simply marked in or phenomenalized by the text.

Paulo's argument highlights the stress that is placed in *Il Moro* on the notion of commemoration, and of memory's relation to death, and Lorenzo suggests that the phrase *memento mori* reminds him of Moro rather than death. For Paulo this is a misreading, and he argues that 'anyone who expounds it [*memento mori*] in its *proper sense* [*proprio senso*] would soon see the cheating happiness of this present life go up in smoke' (E 62/I 158, emphasis mine). Alerting the reader to the possibility of misinterpretation, Paulo lays the foundations for Moro's subsequent refutation of Paulo's own exposition of *The Last Things*. Death for More and for Moro is not a reason for despair, quite the contrary, it is used to ascertain value and to provide a sense of perspective. *The Last Things* is littered with references to sight and to perception, to insight and to blindness and, in a lengthy speech in *Il Moro*, Moro makes a similar connection between perception, reason and the pursuit of happiness:

> I cannot agree with you [Paulo] or with any of the others about happiness, for, although there is no happiness to be found in the things already mentioned, it does not follow that there is none to be found ... Just as the sun often appears behind a mist with a light so ambiguous that you feel you are seeing it and not seeing it at the same time, so reason appears behind the dense fog of our appetite with a light so weak that we grant it recognition in our words and deny it in our deeds.
> (E 66/I 168–9)

Rational, clear sight can enable one to distinguish between the false and the true, between that which *appears* to offer contentment, and that which is an *authentic* route to happiness. *Il Moro* echoes the metaphors of sight of *The Last Things* not only in Heywood's narration but also in Moro's speeches. Thus it is the final end that is privileged, not intention itself but that towards which thought and action are intended. This ultimate, transcendent end is identified by Moro as the 'immediate presence' of God (E 69/I 177).[17] This presence is only attainable once

17 The relationship between the immediate presence of God and language is, of course, what lies behind the Babel story. For the relevance of this to theories and practices of translation, see Jacques Derrida, 'Des Tours de Babel', trans. Joseph F. Graham, in

man has freed himself from this 'imperfect life', and this liberation transcends rationality itself, relying upon an act of faith that is itself more perfect than reason. Thus death is literally the 'end' of life, not only its termination but its goal. We might say: *the end of life is the end of life*.[18]

Until the final pages of *Il Moro*, Moro himself has hardly spoken, entering into the debate only to create and shape a space in which speech is possible, but without himself occupying that space. Moro represents authority and acts as 'surety', and he is deployed and described by Heywood, but is barely present. More's 'voice' is heard through citation of his writings and through Moro's recitation of the Patenson anecdote, but as we have seen even this is a quotation from John Heywood, Ellis's father. The significance of the invocation of *memento mori* in the argument between Lorenzo and Paulo is not that it might function as a reminder of More *or* of death, but that it can sustain both meanings simultaneously without contradiction, serving as a reminder of both death and More, of More's death, of More as dead. We might even say of More as death. In this, Lorenzo the Fool, for whom *memento mori* is a reminder of Moro, sees more than Paulo.

Moro's absence from so much of the text actualizes content on the level of form, since the central theme of the text is the remembrance of death. Heywood's final paragraph makes this explicit. Moro provides the resolution towards which the dialogue has been directed, but the concluding words are Heywood's and he directs the reader's attention out of the text towards its referent:

> And here More stopped, leaving a great admiration in the souls of those who listened to him when they saw how exactly his life corresponded to the words he spoke. Not long after, that admiration was greatly increased by his truly Christian death, when he lowered his head to the very blow of the axe with a happy and open face, reassured by his pure conscience, like one whose great courage faced that final end with more hope of life than fear of death.
>
> (E 70/I 179–80)

Heywood's initial statement here is surely intended to be inclusive – the reader has 'listened' to Moro's words along with the fictional interlocutors. The active form of the dialogue's dialectic positions the reader as a silent, and silenced, interlocutor. In an inverted form of mimesis, Heywood explains that the life

---

Graham, ed., *Difference in Translation* (Ithaca, NY and New York: Cornell University Press, 1985), pp. 165–207; and 'What Is a "Relevant" Translation?', trans. Lawrence Venuti, *Critical Inquiry* XXVII (2001), pp. 174–200.

18 This raises the spectre of suicide, of voluntary death or martyrdom, and thus the problematic Christian inheritance which both rests upon the conscious sacrifice of Christ and at the same time proposes the Mosaic prohibition of murder in any form. On this contradiction, see Georges Minois, *History of Suicide: Voluntary Death in Western Culture*, trans. Lydia G. Cochrane (Baltimore, MD and London: Johns Hopkins University Press, 1999).

corresponds to the words, side-stepping any objections about the absence of any historical moment to which the dialogue could be said to refer. The increase of admiration at the manner of Moro's demise privileges death over life, and the use of *memento mori* is both general and particular – it is an injunction to remember death but also to remember *this* death. More's death is similarly figured as specific and general, both his and also 'truly Christian'. There is no lamentation here, no anger at any perceived injustice, but neither is there any detail or individuation. Like the image of More who takes part in the dialogue, the More/Moro who dies is an approximation.

V

Ellis Heywood's text offers an example of the ways in which different forms of translation may be seen to put to work the representational function of language. The promise of presence that translation makes, like any promise, calls for an act of faith on the part of the one to whom the promise is given, and it is this opening to the sacred, to transcendence, that is at stake in translation. Such a movement towards transcendence always entails a movement away from that being translated, and indeed from the form of the translation itself. From a certain perspective, this might be seen as a movement from materiality to transcendence. Yet the material aspect of translation cannot simply be eliminated, and it is this material element of language (always *a* language, but always more than one language) that is also revealed in translation. This ineliminable materiality can always appear as a form of death, and this is a death which appears at the origin of translation.

Discussing Walter Benjamin's famous essay on translation, Paul de Man speaks of the effect of the act of translation upon the original. In Benjamin's work, the translation canonizes its own version of the original, but in doing so, it reveals that the source text was less stable, less canonical than the supposedly secondary derivation. As de Man states: 'The translation belongs not to the life of the original, the original is already dead, but the translation belongs to the afterlife of the original, thus assuming and confirming the death of the original.'[19] Death is implicit in the act and theorization of translation, but it is also translation which may assure an afterlife, which may give an appearance of life to that which it freezes and silences. *Il Moro* exemplifies this movement of commemoration and annihilation, of a process which produces life-like figures and reveals life as figure, while reminding its readers that this is not an opening to a pathos unrelieved by laughter.

---

19 Paul de Man, '"Conclusions": Walter Benjamin's "The Task of the Translator"', in *The Resistance to Theory* (Minneapolis, MN: University of Minnesota, 1986), pp. 73–105, at p. 85.

Primary texts quoted

Erasmus of Rotterdam, *Praise of Folly* (*Moriae encomium*, 1511), trans. Betty Radice, *Praise of Folly and Letter to Maarten van Dorp* (Harmondsworth: Penguin, 1971; rev. edn 1993).

Hall, Edward, *The union of the two noble and illustrate famelies of Lancastre & Yorke* (1548). *STC* 12721.

Harpsfield, Nicholas, *The life and death of Sir Thomas Moore* (ms. *c*. 1557). ed. E.V. Hitchcock (London: Oxford University Press [Early English Text Society], 1932).

Heywood, Ellis, *Il Moro: Ellis Heywood's Dialogue in Memory of Thomas More*, ed. and trans. Roger Lee Deakins (Cambridge, MA: Harvard University Press, 1972).

[Heywood, John]. *John Heywoodes woorkes* (1562). *STC* 13285.

More, Thomas. *The Yale Edition of the Complete Works of St. Thomas More*, ed. Richard S. Sylvester and others (New Haven, CT and London: Yale University Press, 1963–97).

More, Thomas. *Utopia* (1516), ed. George M. Logan, trans. Robert M. Adams (Cambridge: Cambridge University Press, 1989).

Roper, William, *The Lyfe of Sir Thomas Moore* (ms. c. 1557), ed. E.V. Hitchcock (1935; London: Oxford University Press [Early English Text Society], 1958).

Chapter 7

Translation and the definition of sovereignty: the case of Elizabeth Tudor

Georgia E. Brown

This essay explores the complex interactions between the practice of translation and Elizabethan conceptions of sovereignty. From one perspective, translation into Renaissance English is an assertion of national pride and the power of the vernacular. In the English dedication to the second edition of his Italian–English dictionary, *Queen Anna's New World of Words* (1611), John Florio compares the labour of producing the dictionary to the discoveries of Columbus, as he tells his mistress and pupil, Queen Anne:

> This braine-babe (ô pardon me that title most absolute supreme *Minerva*) brought with it into the world, now thirteen yeers since, a world of words: Since, following the fathers steps in all observant service of your most sacred Majestie, yet with a travellers minde, as erst *Colombus* at command of glorious *Isabella*, it hath (at home) discovered neere halfe a new world.
>
> (sig. ¶12v)

The traffic between languages appropriates the treasures of other cultures for the benefit of the nation, and in the Renaissance, the verb to translate also meant to transport, or remove from one place to another. Nevertheless, while Florio invokes the idea that translation is an assertion of sovereignty, his words to Queen Anne betray the uneasy realization that translation and the nation it glorifies cannot be so easily contained, for if Florio's Columbus figure finds 'neere halfe a new world … at home', then is the nation a composite of alien elements that challenges any claims to purity and integrity?

This study of one of Elizabeth Tudor's translations from French into English argues that translation interacts in complicated and unstable ways with political, religious, sexual and gender categories. By its very nature, translation equivocates. A translation is both English and foreign, both the work of the translator and the work of the author, both a product of contemporary culture and, depending on the source, a product of a previous culture. But the Renaissance also understood translation as an equivocal activity in terms of gender. In the dedication to the first book of his famous translation of Michel de Montaigne's

Essays (1603), which was addressed to the Countess of Bedford and her mother, Lady Anne Harington, the prolific John Florio notes that the very activity of translating is feminine:

> To my last Birth, which I held masculine, (as are all mens conceipts that are their owne, though but by their collecting; and this was to *Montaigne* like *Bacchus*, closed in, or loosed from his great *Jupiters* thigh) I the indulgent father invited two right Honorable Godfathers, with the ONE of your Noble Lady-shippes to witnesse. So to this defective edition (since all translations are reputed femalls, delivered at second hand; and I in this serve but as *Vulcan*, to hatchet this *Minerva* from that *Jupiters* bigge braine) I yet at least a fondling foster-father, having transported it from *France* to *England*; put it in English clothes; taught it to talke our tongue (though many-times with a jerke of the French *Jargon*) would set it forth to the best service I might.
>
> (sig. A2r)

The consequences of such gendered assumptions are even more disturbing than they at first appear because they structure Florio, the translator, as an equivocally gendered figure, one which is both male ('*Vulcan*', a 'foster-father'), and female in that it produces a translation. In fact one of the ironies of the humanist project is that anyone who deals in words runs the risk of feminization, as Florio himself points out in the dedication to *A Worlde of Wordes* (1598):

> Some perhaps will except against the sexe, and not allowe it for a male-broode, sithens as our Italians saie, *Le parole sono femine, & i fatti sono maschii,* Wordes they are women, and deeds they are men. But let such know that *Detti* and *fatti*, wordes and deeds with me are all of one gender.
>
> (sig. A4v)

In Florio's terms there are no longer two distinct genders, but 'one gender'. The predilection of translation for two-in-oneness, for multiplicity in apparent unity, for doubling, is echoed stylistically in the play with doubling and substitution in the dedication to *The Essays*. The dedicatees to each book of the translation of Montaigne come in pairs. When Florio praises his patronesses he uses Montaigne's words, which are themselves quotations from Horace and Virgil, so that voices are subsumed within voices, and these compliments have no absolute point of origin. Moreover, words themselves are doubled or pressed into portmanteau terms which combine active and passive forms: 'To the right honorable my best-best Benefactors, and most-most honored Ladies, *Lucie Countesse of Bedford*; and hir best-most loved-loving Mother, *Ladie Anne Harrington*' (sig. A2r).

The practice of Renaissance translation suggests a different understanding of boundaries that sees them as points of interchange between personal, national and textual spaces. Florio's definition of a translator who exists at the interstices of self and other, and male and female, suggests that queer theory may provide a particularly productive way of analysing the kinds of subject elaborated by the practice of translation. Princess Elizabeth's translation of *Le miroir de l'âme pécheresse* is an example of Christian mysticism which uncovers difference in identity because the author's sense of self, which is assertively and insistently articulated in the text, reveals its dependence on the divine presence from which it can, and cannot, be separated. The sense that identity is not something single or discrete is compounded by the fact that the first-person subject insistently elaborated in Elizabeth's translation also merges elements of the original French author, the reader and, once published, its editors. Queer theory not only supplies the tools for analysing this kind of identity, an identity that cannot ultimately be pinned down; it has made this kind of subject visible, as it challenges the solidarity of identity with the politics of difference. Of course, at the origin of Christian mythology is the story of Adam and Eve – a story that links gender difference to heterosexual desire – but Christianity is also a philosophy of paradox, and paradox, as Rosalie Colie has argued, equivocates.[1] The Princess's text is full of paradoxes, from the hermaphroditic paradox of the man mixed with woman, and the woman mixed with man, to the paradox of being Christ's mother, sister, child and wife simultaneously. It is often claimed that Elizabeth did not subvert the patriarchal order, because she was presented as an exceptional woman, whose extraordinary power and authority proved the rule of female subjection. I want to suggest that Elizabeth both as princess and as queen was subversive precisely because she both embodied and used paradox.

Renaissance studies has privileged Petrarchanism as the discourse in which a new kind of self-conscious subjectivity is fashioned. Since the desiring subject in Petrarchanism is almost always male and the desired object is usually female, one form of heterosexual masculinity has come to stand for early modern subjectivity as a whole, and this individuality is secularized in keeping with a liberal humanist teleology that traces the gradual rejection of the claims of external spiritual authority in the progress to modernity. Translation, queer theory and traditions of mystical devotion challenge this historical teleology and the teleology of the subject – the idea that the subject has a telos, or end, which bounds it as single, pure and stable. Indeed the historical narrative mapped out by Elizabeth's translation of *Le miroir de l'âme pécheresse* is recursive rather than linear, as each edition of the translation in her lifetime reanimates an older, French, Erasmian, Roman Catholic context, even in the midst of English Protestant polemic.

The translation made by Elizabeth which is the focus of this essay is a form of transsexuality which resists the binaries of gender, and the binaries of hetero- and homosexual as it makes various forms of marginalized behaviour the focus of desire. In the case of her translation the mutually constitutive unitary models of individual and national sovereignty are both asserted and undermined. At the

---

1 Rosalie Colie, *Paradoxia Epidemica: The Renaissance Tradition of Paradox* (Princeton, NJ: Princeton University Press, 1966), pp. 5–33.

same time, Elizabeth's translation of *Le miroir de l'âme pécheresse* also suggests the limits of queer theory, as her text occupies a space which is constitutively racialized and nationalized, as well as sexualized. Queer theory emphasizes the constructedness, plurality and ambivalence of sexual identities and challenges any unitary model of identity, but it has tended to ignore race, class and nation as forces that constitute, and are constituted by, sexuality and gender.[2]

In 1544, when she was only eleven years old, Princess Elizabeth translated a French devotional tract into English as a New Year's gift for her step-mother, Queen Katherine Parr. The French original, *Le miroir de l'âme pécheresse*, which was in verse, was written by Queen Marguerite of Navarre, sister of François I, and was originally published in 1531. The choice of text was not only dictated by Parr's own interest in Erasmian devotion and learning, but may also have been a diplomatic compliment to Navarre, who lobbied for English interests in the French court. However, the text may well have had personal resonance for the princess. Elizabeth's mother, Anne Boleyn, had met Marguerite of Navarre when she lived in France, and may even have served in Marguerite's court. The links between the two queens were perpetuated after Anne's return to England by the traffic in scholars which was such a characteristic element of the aristocratic Erasmian movement, which grounded the goal of church and state reform in pedagogical reform. Tutors frequently provided the axis around which politico-religious networks developed. Nicholas Bourbon, a friend of Marot and Rabelais, came under the protection of Anne Boleyn when he lived in England and served as a French tutor in the Carew, Norris, Harvey and Dudley families. He also composed Latin satires against Boleyn's enemies, including Sir Thomas More. When Bourbon's father died in 1535, he returned to France, where he became tutor to Marguerite of Navarre's daughter, Jeanne, the mother of the future Henri IV of France.

Elizabeth's translation, 'Thee Miroir or Glasse of the Sinnefull Soule', which came to be known as *Elizabeth's Glass*, is a typical piece of devotional prose in which the author meditates on her own sinfulness, recognizes God's mercy and strives to purify her soul and bring it closer to God, a goal which is envisioned in erotic terms as a marriage between her soul and Christ. Not only did Elizabeth translate the text, but she copied it out with extreme care, and embroidered the covers of the volume with gold and silver tracery, possibly representing a lovers' knot, surrounding the initials KP, and sewed a hearts-ease in each corner, perhaps

---

2 A very clear overview of the vices and virtues of queer theory is provided by Steven Seidman in the introduction to *Queer Theory/Sociology*, ed. Seidman (Oxford: Basil Blackwell, 1996), pp. 1–29. See also the essays collected in *Fear of a Queer Planet: Queer Politics and Social Theory*, ed. Michael Warner (Minneapolis, MN: University of Minnesota Press, 1993). The point that queer theory needs to enrich its analysis of race and class, while postcolonial theory needs to enrich its analysis of gender, is thoughtfully elaborated in John C. Hawley, ed., *Postcolonial and Queer Theories: Intersections and Essays* (Westport, CJ: Greenwood Press, 2001).

as a compliment to the relationship between her father, Henry VIII, and Katherine Parr. While *Elizabeth's Glass* renegotiates national and personal identities, and her translation is an act of self-determination, Elizabeth very quickly entered into competition with a series of editors for interpretative control of the text. Elizabeth's translation was first published by the Protestant polemicist, John Bale, in 1548. Bale dedicated the text to Elizabeth, included her translation of four biblical sentences into Latin, Greek, French and Italian, a version of Psalm 13, and a conclusion in which he radicalizes Elizabeth's text and represents it as an intervention in the militant Protestant crusade championed by Bale. Bale's text is a longer revised version of the *Glass* which includes passages omitted from Elizabeth's manuscript version, and it seems likely that Bale's edition was a collaborative production, with Elizabeth herself undertaking revisions, perhaps under the instigation of Parr in 1547. The *Glass* was the most widely disseminated of Elizabeth's texts during her lifetime and continued to be published after she ascended to the throne. Bale's edition was reissued in 1590 (without Psalm 13). A new edition of the *Glass* by James Canceller, with a new dedication, conclusion, an acrostic and meditations on Elizabeth's name appeared around 1568, and Canceller's edition was reprinted in Thomas Bentley's *Monument of Matrones* in 1582.[3] Bentley's lavish volume is a celebration of Elizabeth's sovereignty that exploits images of spiritual illumination drawn from the parable of the Wise and Foolish Virgins. It inscribes Elizabeth within a pan-European tradition of female Protestant devotion that includes Navarre and Parr, and continues the process of spiritual renewal instituted by biblical heroines such as Hester.

Elizabeth's piety and learning were cornerstones of her public image, and were essential to the exercise of her power. The publication of *Elizabeth's Glass* facilitates her exercise of government and the editions published after her accession reinforce the myth of learned Protestant devotion, constancy to God and affirm the saintly nature of her youth. The cult of Elizabeth crystallized in the early 1570s and *Elizabeth's Glass* retrospectively confers continuity on Elizabeth's Protestant biography, suggesting that as she was as a child, pious and devout, she is as a queen. She is indeed *semper eadem*, always the same, although the continuity so defined is continuity with the intellectual, Erasmian context of her youth and of her mother, as well as continuity with Protestantism — *semper eadem* was, after all, Anne Boleyn's motto.

Until recently historians have ignored the mutually constitutive relations between England and her foreign neighbours. Yet, as Patrick Collinson reminds us, English Puritanism can only be understood in relation to developments in

---

3 The British Library possesses another edition (C.38.c.57) based on Canceller's that lacks the title-page and signature A. The 1568? edition has the small 16mo format of books of devotion. Neither the dating of, nor indeed the number of, editions by Canceller has been settled, and catalogues remain confused.

France and the Low Countries.[4] Elizabethan attitudes to France exist in a complex predicament of relation and need to be read in relation to Scotland, home of Mary Queen of Scots, the widow of François II, and in relation to Spain. The different versions of Elizabeth's translation suggest how an identification with French culture is remodelled in response to changing political, religious and hermeneutical contexts, with the result that, while *Elizabeth's Glass* defines both France and England, neither nation is the same thing in all periods. Between 1570 and 1582, Elizabeth conducted serious, but spasmodic, marriage negotiations with the Duke of Anjou, and then his younger brother, the Duke of Alençon. In this context the editions of 1568 and 1582 could either be read as offering support to the negotiations, by affirming England's Frenchness, or as implicit criticisms of the negotiations which remind Elizabeth of her own reformist inheritance – an inheritance that was threatened by marriage to a Catholic Frenchman. In the former reading, France, as represented by Anjou and Alençon, is identified with Navarre's context; in the latter reading, France, as represented by the brothers, is dissociated from Navarre's context. The edition of 1590 may respond to renewed interest in French affairs after the murder of Henri III in August 1589, which provoked civil war between his heir Henri of Navarre, Marguerite's grandson and a Protestant, and the Catholic League, supported by Spain. Elizabeth sent money, arms and men to support Henri, and the republication of Bale's edition, with its radical Protestant apparatus, may have served as a rallying cry, reminding its readers of the plight of French Protestantism and the long-standing reformist communion between the two countries.

Marguerite of Navarre herself functions in varied ways in Renaissance culture. She is a model of humanist learning and eloquence, and one of her letters appears in Aldus Manutius the Younger's *Lettere volgari di diversi nobilissimi huomini* (1564), the kind of hagiographic anthology that popularized humanism across Europe. However, Marguerite, her text and *Elizabeth's Glass* all underwent a retrospective process of radicalization in the sixteenth century. Although it emphasizes grace and free will, there is nothing necessarily Protestant about *Le miroir de l'âme pécheresse*, and Marguerite remained a Catholic, albeit a supporter of the French Evangelical movement. *Le miroir* appeared in 1531 without fuss, but the second edition of 1533 was condemned by the Sorbonne in October of that year, and then acquitted after the intervention of her brother in November. It was published by Antoine Augereau, who was later burnt as a heretic after the Affaire des Placards of 1534, which marked the end of François I's openness to reform. Marguerite's dispute with the Sorbonne entered the annals of Protestant history when Calvin relayed the incident to François Daniel, in a letter dated October 1533, and this version was more widely publicized by Théodore de Bèze, in his *Histoire ecclesiastique des églises reformées au*

4 Patrick Collinson, *The Elizabethan Puritan Movement* (1967; Oxford: Clarendon Press, 1990), pp. 71–83 and 109–11.

royaume de France (1580).[5] As *Elizabeth's Glass* is edited by Bale, Canceller and Bentley, it too is radicalized, but it is ironic that it is a Roman Catholic French tract that plays a part in the constitution of the Protestant English nation.

In *Elizabeth's Glass*, the business of translation is both passive and active, both a reflection of Elizabeth and the actual means by which she is fashioned into a soul fit to be the Bride of Christ. As she explains in her dedication:

> The which book is entitled, or named, *The Mirror or Glass of the Sinful Soul*, wherein is contained how she (beholding and contemplating what she is) doth perceive how of herself and of her own strength she can do nothing that good is, or prevaileth for her salvation, unless it be through the grace of God, whose mother, daughter, sister, and wife by the scriptures she proveth herself to be.
>
> (p. 111)[6]

The act of looking outwards is simultaneously an act of introspection, which 'proves' Elizabeth. In other words, it not only gives evidence of her integrity and virtue, it also whets, files and moulds the princess as one would prove a piece of metal. Thus in *Elizabeth's Glass* the activities of reading and rewriting are integral to her self-definition: they are the very processes by which she comes into being. The text, particularly the manuscript text of *Elizabeth's Glass*, plays with the idea of origins and imprints in further ways. The *Glass* is, according to the dedication, labour that is 'as well spiritual as manual' (p. 112). In this pun on the idea of a spiritual manual, Elizabeth also alludes to the manual labour that went into copying and then embroidering her translation for Katherine Parr. The copy of herself that Elizabeth sends Parr is precisely that, something that is unique to Elizabeth, and bears her manual imprint, a visual assertion of her character.

The princess is in the process of spiritual and social refinement in the self-originating work of translation. In this respect, her text not only challenges any dismissal of translation as unoriginal, it also challenges criticism by feminist

5 The most detailed and reliable studies of the history of Navarre's *Miroir*, and of its relationship to Elizabeth's translation are Renja Salminen, ed., *Le miroir de l'âme pécheresse* (Helsinki: Suomalainen Tiedeakatemia, 1979), and Saara Nevanlinna, 'The first translation of a young princess', *Proceedings from the Third Nordic Conference for English Studies*, ed. Ishrat Lindblad and Magnus Ljung (Stockholm: Amqvist & Wiksell International, 1987), I, pp. 243–56.

6 All quotations from the manuscript version and from Bale's additions are from *Elizabeth's Glass*, ed. Marc Shell (Lincoln, NE: University of Nebraska Press, 1993). There have been few studies of *Elizabeth's Glass*. Apart from Shell's introduction, the most stimulating study is John King, *Tudor Royal Iconography* (Princeton, NJ: Princeton University Press, 1989), pp. 54–116 and 201–66, which is particularly interesting on the Henrician intellectual context and the context of Bentley's edition. Anne Lake Prescott, 'The Pearl of the Valois and Elizabeth I', in *Silent but for the Word*, ed. Margaret Patterson Hannay (Kent, OH: Kent State University Press, 1985), pp. 61–76, takes a psychological approach to *Elizabeth's Glass*.

students of the Renaissance that has given the study of translation a place, only in so far as it is symptomatic of the restrictions that governed female behaviour. While Tina Krontiris has demonstrated that translation, particularly the translation of devotional works, was an acceptable form of female activity in the Renaissance, not only because the holy subject matter legitimized the undertaking, but also because translation itself was thought to be a modest enterprise in which the self did not claim priority, her nuanced analyses of how this dictum actually works through the specificities of a particular translation have been ignored in the tendentious claims made by some feminist scholars that women's translations in the Renaissance are more literal than men's.[7] Indeed Elizabeth's own translations are usually dismissed as bad and/or excessively literal, and yet in 1598 she chose to translate a passage from Horace's *Ars poetica* that explores the issues of originality and good translation and suggests that she thought self-consciously about her own practice.[8] In her translation of *Le miroir*, Elizabeth follows the text closely, sometimes adding words for rhetorical effect or clarity, at other times confusing the syntactical relations of what is a very difficult source. Translation always raises the issues of freedom and literality, and the extent to which these are to be reconciled with the demands of source and audience. Translation, commenting and glossing are all modes of textual exposition, and the issue of literality is linked to stylistic ideologies and exegetical controversies that are inflected by Renaissance calls for spiritual reform. The Erasmian reform movement which provides the context for both Marguerite's *Miroir* and *Elizabeth's Glass*, advocates a move towards simplicity and plainness, because it sees language as a bearer of meaning, not of proliferation and deferral.

Issues of literality, originality and sovereignty in female translation need a more nuanced consideration than they have received. Translations like *Elizabeth's Glass* were also essential tools in learning a language, and the aims and methods of language acquisition vary. Renaissance language manuals are heavily practical and emphasize the ability to read and speak French. They devote a lot of their space to explaining pronunciation, and present the language ready for use, by offering vocabulary in the form of contextualized dialogues. Giles Du Wes's *Introductory for to learn to read, to pronounce, and to speak French* (1532?) is characteristic of Tudor manuals. Du Wes was tutor in French to Henry VIII, and his *Introductory* was compiled at the request of another of his royal pupils, Elizabeth's half-sister, Mary. As the title suggests, the aim was to read and speak French, and the first book is devoted to grammar and vocabulary,

---

7 Tina Krontiris, *Oppositional Voices* (1992; London: Routledge, 1997), pp. 20–21. The claim that women's translations are more literal than men's is made by Mary Ellen Lamb, 'The Cooke sisters: attitudes toward learned women in the Renaissance', in Hannay, ed., *Silent but for the Word*, pp. 107–25, at p. 124.

8 See, for example, Maria Perry's dismissive comments in *Elizabeth I: The Word of a Prince* (London: The Folio Society, 1990), pp. 31–3.

while the second book consists of a series of practical examples in the form of letters and dialogues in French with interlinear English translations. The dialogues are tailored to the realities of Mary's life and interests, and include such issues as the proper way to receive a messenger from a prince and an exposition of the Mass. (As a point of comparison, French manuals aimed at the merchant class, include dialogues set in taverns, or commercial exchanges about the price and quality of cloth.) Elizabeth made her translation fourteen years after the publication of John Palsgrave's *Lesclarcissement de la langue francoise* (1530), the first large-scale, systematic attempt, in either French or English, to codify the French language. Palsgrave's grammar attempts to classicize French by drawing up a set of rules that represent it as the equal of Latin or Greek. While still privileging pronunciation, Palsgrave's emphasis on rules marks a movement away from learning by imitation and doing. Nevertheless, before the ascendancy of codification, which was still in its infancy with Palsgrave, grammatical accuracy was not as highly prized by Tudor language teachers as it is by us, and it remained secondary to pronunciation, even for Palsgrave. Given such aims, even a literal translation that was not written in fluent English, or one that included mistakes, would fulfil the practical aims of language teaching to achieve communication in French.

The origins of Elizabeth's text are both divine and earthly, but when she does acknowledge the earthly origins of her text, those origins are predominantly female – lying either in Elizabeth herself, as she pursues the self-originating and self-authenticating processes of authorship, or in a community of female authors who inspire the text, specifically Queen Marguerite of Navarre and Queen Katherine Parr. *Elizabeth's Glass* inscribes the princess within a community of reform-minded, royal authoresses, privileging matrilineage over patrilineage, spiritual and intellectual inheritance over the inheritance of blood, and constructs a collaborative model of reading and writing. In her preface to the *Glass*, Elizabeth's witty turn on the word matter undermines the preconceptions of gender that link spirit and form to masculinity, and matter and formlessness to femininity. In her subversion of Aristotelian distinctions, matter becomes meaning, and men and women are equally weak:

> If thou dost read this whole work, behold rather the matter and excuse the speech, considering it is the work of a woman which hath in her neither science nor knowledge but a desire that each one might see what the gift of God doth when it pleaseth Him to justify the heart of a man. For what thing is a man (as for his own strength) before he hath received the gift of faith whereby only he hath the knowledge of the goodness, wisdom and power of God?
>
> (p. 113)[9]

---

9 Although Elizabeth's preface claims that the text is 'the work of a woman', Elizabeth was only a twelve-year-old girl when she wrote it, and her persona is distanced from Navarre's by the play of age as well as the play of gender.

The princess assumes both male and female gender: this is the work of a woman who has the heart of a man, and men are now feminized matter. But she also confuses categories by assuming different generational identities simultaneously, she is both 'mother, daughter, sister and wife', as she has already noted in the dedication (p. 111). She transgresses earthly customs as her soul desires to be overwhelmed by God – 'ravished' (p. 132) is one of the terms used. But God, who has both masculine and feminine characteristics, is desired by a subject which itself displays both masculine and feminine characteristics. Moreover, God as the father, brother and husband desires her as sister and daughter, as well as wife. In *Elizabeth's Glass* what is excluded from identity and is therefore stigmatized does indeed become the focus of desire in incest and same-sex desire.

Although Christianity condemns same-sex relations as sodomitical and early modern culture relates sodomy to a host of social, sexual and political transgressions, the text presents same-sex relations and the transgressions of gender as models of spiritual perfection. At the same time, it prevents us from reading out the sexual, particularly when *Elizabeth's Glass* is read in the context of the accusations of multiple adultery, incest and bestiality made against Elizabeth's mother, Anne Boleyn, and her political and religious allies in 1536. Perhaps it is not surprising, given Princess Elizabeth's unhappy biography, that her text is particularly acute at unravelling the definitions of sexuality and gender and their points of intersection with networks of social, familial and political power. Elizabeth had been declared a bastard in 1536, but her text protests the marginal space to which she had been consigned, and equivocates between private and public realms. It is a monstrous text which indulges in preposterous logic. Indeed, it is a self-assertive text, but that self-assertiveness depends on transgressing the models through which subjectivity is normally defined. This is a text that dares to speak secrets and challenges interlocking networks of power, appropriating its own unstable forms of authority: 'Shall or dare I tell it? May I pronounce it without shame? Alas, yea, for my confusion is to show the great love of my husband', cries the sinner (p. 127). The only restrictions on individual autonomy are spiritual ones; in every other sense the individual is self-determined. Besides, as the princess archly reminds us, the service of God is perfect freedom, because God is perfect love. He is purer and more constant than any earthly husband, father, lover or brother, mother or child:

> Keep my heart then, my brother, and let not Thy enemy enter in it. O my father, brother, child, and spouse, with hands joined, humbly upon my knees, I yield Thee thanks and praise that it pleaseth Thee to turn Thy face toward me, converting my heart and covering me with such grace that Thou dost see no more evils and sins.
>
> (p. 122)

Bale's edition seeks to politicize the *Glass*, and renders it more conservative, and less subversive of patrilineage than Elizabeth's original, partly because he produces a printed text which needs to be policed more carefully than a manuscript which is aimed at an elite, courtly readership. His assertion of patriarchy is aligned with virulent anti-Catholicism, and much greater anxiety about various kinds of contamination, including hostility to the French, than is exhibited by Canceller or Bentley. Bale was an astute reader of Elizabeth's text and recognizes its interest in origins and in female virtue. But Bale immediately undermines Elizabeth's emphasis on matrilineage, defining her worth in relationship to men at the very opening of his rededication : 'To the right virtuous and Christianly learned young Lady Elizabeth, the noble daughter of our late sovereign King Henry the Eighth'. Orthodox patriarchal responses to the question of a woman's chastity are to affirm or deny it. Here Bale implicitly affirms Anne Boleyn's chastity and thus the legitimacy of her daughter. Elizabeth's response in the *Glass* is to question chastity as a stable principle of definition, through Christ, a husband–father who forgives his bride even though she has 'committed fornication' with 'false lovers' (p. 130). If one can forgive the lapse of chastity and still see one's wife as legitimate, then the polarities on which the Renaissance understanding of gender is constructed are themselves undermined. On the contrary, Bale emphasizes Elizabeth's blood in his dedication and spends much time defining 'right nobility' (p. 83) as a condition that is both inborn, stemming from Elizabeth's inheritance, and acquired, stemming from Elizabeth's noble actions. Courtesy, gift-giving and learning are all attributes of nobility Bale claims (p. 84) and are all displayed by the *Glass*. In the conclusion, Elizabeth's education is upheld 'as an example to be followed of other noble men and women concerning their children' (p. 95), so that, in addition to the imitation of Christ, the imitation of Elizabeth is set up as the way to instil the nation with the values of cultivated Protestantism.

Within the context of his discussion of nobility in the dedication, Bale also starts to develop the idea of English fair play, a natural regard for equality which is associated with Protestantism and stands in opposition to the arrogance of the 'monstrous' nobility of Rome, with its 'pontifical lords, spiritual sirs and ghostly fathers' (pp. 84–5). In the end, Bale presents legitimacy as a conflation of social, spiritual and familial factors, and whatever authority Elizabeth gained by the act of authorship, Bale tries to control by reinterpreting and refashioning her text and therefore the princess herself. He prescribes her as a character enfolded in his text: 'Most lively in these and such other excellent facts express ye the natural emphasis of your noble name. Elizabeth in the Hebrew is as much to say in the Latin as *Dei mei requies*; in English, The rest of my God' (p. 91). Yet, in spite of his revisions, her attack on gender distinctions in the body of the text remains. Often, in Elizabeth's translation, the gendered subject is unstable, and while this may be the result of translating French, where all nouns are gendered, it has the effect of undermining the oppositions on which we depend for the construction of gender. In this way Bale's dedication sits uneasily with the tendencies of Elizabeth's text. In fact, when Bale comes to the crux of his attack on the Roman Catholics, the attack on transubstantiation, his words betray anxieties about the sort of conflation of gender that Elizabeth exploits. He attacks transubstantiation because it is 'more than Luciferian presumption' (p. 86) to claim that a priest can make God, and the consequence of the Catholic claim is to turn men into sexual monstrosities, into women who bear Christ: 'A priest may every day both beget Him and bear Him, whereas his mother Mary begat Him (bore Him they would say) but once' (p. 86). By 1548, Elizabeth as cultural genetrix is already in competition with male authors for control of her texts.

In spite of its equivocations, in the context of Bale's nationalistic edition, Elizabeth's translation represents the standard for good writing. As Juliet Fleming points out, the vernacular, or mother tongue, and especially an idealized vernacular, had associations with the feminine that went back to Cicero's remarks in *De oratore* that the quiet and sequestered life of Roman women preserved their language from the contaminations of fashion and business, so that the purest form of Latin was spoken by chaste women.[10] Proper style for Bale is a style that avoids the 'gorgeously garnished ... rhetorics' (p. 85) of the scholastics because God favours the plain style, as he notes in his conclusion: 'He that is here familiarly commoned with regardeth no curiosity, but plainness and truth' (p. 93). What Bale describes as the 'homely speech' (p. 93) of women is something spoken from the heart, a sign of the integrity of the speaker, and female verbal style becomes a model for English Protestant style. Bale's contemporaries, on the other hand, frequently associate plainness with the stoic ideal of English masculinity, and Protestant writers, like John Knox, resist models of female authority. What is so striking about Bale's catalogue of English heroines in his conclusion is not only that he praises women as rulers, authors, warriors and civilizing forces, but it is these godly women who link the Reformers to England's past, who have preserved true Englishness from Roman Catholic interference, and who embody the principles of Protestant nationalism. Hilda, for instance, 'a noble woman both godly, wise, and learned, not only disputed in the open Synod at Streneshalce in the north country against the prelates concerning their newly found out celebration of Easter and their crown shaving, with other ceremonies, but also wrote a treatise against bishop Agilbert, a Frenchman, the busiest among them' (p. 100).

Humanism moralizes the relationship between inner and outer discourse so that a good man is supposed to speak well, but the relationship between moral worth and eloquence is emphasized in discussions of royal language. In a letter addressed to James VI, written in August 1583, Elizabeth advises her cousin: 'Among your many studies, my dear Brother and Cousin, I would Isocrates' noble lesson were not forgotten, that wills the Emperor his sovereign to make his words of more account than other men their oaths, as meetest ensigns to show the

---

10 See Juliet Fleming, 'Dictionary English and the female tongue', in *Enclosure Acts: Sexuality, Property and Culture in Early Modern England*, ed. Richard Burt and John Michael Archer (Ithaca, NY: Cornell University Press, 1994), pp. 299–302.

truest badge of a Prince's arms' (*Letters*, p. 159). Not only does Elizabeth lay claim to the godlike power of a language where signified and signifier coalesce, she also claims knowledge of the other, non-sovereign kind of language with its flattery and lies, as she delivers a sly rebuke to James for failing to show her true friendship. For a sovereign, word and deed are the same thing so that language is embodied or literalized in the person of the queen. This understanding of language is exemplified in the acrostic James Canceller included in his edition of *Elizabeth's Glass* which turns Elizabeth's name into the generic name of virtue:

E Embrace Vertue
L Love perfectly
I Imitate Christ
Z Zelously pray
A Aske heavenly giftes (sig. G8v).

Elizabeth becomes an act of language that projects moral virtue, as word and referent are bonded through her moral character. This is the character of Elizabeth as a letter, and in the Theophrastan sense – the poem really does contain the virtue Canceller describes as it becomes her glass, the reflection of her true self and reconnects *res* and *verba*. A similar understanding of language motivates Bale's Hebrew–Latin–English pun on Elizabeth's name as signifying 'The rest of my God' (p. 91). Moreover, such multilingual puns suggest a culture that is acutely receptive to the simultaneity of different codes, and the simultaneity of different languages, an observation that may be reinforced by the dominance of the interlinear format in Tudor language manuals, where the eye slips easily between a line of French and a line of English. The multilingual pun plays with a language as a sound system, similarly an acrostic plays with a language as a visual system. In both cases, meanings develop from the formal nature of the words which generates connections and ideas. Elizabeth's translations not only appropriate the world as Florio's 'Colombus' appropriates new wealth, they actually transform the word into the world, they transform the name into a thing. Bale's advice that we should all imitate Elizabeth's style homogenizes English and works with the Tudor drive to centralization by making the princess and the court the universal standard of English, he also understands the imitation of her style as civilizing: the reproduction of the particular language exemplified by her translation will create order, and not merely reflect it. Meaning is an effect of language, not something preserved behind words, and the nation is built by the dissemination of Elizabeth's words through the land.

Elizabeth's translations are part of an ongoing dialogue with models of learned sovereignty that were not only elaborated by Marguerite of Navarre, but also by Elizabeth's European contemporaries, such as Henri III, and especially her cousin and potential heir, James VI of Scotland. The idea that Elizabethan England was an island entire of itself is a myth. James presented himself as a prince who would glorify Scottish literature by promoting the vernacular and by defining the modes of good writing. The young king became a political force in Scotland from the mid-1580s, and he elaborated his theories of sovereignty in a succession of publications that define political ideology in linguistic and stylistic terms. In his *Schort Treatise,* published with *The Essayes of a Prentise, in the Divine Art of Poesie* (1584), James discusses poetry and the rules of versification in order to establish Scottish poetic, linguistic and national autonomy, by differentiating Scots from English. As the first critic to define rules for Scots rhyme, rhythm and stanza formation, or so he claims, James becomes the source of Scots poetry, a role that he played out in the informal poetry school that he set up at court, which included William Fowler, William Alexander and Stewart of Baldynneis. James promotes invention, in the *Schort Treatise*, arguing that, 'sen *Invention*, is ane of the cheif vertewis in a Poete, it is best that ze invent zour awin subject, zour self, and not to compose of sene subjectis' (sig. M2v). He is particularly critical of translation because, 'ze are bound, as to a staik, to follow that buikis phrasis, quhilk ze translate'. Autonomy is a sign of sovereignty for James, and that autonomy is threatened by translation.

The problem of translation is compounded for a virgin queen by the fact that translation is potentially a form of vulgarization, which makes select knowledge freely available, and also a form of prostitution. Florio is acutely aware of the intersections of class and sexual ideologies in definitions of translation, but defends the practice as the universal condition of all knowledge, in the preface to Montaigne's *Essays*. 'From translation all Science had it's [*sic*] of-spring' (sig. A5r), he notes, because knowledge is always mediated, transformed, and second-hand, and he sets out to undermine the interlinked negative class and sexual connotations of translation:

> Why but Learning would not be made common. Yea but Learning cannot be too common, and the commoner the better. Why but who is not jealous, his Mistresse should be so prostitute? Yea but this Mistresse is like ayre, fire, water, the more breathed the clearer; the more extended the warmer; the more drawne the sweeter.

The nature of translation in *Elizabeth's Glass* is further complicated by the fact that different languages seem to have different gender associations. In Renaissance England, French connotes love, good taste and social refinement, and while the general populace viewed France with suspicious hostility, knowledge of French was widespread among the gentry and aristocracy.[11] Translation focuses attention on the conventional aspects of language, on idioms, on the impact of context and time on words. It tends to link language to the temporality of human customs, but in sixteenth-century England, the mutability highlighted by translation was exacerbated and epitomized by French. In

11 See Kathleen Lambley, *The Teaching and Cultivation of the French Language in England during Tudor and Stuart Times* (Manchester: Manchester University Press, 1920), pp. 61–85 and 117–18.

Lesclarcissement de la langue francoise, Palsgrave points out that French is difficult to control as it is unstably gendered. Some French words like 'exemple' have masculine and feminine forms (sig. M3r), others change gender depending on whether they are singular or plural (sig. M4r–v)! Such slippery terms include 'evangille', which is masculine in the singular and feminine in the plural, and 'affaire', which is feminine in the singular and masculine in the plural. It would seem that equivocation is particularly characteristic of French. For Sir James Melville, the envoy from Mary Queen of Scots in 1564, Elizabeth's French was not idiomatic precisely because it did not equivocate, leading her to misinterpret one of Mary's letters because she was too straightforward: 'albeit hir Majestie culd speak asgud Frenche as any that had never bene out of the contre, ... yet sche laiketh the use of the Frenche court langage, whilk wes frank and schort, and had oft tymes twa significations, quhilk discreit and famylier frendis tok alwayes in the best part' (p. 117).

In Renaissance attitudes to French, fear of the instability of language intersects with fears of sexually active women and even effeminized men. Henri III was famed for his eloquence and notorious for the band of male favourites, the so-called 'mignons', with whom he surrounded himself. 'French hath long time beene termed the language of Ladies', Florio notes in the dedication of Book III of Montaigne's *Essays* to Lady Elizabeth Grey and Lady Mary Nevill, and his band of six patronesses epitomizes the association of French with femininity and courtliness. Nevertheless, as he implies in the preface where he describes the genius of French as 'Venus' (sig. A5v), femininity and courtliness have the potential to distract with dangerous Venerean pleasures. This fear is echoed in John Eliot's *Ortho-Epia Gallica* (1593), a curious mixture of language manual and jest-book, with prefatory material very much in the irreverent, dynamic and copious manner of Nashe. In his preface 'To the Gentlemen Readers' (sig. B2v), he calls French the most 'ticklish' of all tongues, pinpointing not only the difficulty of pronunciation, but its sexual promiscuity. In his 'Epistle to the learned professors of French', Eliot affects gibberish, coins words, portmanteau terms and lists of synonyms and epithets, all to introduce his countrymen to the 'curious and courtesan French tongue' (sig. A4r), with an Anglo-French pun on courtesan, as courtly lady and prostitute. He connects race and sexuality, as French is constructed as the fetishized, sexually promiscuous other that stands in for the object of a generalized desire for the possession and appropriation of French riches. The association of sexuality with courtliness is precisely the association that is made by critics of Elizabeth's court, from George Gascoigne in 'The Adventures of Master F.J.' (1573) to Edmund Spenser in his presentation of Acrasia in Book II of *The Faerie Queene* (1590) as a desirable but dangerous lady who disarms and emasculates her knights. Elizabeth, it was feared, spread a dangerous femininity among her male courtiers and so it is highly appropriate that she should be skilled in the eroticized and equivocal language of French. During her reign, Elizabeth's fluency in French has the potential both to assert and deny her authority as it feeds into, and is fed by, hostility to her style of government.

Translation toys with the cultural prescriptions governing both genders. The crossing it produces involves the transfer of knowledge and labour across borders, which also has the potential to cross in the sense of breaking boundaries and contaminating. Elizabeth's conception of her sovereignty is fashioned from attitudes acquired in her youth in which French culture plays an important and continuing role. *Elizabeth's Glass* records difference in identity in all sorts of ways, in the issue of gender, but also in denominational, national and temporal identities. The interior, spiritual, contemplative life of medieval piety persists in *Elizabeth's Glass,* albeit in modified form, but one of the things translation does is raise questions about the meaning and viability of periodization through its temporal equivocations. The sovereignty defined in her translation is not purely English, or purely Protestant, as the text moves across national and linguistic borders as well as epistemologies of gender. *Elizabeth's Glass* suggests that we should redraw the map of the emerging English subject as a space of continuing mediations and confrontations with alien elements, since sexual, gender, social, national and linguistic stratifications are interlinked in multiple and unstable ways.

Primary texts quoted

Eliot, John, *Ortho-Epia Gallica. Eliots Fruits for the French 1593*, Scolar Press Facsimile (Menston: Scolar Press, 1968).

Elizabeth I, *Elizabeth's Glass*, ed. Marc Shell (Lincoln, Nebraska: University of Nebraska Press, 1993).

Elizabeth I, *The Letters of Queen Elizabeth*, ed. G.B. Harrison (London: Cassell, 1935).

Florio, John, *A Worlde of Wordes* (1598). *STC* 11098.

Florio, John, trans., *The Essays* (1603; Menston: Scolar Press, 1969).

Florio, John, *Queen Anna's New World of Words* (1611; Menston: Scolar Press, 1968).

James VI, *The Essayes of a Prentise, in the Divine Art of Poesie* (Edinburgh, 1584). *STC* 14373.

[Melville, Sir James], *Memoirs of his own Life by Sir James Melville of HalHill* (Edinburgh: The Bannatyne Club, 1827).

Palsgrave, John, *Lesclarcissement de la langue francoise* (1530; Menston: Scolar Press, 1969).

Chapter 8

Italian weeds and English bodies: translating 'The Adventures of Master F.J.'

Amina Alyal

When George Gascoigne published *The Posies of George Gascoigne Esquire* in 1575, he included 'The pleasant Fable of Ferdinando Jeronimi and Leonora de Valasco', translated, he claimed, from the Italian. It had first appeared two years earlier as 'A Discourse of the Adventures passed by Master F.J.' in the anonymous *A Hundreth Sundrie Flowres*, in fact, the first edition of the *Posies*.[1] The 'translation' was indeed more consciously Italianate than the earlier version, which had been presented as the actual story of a young Englishman, F.J., and his affair with the married Elinor, recorded in a range of modes, including letters, poems and reported anecdote. It had a mixed reception, causing as it did speculations about the characters' identities and protests about indecency. But while in the second version Gascoigne acknowledged authorship of the volume generally, he denied direct responsibility for the story of F.J., giving as his source the fictional Italian, 'Bartello'. Why he should pretend his story was a translation, why from the Italian, why he should simplify the narrative structure and include it in the section entitled 'Weedes' in the *Posies*, are all questions that uncover Reformation attitudes to romantic fiction. The toning down of sexual adventurousness in the second version parallels the more controlled narrative structure, so that excess, both of form and of matter, seems to be the subject of reform. By examining the process of transition from one version to the other, it is possible to trace the ways in which *inventio* is arbitrated and textual depravity encoded as translation in response to censure.

Ostensibly, the narrative simply accommodates the writing of a series of poems. 'The Adventures' is a roughly chiselled space, *La Vita Nuova* in a setting reminiscent of Gawain's sojourn in the house of the Green Knight. The text

---

1 References to Gascoigne's *A Hundreth Sundrie Flowres* (1573) are to the text edited by G.W. Pigman III (Oxford: Clarendon Press, 2000) in the form, e.g., H23; references to Gascoigne's *The Posies of George Gascoigne Esquire* (1575) are to the text edited by John W. Cunliffe (Cambridge: Cambridge University Press, 1907), in the form, e.g., P433.

explores, often subversively, *questioni d'amore*, Petrarchan poetry, highborn adultery, chivalry, ribaldry and psychological interrelationships. It is also the site of subtle explorations of literary creativity and the role played by readers and narrators. Conversations are observed, interpreted and misinterpreted, moulded into poems; stories are offered for interpretation so as to expose the bias of the interpreter. Elinor is described as 'deciphering' her thoughts in the act of writing them down (e.g. H152–3). It is as if the act of translation itself is under scrutiny, even in this first version – both in the sense of putting the same thing into different languages, and in the sense that Peter Quince uses it of Bottom, of a radical metamorphosis into something else. Events are translated into verse, thoughts into writing, incidents into variable opinion. Literary creation, of one sort or another, is a constant activity, and interpretation, both of events and of tales, shown to be a subjective and fluid process. Susan Staub has noted this characteristic of the text: 'Instead of grounding the tale in the objectivity of history, as G.T. might wish, the work becomes steeped in a multiplicity of subjectivities.'[2]

This emphasis on creativity and interpretation, on readership and authorship, is reflected in the structure of 'The Adventures'. The narrative is mediated through five named levels of interpretation, including an implied reader, in a manner not unusual in Tudor prose collections.[3] One H.W. passes on the book he has received from his friend G.T., who had it from *his* friend F.J. and others. The Printer, offering the book to the reader, finds himself to be a reader as well, and makes his own interpretations of what G.T. and H.W. say about their wish for the work to remain secret. G.T. himself never lets a poem pass without a commentary; for example: 'This Ballade, or howsoever I shall terme it, percase you will not like … and for my part, if I were not parciall, I woulde saye more in commendacion of it than nowe I meane to do, leaving it to your and like judgementes' (H3). This experimental approach, with its emphasis on revision, is evident in the self-consciousness of G.T.'s comment that 'I did with more labour gather them into some order, and so placed them in this register' and the Printer to the Reader writes of the pieces in the whole volume that it is not necessary to 'take them up in such order as they are sorted: But you may take any one flowre by itselfe, and if that smell not so pleasantly as you wold wish, I doubt not yet but you may find some other which may supplie the defects thereof' (H145). Gascoigne, George E. Rowe argues, is through the fumbling analyses of G.T. attempting to give readers instruction, portraying G.T. as 'a bad reader' in

2 Susan C. Staub, '"According to My Source": Fictionality in *The Adventures of Master F.J.*', *Studies in Philology* LXXXVII (1990), pp. 111–19, at p. 18.

3 See Paul Salzman, *English Prose Fiction, 1558–1700: A Critical History* (Oxford: Clarendon Press, 1985), pp. 14–19 and Constance C. Relihan, *Fashioning Authority: The Development of Elizabethan Novelistic Discourse* (Kent, OH and London: Kent State University Press, 1994), pp. 35ff.

Renaissance terms.[4] The implied reader is certainly, in Wolfgang Müller's words, 'an active participant' in the narrative process.[5] The issue of shifting interpretation is a pressing one at this time, when, as David Kastan notes, the translated Bible meant that a worrying potential for multiple interpretations threatened to obscure the desired unity of faith.[6] Thus interpretative conjecture is an integral part of 'The Adventures', readership being presented as another aspect of authorship.

The charge that the tale was a *roman à clef* apparently called for an elaborate strategy in defence, rather than a simple insistence that the story was invented. This in itself is a telling reflection of contemporary concerns about fiction that become clear in the unravelling of the process by which 'The Adventures' becomes 'The pleasant Fable'. 'The Adventures' is merely presented as the 'history' of one of the 'sundrie gentlemen' whose works have been arranged to the best of G.T.'s ability in the *Sundrie Flowres*, F.J.'s poems being the ones at the beginning (possibly those following 'The Adventures', with the motto '*Si fortunatus infoelix*' [H145], which could explain the initials F.J.).[7] It is only in the restructuring as 'The pleasant Fable' that it becomes a discrete piece of work, as R.W. Maslen notes, '[modifying] the emphasis on anarchic inventiveness which characterized the first'.[8]

'Bartello', the supposed author of the 'source', is generally agreed to be fictitious, although there is one reference to an Italian author of that name in a seventeenth-century text. The strongest argument for his being a fake is, however, the existence of 'The Adventures', which plainly is not a translation from an Italian romance. But 'Bartello' is frequently referred to in 'The pleasant Fable', and the setting is altered; the secretary's trip is to Florence, for example, replacing London in the original. Naming is simplified: the mysteriously initialled 'F.J'. becomes plain 'Ferdinando de Jeronimy'. Similarly, Dame Pergo is introduced in 'The Adventures' as 'an old courtier, and a wylie wench, whome for this discourse I will name *Pergo*, least hir name natural were too brode before,

---

4 George E. Rowe, 'Interpretation, Sixteenth-Century Readers, and George Gascoigne's "The Adventures of Master F. J."', *English Literary History* XLVIII (1981), pp. 271–89, at p. 279.

5 Wolfgang G. Müller, 'The Modernity of the Second Version of George Gascoigne's Master F.J.', in Wolfgang Görtschacher and Holger Klein, eds, *Narrative Strategies in Early English Fiction* (New York and Salzburg: Edwin Mellen Press, 1995), pp. 87–102, at p. 95.

6 David Scott Kastan, '"The noyse of the new Bible": Reform and Reaction in Henrician England', in Claire McEachern and Debora Shuger, eds, *Religion and Culture in Renaissance England* (Cambridge: Cambridge University Press, 1997), pp. 46–68.

7 See Anthony Brian Taylor, '"The Adventures of Master F.J." and *Twelfth Night*', *Notes and Queries* n.s. XLV (1987), pp. 331–3.

8 R.W. Maslen, *Elizabethan Fictions: Espionage, Counter-Espionage, and the Duplicity of Fiction in Early Elizabethan Prose Narratives* (Oxford: Clarendon Press, 1997), p. 120.

and might not drinke of all waters'; and in 'The pleasant Fable' as 'an old courtier, & a wilie wenche, named *Pergo*' (H191; cf. P428). In the first version, possibly to assist in the illusion of the documentary, the naming is self-conscious, revealed as a process of judgement; in the second it is presented unambiguously.

Similarly, the intricate accumulation of narrators at the beginning, and the continued presence of G.T., are all cut in the second version, which becomes a single narrative by an unnamed narrator. The transition creates the illusion of simplicity; in 'The Adventures' G.T. constantly referred to F.J. as a source for his information, and this is replaced by references to Bartello. For example, in 'The Adventures', G.T. describes the secretary, a rival for the love of Elinor, thus:

> [A]nd to make my tale good, I will (by report of my very good friend *F.J.*) discribe him unto you. Hee was in height, the proportion of twoo *Pigmeys*, in bredth the thicknesse of two bacon hogges, of presumption a *Gyant*, of power a Gnat, Apishly wytted, Knavishly mannerd, and crabbedly favord, what was there in him then to drawe a fayre Ladies liking?
>
> (H153; cf. P392)

In 'The pleasant Fable' the same words come courtesy of Bartello. In the first version, G.T.'s description of the rival's appearance and nature is pluralistic, in that it has the voice of G.T., apparently attempting an objective reporting of fact, citing his source, F.J.; then it has, unmistakably, F.J.'s angry and jealous view of the secretary; it also has an authorial voice coolly supervising the whole thing (an authorial voice which is possibly G.T., being disingenuous, or, as Staub suggests, a version of Gascoigne, being ironic at G.T.'s as well as F.J.'s expense).[9] In the second version, we have merely an amusing description of the secretary. Similarly, the poems are presented as they are, with little or no suggestion that they could have been different – whereas in the first version their stasis is each time undermined by the speculative commentary of G.T., as if they are merely in a protean state of variable composition and interpretation. So while throughout 'The Adventures' there is a disquieting proliferation of voices, in 'The pleasant Fable' all is reassuringly smooth. There is one source, one narrator, one set of characters, an appearance of greater cohesion and transparency, and the filo-pastry effect of the 'The Adventures' is flattened out.

Gascoigne denied speculations that 'The Adventures' was a *roman à clef*. But conjecture did not die with his disclaimer. Throughout the twentieth century, there have been attempts to decipher the clues and uncover the real-life provenance of the story, whether it is seen as autobiography or as scandalous gossip. (C.S. Lewis remarked drily of the controversy: 'It is always difficult to convince unimaginative readers that anything is invented').[10] This kind of critical

9 See Staub, '"According to My Source"', p. 115.

10 C.S. Lewis, *English Literature in the Sixteenth Century* (Oxford: Clarendon Press, 1954), p. 269.

questing testifies to the highly convincing documentary construction of 'The Adventures' and of the *Sundrie Flowres* as a whole, but misses the point of why that illusion was created in the first place. That it is an illusion is clear when a close look at 'The Adventures' reveal cracks in the biographical façade: frequently, G.T. tells us things ostensibly from the account of F.J., which F.J. could not possibly have known. These discrepancies have been variously interpreted by critics.[11] The tale's place in the history of the novel has been debated, and it has been read as satire.[12] But such readings equally miss the precise nature of the difficulties Gascoigne was in when he tried to write a work of fiction at this point in history.

It took a revolution in reading practices to look at the possible theoretical purpose behind the technical constructions. Focus on the story's literary rather than literal nature and on its self-conscious artifice is developed by more recent debate on the experimental structure, so that it is read as a theorized experiment with the implications of interpretation and the structures of fiction. Prouty in 1942 sees 'the interpolated stories' as 'a structural weakness' whereas Staub in 1990 thinks 'storytelling is a the real subject of the tale'.[13] The text apes the construction of a report of actual occurrences, in the style of the writers of popular pamphlets on wonders at this period – with the same citation of witnesses, use of sources and accumulation of relevant documents.[14] The effect is to obscure the inventiveness that is actually taking place – in view of the response, too successfully. But the same impulse that led to the raising of this complex edifice led also to the second disguise as a translation. In neither incarnation could the tale be presented simply as a product of the author's imagination.

To do that would be to fall prey to the kind of disapproval that was also shown towards the sexual elements in 'The Adventures'. In the outcry over sexual licentiousness, the response to 'The Adventures' mirrored contemporary attitudes to 'poetry', otherwise termed 'poesie', or indeed to the activity rather than the

---

11 See especially Relihan, *Fashioning Authority*, p. 22; and Ronald C. Johnson, *George Gascoigne* (New York: Twayne Publishers, 1972), p. 120.

12 The debate may be followed in these works: C.T. Prouty, *George Gascoigne: Elizabethan Courtier Soldier, and Poet* (New York: Columbia University Press, 1942), p. 201; Johnson, *George Gascoigne*, pp. 121, 124ff.; R.S. White, 'Functions of Poems and Songs in Elizabethan Romance and Romantic Comedy', *English Studies* LXVIII (1987), pp. 392–405; A.C. Hamilton, 'Elizabethan Romance: the Example of Prose Fiction', *English Literary History* XLIX (1982), pp. 287–99; Salzman, *English Prose Fiction*, p. 24; Johnson, *George Gascoigne*, pp. 124ff.

13 Prouty, *George Gascoigne*, p. 209; and Staub, '"According to My Source"', p. 117. See also Müller, 'Modernity', pp. 91–2.

14 See David Cressy, *Travesties and Transgressions in Tudor and Stuart England: Tales of Discord and Dissension* (Oxford: Oxford University Press, 2000), pp. 23 and 35.

product: 'poesis', literary making.[15] What is alarming about sexual activity is also alarming about textual extravagance.[16] It is significant that the simplified narrative presentation in the second version parallels a simplified treatment of sexual activities. Gascoigne cut three offending passages from 'the pleasant Fable': the initial lovemaking in the gallery; the episode of F.J. composing verses about the horns of the cuckolded husband; and the rape of Elinor by F.J. In 'The Adventures' both Elinor and F.J. show themselves to be prey to unpredictable sexual desire, which leads them into disorderly acts, such as the rape, and the married Elinor's affairs with F.J. and the secretary. Reformation policing of sexuality, as Lawrence Stone tells us, consisted mainly of a narrowing down of the definition of the sexual act itself as well as of marriage laws.[17] So long as the libidinous impulse could be contained, it could be countenanced within a rational and godly society. St Augustine's theory of Edenic sex provides an example of the influences brought to bear in the Reformation: for St Augustine it is the abandoned pleasure of fallen lust that poses problems. He posits a lack of shame before the Fall, an absence of appetite, and ideally wishes the unruly member to 'serve the will' like the hands and feet (II. 14. xiv–xix). He sees the battle between lust (including but not exclusively sexual lust) and will as a constant feature of humanity after the Fall. Sir Philip Sidney makes a similar point in *Apology for Poetry* [1595]; ms. c. 1580), when he talks about the 'infected will' inherited by mankind (p. 101), and George Puttenham in his *Art of English Poesy* (1589) when he discusses depraved and wholesome imaginations (pp. 19–20). It became a common Protestant argument.[18]

Gascoigne himself makes the connection between writing and sex, for example in connection with Elinor's secretary, who is significantly also her lover, F.J. offering to 'lend his mistress such a pen in her secretary's absence as he should never be able at his return to amend the well-writing thereof' (H267). The sixteenth century is, as Jeffrey Masten points out, 'a discursive world where men often figured texts as compliant women';[19] to take the analogy further, the act of

15 George Puttenham quotes the Greek infinitive *poiein* as the origin of 'poet' (p. 3): the more usual Latinate form, deriving from Horace, is 'poesis', used by Gascoigne himself. Cf. Sidney, *Apology*, pp. 50, 99. See also Ernest B. Gilman, *Iconoclasm and Poetry in the English Reformation* (Chicago and London: University of Chicago Press, 1986), p. 1.

16 See Patricia Parker, *Literary Fat Ladies: Rhetoric, Gender, Property* (London: Methuen, 1987).

17 Lawrence Stone, *The Family, Sex and Marriage in England 1500–1800* (1977; rev. edn Harmondsworth: Penguin, 1979), pp. 311–15.

18 See John N. King, *English Reformation Literature: The Tudor Origins of the Protestant Tradition* (Princeton, NJ: Princeton University Press, 1982), p. 146; Gilman, *Iconoclasm*, p. 11.

19 Jeffrey Masten, *Textual Intercourse: Collaboration, Authorship, and Sexualities in Renaissance Drama* (Cambridge: Cambridge University Press, 1997), p. 8.

wrestling in composition with the text can be symbolized as a sexual experience. It is as if the unpoliced sexuality the characters indulge in mirrors the pleasurable, irresponsible fiction that the various narrators (and various authors) produce. 'The Adventures' seems to indulge both, while trying to contain them within conventional forms and conduct, albeit somewhat unsuccessfully. Wild fiction is harnessed in poems, supposed evidence, letters, formal conversation, allegorical tales; and yet ultimately there are so many different forms that the effect is of exuberant excess, rather than formal restraint. Both fiction and sexuality are perverse and extravagant in the first version of the tale, and are curtailed and simplified in the second, the supposed 'translation'.

Sensual temptation, appetite, intractability are perceived as problematic for humanity. And the appetitive is also characteristic of literary creation, or 'poesis'; Sidney was not the only one to raise the issue of the 'the serpent's tale of sinful fancy' (p. 123). His accompanying image of the 'siren's sweetness' is an echo from Stephen Gosson and Roger Ascham, both writers who worried about the seductiveness of literary creation, and indeed mainly Italianate literary creation. In his *School of Abuse* (1579), Gosson talks about how poets fix the mind at the level of the delighting words, where the 'wanton' images 'run riot' (p. 20) – and consequently, as Andrew Hadfield says, 'the signifier of the allegory has served to delight the senses of the reader or playgoer so that the allegorical signified does not register in the mind'.[20] The intractability of literary creation is also treated by Gosson: 'If you inquire howe many such poets and pipers wee have in our age, I am persuaded that every one of them may creepe through a ring, or dance the wild morris in a needles eye' (p. 27). Poets are perfidious shape-shifting little folk who refuse to follow the rules, cannot be counted or labelled. Protean activities of any kind were viewed with a particularly strong mistrust at this period, be they performed by papists, Puritans, men who dress as women, or, indeed, poets.[21] In addition to the slipperiness of the form, Gosson's sense of poetry's appeal to the sense is figured in food imagery – he likens poets to cooks and poetry to over-rich banquets. Poets are poisoning basilisks, poetry honey disguised as poison, or the poison in the well. And of course the cross-over between poetry and flowers as the referents of 'poesie' fully supports the metaphor of the senses: Gascoigne talks about the 'smell' of his work – on the title-page of his *Sundrie Flowres* (P1), the flowers are bound up in one small 'poesie' (H1). This is further developed by the shift of title to *Posies*; the

---

20 Andrew Hadfield, *Literature, Politics and National Identity: Reformation to Renaissance* (Cambridge: Cambridge University Press, 1994), p. 117. See also Gilman, *Iconoclasm*, p. 1.

21 See Kristen Poole, *Radical Religion from Shakespeare to Milton: Figures of Nonconformity in Early Modern England* (Cambridge: Cambridge University Press, 2000); and Laura Levine, *Men in Women's Clothing: Anti-Theatricality and Effeminization, 1579–1642* (Cambridge: Cambridge University Press, 1994).

significance of the Greek derivation of 'anthology' from 'flower-collecting' is obvious. In an age of reform, when sensuous excess was always the problem, in the flesh and on the page, when censorious comment and legislation were levied alike at works of fiction and at sexual licence, it is not altogether surprising that the two topics should preoccupy the author's mind with equal intensity in a single work.

What is somewhat suprising is that Gascoigne should choose an Italian tale as the spurious original, that he should, subjected to charges of lewdness, resort in defense to Italy, widely perceived as the very home of harmful naughty tales in English Reformation ideology. Views of Italy are perhaps best typified by Ascham in his *Scholemaster* (1570), as a place of heresy and sensuous indulgence, producing stories that lead the reader into sin and even atheism (p. 20). Aretino, for example, became 'an emblematic figure of Italian vice'.[22] Italy is the source of the 'fictions' of Papistry, as well as of the prose romances reproduced in contemporary English anthologies. There is a clearly expressed fear that these tales undo the good work of the Reformation: 'Mo papistes be made by your mery bookes of *Italie*, then by your earnest books of *Louain*', writes Ascham, warning that 'subtle and secrete Papistes at home procured bawdie bookes to be translated out of the *Italian* tonge' (p. 3). Gosson endorses this view: 'Compare *London* to *Rome*, and *England* to *Italy*, you shall finde the Theaters of the one, the abuses of the other, to be rife among vs' (p. 34). So current is this view of Italian danger at the time 'The Adventures' was published that Maslen even sees Gascoigne as perversely courting censorhip by producing in the two versions of 'The Adventures' a threatening study of Catholic infiltration in the state.[23] Perhaps even more perversely, the pseudo-Italian version of the tale is the expurgated one.

But Gascoigne's allusion to Italy does not only conjure up Ascham and Gosson. There were two images of Italy in Tudor England, and sometimes one gained precedence over the other. On the one hand, there was the Italy of Machiavelli, the Borgias and the papist threat, the Italy of deceiving tales – on the other there was the Italy of Castiglione and Petrarch, the courtly, literary Italy of 'pleasant fables'. Appreciation of Italy's elegant style is shown by Puttenham and Sidney, writing slightly later than Ascham and Gosson. Sir John Harington, translator of Ariosto, is similarly positive. Ariosto is a good example of the dual image of Italy: condemned for his naughty stories, he was none the less often held up as an example of great literature to be imitated. Harington in the preface to his translation of *Orlando Furioso* (1591), wonders provocatively if he is

---

22 Michael J. Redmond, '"I have read them all": Jonson's *Volpone* and the Discourse of the Italianate Englishman', in Michele Marrapodi, ed., *The Italian World of English Renaissance Drama: Cultural Exchange and Intertextuality* (London: Associated University Presses, 1998), pp. 122–40, p. 130.

23 See Maslen, *Elizabethan Fictions,* pp. 114–57; and Cressy, *Travesties*, p. 23.

dealing with instructive literature or merely 'Italian toys' (p. 220). Gascoigne seems to be divided about Italy. In the 'Certayne Notes' he declares his preference for native English words over 'Inkhorne' terms and foreign influences (p. 465); but he is avowedly writing it for an Italian, Edouardo Donati, and, as his anthology demonstrates, frequently translates from the Italian, for example Ariosto's *I Suppositi* (a text he places in the more wholesome 'Hearbes' section of his *Posies*).

There is some truth in Lewis's pronouncement that Gascoigne was 'a transitional poet – one in whom we see the Golden quality coming to birth'.[24] Gascoigne wrote in the early 1570s, just after Ascham and a little before Gosson. In this post-Edwardian, post-Marian period, Reformation propaganda was still acrimonious. Ascham's view of the time before Henry VIII's Act of Supremacy was widely held: in that dark age 'Papistrie, a standyng poole, couered and ouerflowed all England', and the most popular literature was the 'mans slaughter and bold bawdrie' of *Le Morte d'Arthur* (*Scholemaster*, pp. 3–4). In the next decades, anti-Italian fervour continued to be expressed, for example in Gabriel Harvey's denunciation in *Pierce's Supererogation* (1593) of the 'Inglishe horrel-lorrel' who 'attempt[s] to putrify gentle mindes with the vilest imposthumes of lewde [Italian] corruption' (p. 259).[25] But there was conversely some rediscovery, led by Sidney and Puttenham, of the Italianist poetic work of the reign of Henry VIII. Puttenham's celebrated paragraph on the 'courtly makers' (pp. 62–3) – Wyatt and Surrey and others – crystallizes this movement, although it was to fade in the seventeenth century, and for a long time after that.[26] But Gascoigne seemed to be struggling to reinstate Italian literature as a model for imitation just before the main current changed in the same direction. In this he reflects royal inclinations; indeed Ascham's tract is curiously at odds with the fact that he was tutor to the learned Elizabeth, who translated Petrarch, and for whom Gascoigne wrote a poem in four languages, including Italian. Elizabeth took after father and grandfather in welcoming Italians at court.[27]

Gascoigne's connection of the story with Italy thus cites itself within a

---

24 Lewis, *English Literature*, p. 269.

25 See William Nelson, *Fact or Fiction: The Dilemma of the Renaissance Storyteller* (Cambridge, MA: Harvard University Press, 1973), p. 50, 75ff; and King, *Reformation Literature*, pp. 144ff.

26 Hadfield, *National Identity*, pp. 1–2; see also Reed Way Dasenbrock, *Imitating the Italians: Wyatt, Spenser, Synge, Pound, Joyce* (Baltimore, MD and London: Johns Hopkins Press, 1991), pp. 1–2.

27 See Teresa Bela, 'The Knight and His Queen: Poetry and Politics in the Life of George Gascoigne', in Wojciech Kalaga and Leszek Drog, eds, *PASE Papers in Literature: Proceedings of the Seventh Annual Conference of the Polish Association for the Study of English* (Katowice: PACE, 1999), pp. 19–29, at pp. 25–6; and Lewis Einstein, *The Italian Renaissance in England* (New York: Columbia University Press, 1983), p. 185ff.

dynamic controversy the main thrust of which, within the space of a few decades, switched from anti-Italian to pro-Italian critical argument, and back again. In this context, the tale explores a number of interlinked topics. There is the concern with readership as authorship; there is the problem with sensuous excess; and there is, further, the troubled status of prose fiction, especially taken in conjunction with the puritanical perception of poetry as lies.

In the late sixteenth century, as has frequently been observed, prose fiction was in its infancy and of uncertain status in the literary establishment. As Constance Relihan reminds us: '"fiction" is not a term its early practitioners or their readers used. Instead they termed their work "pamphlets", "histories", "romances", or, as in Sidney's *Defense*, "poetry"'.[28] These are the 'fond bookes' about which Ascham expressed concern, 'of late translated out of Italian into English, sold in euery shop in London ... inticing men to ill liuing' (*Scholemaster*, p. 3). David Margolies likens them to 'early cinema', in that they were ephemeral entertainment, and adds: 'The Elizabethan novelist had to find or make a place for himself in a society that did not naturally provide him with one.'[29] The lack of definition is illustrated by the catch-all term 'poet', which could be equally applied to writers of prose 'pamphlets', doggerel verse, or poetry of literary merit.

The newness of the form of prose fiction partly explains the experimental form of 'The Adventures'. The mix in the work of poems with a prose narrative can be explained as a means of ensuring status denied to purely prose works. Gascoigne presents his work ambitiously, as can be seen from the title-page of the *Sundrie Flowres*. Here the names of the imitated authors are mentioned prominently, as the aspiration and the marker of excellence; the claim is made for the work's being 'bothe pleasaunt and profitable'; and lastly, there is Gascoigne's posy, or one of his posies, 'Meritum petere, grave', which roughly translates as 'To seek merit is a serious matter'.[30] The work is '[g]athered partely (by translation) in the fyne outlandish Gardins of Euripedes, Ovid, Petrarcke, Ariosto, and others: and partly by invention, out of our owne fruitefulle Orchardes in Englande'. Gascoigne establishes his credentials as a properly learned author, in the best tradition of Renaissance *imitatio*. 'Invention' is relegated to second place, as is the home-language of the work itself.

He is doing for the emerging novella form what Sidney and others were to do for verse: attempting to give it literary status. Literary status is partly gained by

---

28 Relihan, *Fashioning Authority*, p. 3.

29 David Margolies, *Novel and Society in Elizabethan England* (London and Sydney: Croom Helm, 1985), pp. 2, 19. See also Margaret Spufford, *Small Books and Pleasant Histories: Popular Fiction and its Readership in Seventeenth-Century England* (London: Methuen, 1981).

30 I am grateful to Peter Biller and Peter Happé for advice on Gascoigne's motto.

antecedent – Bartello recalls Bandello, whose *novelle* make up a quarter of Painter's collection. And so we are reminded that this form already has an established tradition, of sorts; the Italian connection borrows lustre from the soon-to-be prevailing view of Sidney and others that English inventiveness and an English style must owe much to continental imitation. The Italian names signal an adherence not so much to a classical past (although that is there as well) as to a current, vernacular tradition closer to home. In the body of the text, H.W. promulgates English, and Gascoigne returns to the question in his more authoritative *Posies*, the Collected Works that lend *gravitas* to an author: he promotes 'olde English wordes' in the interests of demonstrating 'that it is not unpossible eyther in Poemes or in Prose to write both compendiously, and perfectly in our Englishe tongue' (P5). This is part of a growing movement at this time, expressed most lucidly perhaps by Richard Carew in his essay 'On the Excellency of the English Tongue' (1595–96), who wants to ransack European languages in search of qualities that might enrich English, 'and soe (like bees) gather the honye of their good properties and leaue the dreggs to themselfes' (pp. 292–3). These writers are trying to grow out of what Lord Morley in his translation of Petrarch's *Tryumphes* (1553–56) called disparagingly the homegrown 'dongehill matter' of the 'tale of Robyn Hoode' (p. 77), and create instead a golden world, a new and contemporary Arcadia, exotic in provenance but European rather than classical. In the interim between the *Sundrie Flowres* and the *Posies*, Gascoigne became more confident in his claims to literary greatness. Whereas in the *Sundrie Flowres* the anthology is termed 'trifles' and 'Pamphlets' (by H.W. and G.T.), in the *Posies* Gascoigne writes under his own name that he wishes not to produce the 'ydle Bookes and wanton Pamphlettes' which are 'forbidden' by the reverend divines, and in support of this plea to be taken seriously declares that he made not 'one grote or pennie' from the publication of the *Sundrie Flowres* (P4).

This aim of producing serious literature is reflected in the alteration made to the ending of the 'The pleasant Fable'. In 'The Adventures' G.T. abruptly becomes tired of his story, and breaks off with 'It is time now to make an end of this thriftless history' (P452–3), meandering, brilliantly unclosed, into what appear to be some jottings on his use of synonymous names for the characters, as compared with other writers' styles. He then drifts into introducing the other poems of the *Sundrie Flowres*, which continue to have a commentary, presumably from G.T. Here Gascoigne actually appears among the poems, as one of G.T.'s 'sundrie gentlemen', thus almost becoming a fictional character himself in his own work. The ending of 'The pleasant Fable' is quite different. It has closure, it has a moral. But it is an ending worthy of Voltaire, and its moral revolts against the evidence. Frances dies of unrequited love, while F.J. and Elinor continue quite happily to pursue their dissolute lives; nevertheless, the moral, we are told, is that 'wicked lust' brings confusion to all who touch it, including the virtuous, and the narrator hopes that the story will be an 'ensample to warn the youthful reader from attempting the like worthless enterprise' (H263). He continues chattily about the poverty of his 'translation', and asks 'the gentle reader rather to take example of reformacion therein, then to finde fault at the homely handling of the same'. The onus, once again, is on the reader to read responsibly, rather than on the writer who writes the naughty stories or the halting prose. This point is further reinforced by the three sections into which the *Posies* is divided: 'Flowres', 'Hearbes' and 'Weeds'. The Flowres are 'more pleasant than profitable', the Hearbes 'morall discourses and reformed inventions ... more profitable than pleasant' and the Weeds 'right medicinable ... none so vile or stinking, but that it hath in it some virtue if rightly handled'. He ends his introductory epistles: 'I pray thee to smell unto these Posies, as *Floures to comfort*, *Herbes to cure*, and *Weedes to be avoyded*. So have I ment them, and so I beseech thee Reader to accept them. Farewell.' And so the author bows out, scripting his own death. The mutual translation of reader and author is complete; and the reader is explicitly directed to employ a critical discernment when learning from the text.[31]

This is an Augustinian dictum, which perhaps received at the hands of Elizabethan courtly writers a somewhat irreverent treatment. In the moralized ending, Gascoigne is doing what Harington and others did, perhaps in the knowledge that protestations about profit would simply add to the titillation which was sought in texts: Harington is aware, as he presents his worthy apology for Ariosto's ribaldry, that some readers will be 'half offended that I have not made some directions that you may finde out, and read them immediately'. Tongue in cheek, he advertises his wares by asking readers 'I beseech you ... to read as my author ment them, to breed detestation and not delectation. Remember, when you read of the old lecherous friar, that a fornicator is one of the things that God hateth' (*Orlando*, p. 214); and he asks, echoing Chaucer, and indeed Gascoigne, that if a tale is too saucy to stomach, 'turne over the leafe and let it alone'.[32]

But Gascoigne's exhortation to the reader is even more suggestive, in the context of contemporary attitudes to prose fiction. Again and again, in both versions, the image of the 'industrious bee' is offered as a model for the reader, gathering honey where the 'malicious spider' only gleans poison. This is an image from classical antiquity, taken up by Petrarch and others, and is originally a model of successful imitative writing; to use it in the context of reading – and Gascoigne was not the only one to do this – puts the reader on a level with the writer in the creative exercise. Both are equally authors of the text – and of how the text is measured in its cultural context. Gascoigne asks, by doing this, that

---

31 See Rowe, 'Interpretation', p. 278.

32 See also Augustine, *City of God*, II. 14. xxiii.; Geoffrey Chaucer, 'The Miller's Prologue' in *The Riverside Chaucer*, edited by Larry D. Benson (Oxford: Oxford University Press, 1987), lines 3176–7; Gascoigne, H142, 180.

'pamphlets' are reassessed, in effect 'translated' by the reader into valued works of literature.

This is important when the text in question is merely a 'weed', a suspect invention without even the authority leant to it by a classical source. 'Invention' is a problematic concept. In 'Certayne Notes' Gascoigne discusses 'invention' and clearly it has there the accepted Renaissance meaning of a concept, a starting-point upon which a composition is based, rather than a creative construct. In 'The Adventures' G.T. discloses the 'occasion' which sparked a piece of writing, and this 'occasion' has almost the same sense as Gascoigne's 'invention'. The 'occasion' bases the writing in a factual rather than imaginative world; and where Gascoigne is on shaky ground is that his 'occasion' is actually invented (in the modern sense of the word), rather than drawn from life or from an imitated model. As Nelson has demonstrated, the 'endemic' propensity for faked documentary sources in Renaissance texts suggests 'that the accepted decencies forbade an author, not to make up stories, but to admit that he had'. It seems that Gascoigne was attempting to negotiate an acceptance of purely creative stories, but had to do so cautiously.[33] The second version of the tale is in all senses less depraved than the first – if we consider the Latin derivation from *pravus* ('crooked'). The moral crookedness of 'The Adventures' is straightened out in 'The pleasant Fable', and the inventiveness is apparently less crooked, since he presents it more acceptably as a 'translation'.

That is of course where the image becomes unstuck – because it is not a translation, but an original story, with an invented source. Gascoigne lies, ingeniously and too successfully in 'The Adventures', and again smoothly and invisibly in 'The pleasant Fable' with the translation story – where he produces an even more deviously crooked fabrication. With the loss of G.T.'s constant qualification of the poetry, what is also lost is the reference to actual sources for some of the poems. The correct attribution to '*Ariostoes* xxxi. song' of the poem 'What state to man' is simply cut in 'The pleasant Fable', as is the reference to an 'Italian' original of 'The stately dames of Rome' (for which there is a variety of possible sources). Ariosto's story of Suspicion is inaccurately ascribed to Bartello. The result is that Bartello is credited with *inventing* poems that are in fact *translations* from Ariosto, Petrarch, or Du Bellay; and because Bartello is a figment of Gascoigne's imagination, what in reality is happening is that Gascoigne is convolutedly claiming to have written material that was written by other poets. 'The Adventures' is nowhere near as mendacious as 'The pleasant Fable'.

All these lies are set in motion to conceal the other lying in which he is

---

33 Nelson, *Fact or Fiction*, pp. 26, 27. See also Staub, '"According to My Source"', p. 116; and Amina Alyal, *Changes of Mind: Imitation and Metamorphosis in the Work of Petrarch, Shakespeare, and Their Contemporaries* (doctoral dissertation, University of York, 1997), pp. 138–9. Lewis, *English Literature*, p. 271.

engaged: the lying of his calling, Sidney's 'serpent's tale' (*Apology*, p. 123) and Ascham's 'enchantments of *Circes*' (*Scholemaster*, p. 2), in other words, the exercise of his art as a poet. This is of course why Gascoigne camouflaged his creativity in the first place with the meticulous simulation of historiographical processes, as Staub argues: 'The poet uses these devices to evade responsibility for the text and disarm those who criticise poetry as the father of lies.'[34] But paradoxically, he is in this way falling foul of those Augustinian critics who preferred stories that were obviously untrue, such as Aesop's fables, to stories that mislead by convincingly faking truth.[35] Sidney picks this up as a central argument when he says, 'The poet is the least liar, because he nothing affirmeth, he never lieth' (p. 123). Sir Thomas Hoby, in his translation of Coignet's *Politique Discourses* (1585), however, on the other side of the argument, accuses poets of 'cleane disgyuising the truth' that 'they might the more delight' (pp. 159–61). In a long passage about 'their lying and wanton discourses', he seems to equate lewdness with lies – as if they are not easily distinguishable. Gosson's emphasis on the 'wanton' quality of words seems to detect a wantonness both of form and of content; inventiveness and decadence go hand in hand. Gascoigne embraces this opposition view, and does not attempt to defend poets from the charge of lying, as so many poets did. His 'Certayne Notes' do not touch on this. Gascoigne 'affirms' where Sidney would not: rather than produce a patently fantastical *Arcadia*, he writes a tale which in both versions attempts a scrupulous verisimilitude. His texts explore what it is to lie, in other words to construct fictional works. Müller for example draws attention to the tricky moment in 'The pleasant Fable' when F.J.'s report is replaced by the obscure phrase 'mine aucthor dreameth': 'The description ... is presented not as a result of actual observation, but of the author's imagination, called "dreaming" here' (H197; cf. P433).[36]

In the two versions of 'The Adventures of Master F.J.' Gascoigne negotiates inventiveness, the treacherous, intractable, sensuous *poesis*, by alluding to papist Italy, with all its very similar associations. In referring simultaneously to both images of Italian literature current at the time, his work achieves a fusion of the associations of each: elegance and style coupled rudely with licentiousness and lies. The fusion is achieved in a work in the English tongue, which is becoming increasingly associated with plainness, with control, with truth-speaking.[37] Thus when Gascoigne says he has 'translated' his second version 'from the Italian',

34 Staub, '"According to My Source"', p. 114.

35 See Nelson, *Fact or Fiction*, pp. 14–15.

36 See Müller, 'Modernity', p. 93.

37 See King, *Reformation Literature*, pp. 18, 144; and Andrew Hadfield, 'The "sacred hunger of ambitious minds": Spenser's savage religion', in Donna B. Hamilton and Richard Strier, eds, *Religion, Literature and Politics in Post-Reformation England, 1540–1688* (Cambridge: Cambridge University Press, 1996), pp. 27–45, at p. 29.

when he has merely reworked it from the first, it is as if that phrase 'the Italian' becomes a metaphor for the creative process illuminated in 'The Adventures' and figured forth by the disorderly sexuality contained in 'poesie'; and his 'translation' is his trimming and shaping of it in 'The pleasant Fable'. The first version is like a draft, whose narrative, as Maslen notes, 'takes G.T. by surprise', and the second is the edited final version.[38] In both versions of the tale, Gascoigne was being overly inventive, and ultimately had to 'translate' his inventiveness into a more palatable form.

Fiction comes primarily, in the minds of reforming critics, from Italy and its seductive tales. Fiction, like papistry itself, like sensory indulgence, is perceived as unreliable and dangerous; in this context, translation is a more godly activity than original composition. It is almost as if Italians might commit the sin of invention, but this once done could then be used by honest English Protestant writers, who would not themselves be guilty of indulging their fallen fantasy. Italian material might be expected to contain immoral fiction, but also had the reputation of a much-sought-after polish and sophistication; this, if translated safely into English prose, could only enrich literary endeavour. Gascoigne's attribution of the story to the Italian and its disguise as a translation can be read as a strategy to fend off accusations of a too successful inventiveness, as well as of a too unbridled sensuality. The structure of the *Posies* conceals at least one significant pun. The story is in a sense *dressed* in the 'new patched cote' (or indeed *weeds*) of an Italianate veneer so as to deflect perception from the very Englishness and newness of the tale.

Primary texts quoted

Ascham, Roger, *The Scholemaster* (1570), exc. in Smith, *Elizabethan Critical Essays,* I.

Augustine, *City of God* ['De civitate dei'], trans. John Healey (1610), ed. R.V.G. Tasker and Sir Ernest Barker (London: J.M. Dent & Sons, 1945).

Carew, Richard, *The Excellency of the English Tongue* (ms. 1595–96), in G. Gregory Smith, ed., *Elizabethan Critical Essays* (Oxford: Clarendon Press, 1904), II.

Gascoigne, George, *A Hundreth Sundrie Flowres*, ed. G.W. Pigman III (Oxford: Clarendon Press, 2000).

Gascoigne, George, *The Posies of George Gascoigne Esquire* (1575), ed. John W. Cunliffe (Cambridge: Cambridge University Press, 1907).

Gosson, Stephen, *The Schoole of Abuse* (1579), ed. Edward Arber (Westminster: A. Constable and Co., 1895).

38 Maslen, *Elizabethan Fictions*, p. 133.

Harington, Sir John, 'A Preface, or rather a Briefe Apologie of to his trans. of Ludovico Arisoto, *Orlando Furioso*' (1591), ed. Smith, *Elizabethan Critical Essays,* II.

Harvey, Gabriel, *Pierce's Supererogation* (1593), exc. in Smith, ed., *Elizabethan Critical Essays,* II.

Hoby, Sir Edward, trans. Martin Coignet, *Politique Discourses vpon Trueth and Lying* (1586). *STC* 5486.

Morley, Henry, Lord, trans., Francesco Petrarca, *Tryumphes of Fraunces Petrarcke* (1553–56), ed. D.D. Carnicelli (Cambridge, MA: Harvard University Press, 1971).

Puttenham, George, *The Art of English Poesie* (1589), exc. in Smith, *Elizabethan Critical Essays,* II.

Sidney, Sir Philip, *An Apology for Poetry* (1595; ms. *c.* 1580), ed. Geoffrey Shepherd (Manchester: Manchester University Press, 1973).

Chapter 9

Sir John Harington and the poetics of Tudor translation

Massimiliano Morini

Since its first appearance in 1591, Sir John Harington's translation of Ludovico Ariosto's masterpiece, *Orlando Furioso*, in 'English Heroical Verse', has divided readers and critics as to its quality. Ben Jonson, who was faithful to the early humanistic idea of precise, scholarly rendering, found it 'under all translations [...] the worst', whereas Francis Beaumont thought that Ariosto 'instructed by M. Harrington doeth now speak as good English as he did Italian before'.[1] In the twentieth century, this most famous among all sixteenth-century verse translations continued to elicit quite varied comments: while Robert McNulty, in the most recent edition of the text, opens his introduction with the triumphal assertion that 'even in an age famous for translation Sir John Harington's *Orlando Furioso in English Heroical Verse* stands out from its honoured fellows',[2] F.O. Matthiessen, the author of a fundamental book on Elizabethan prose translation, writes that 'such works as Golding's Ovid and Harington's Ariosto neither suggest the qualities of the original, nor possess exceptional poetic merit in compensation'.[3]

The disagreement is due to the fact that each age, and each commentator, brings to the text its or his or her own critical attitudes to poetry in general, and a definite idea of what a good translation should be – and to the twentieth-century scholar, it is mainly a matter of philological precision. As a consequence, though agreeing that the poem as it stands in English is an invaluable document of the social and literary environment of the day, most if not all contemporary critics have tended to concentrate on the mistakes, or, more neutrally, on the deviations from the original to be detected in the translated text. Depending on each critic's degree of appreciation of Harington's achievement, these deviations have been treated either as strengths or as weaknesses; but, despite notable individual

1 D.H. Craig, *Sir John Harington* (Boston: Twayne, 1985), p. 42.

2 Robert McNulty, ed. Sir John Harington, *Ludovico Ariosto's Orlando Furioso: Translated into English Heroical Verse* (Oxford: Clarendon, 1972), p. ix.

3 F.O. Matthiessen, *Translation: An Elizabethan Art* (1931; New York: Octagon, 1965), p. 5.

contributions,[4] we still lack a coherent explanation of the reasons why those deviations were produced, or, to paraphrase Matthiessen, of the means by which Ariosto came to England,[5] was naturalised, and became an English poet of moderate though not negligible powers. In other words, what did Harington try to make out of the *Orlando Furioso*? Where does Harington's translation stand in the debate, characteristic of the sixteenth century, between literalism and freedom? What does the *Orlando Furioso in English Heroical Verse* tell us of the conflicting views of translation at the end of the sixteenth century?

In what follows, I propose to study Harington's translation both in itself, and as a key to a better understanding of the poetics of sixteenth-century translation. The English *Orlando Furioso* is particularly suited for such an operation, not only because it sums up in itself so many habits of its age, but also because it stands mid-way between older, medieval practices of translation and more modern, humanistic ones, which had been circulating in Europe for almost two centuries, but which became the rule for secular translation in England only towards the middle of the seventeenth century.

In order to understand the significance of the English *Furioso* in the context of late sixteenth-century translation theory and practice, Harington's deviations from his original ought to be classified according to the reasons which produced them, rather than to their immediate literary consequences. Of course, this does not merely or necessarily imply searching Harington's life and opinions for information about his ideas and practice as a translator; on the contrary, it is to the text itself that one must turn in order to understand the reasons of its existence and form, which are, so to speak, embedded in its very lines. Accordingly, Harington's alterations can be classified along three lines: first, the changes he made in order to 'demonstrate' that the *Furioso* was an epic poem; secondly, the way he tried to turn, at least in part, Ariosto's work into his own; and thirdly, the alterations, conscious or not, which made Ariosto's work acceptable as English courtly poetry.

I

In trying to show that the *Orlando Furioso* was a true epic in the tradition of Virgil, Harington drew upon a debate which had begun in Italy immediately after the publication of Ariosto's poem, and which was still alive at the end of the century. Whereas Ariosto's Aristotelian detractors attacked him because of his deviations from the epic norm, there were divisions among his advocates. Some

4 See especially Daniel Javitch's *Proclaiming A Classic: The Canonization of Orlando Furioso* (Princeton: Princeton University Press, 1991), pp. 134–57.

5 Matthiessen writes: 'A study of Elizabethan translations is a study of the means by which the Renaissance came to England' (*Translation*, p. 3).

of them, like G.B. Pigna, praised him for his adherence to those very norms, and hailed the *Furioso* as a modern equivalent to the Greek and Latin classics, Virgil in particular; while some others, like Giovanbattista Giraldi, extolled the novelty of the poem, and defended it as the masterpiece of the new chivalric genre.

Since he needed to demonstrate that what he had decided to 'English' was a work of serious, ethically acceptable literature, Harington chose to align himself with those who praised Ariosto for his derivation from Virgil. In order to do so, it was not enough to declare, in the preface, that 'it seemeth my author doth follow [the *Aeneid*] as appeares both by his beginning and ending' (p. 10). It was also necessary to alter the original so as to make it more serious and more compact – seriousness and compactness being two of the main features of epic poetry. Harington, as a translator, had a very important advantage over Ariosto's Italian commentators: he could change the original more or less at his will, though he was conscious that many of his readers, as connoisseurs of Italian literature, would probably be aware of at least the most evident alterations.

To be sure, the *Furioso* had very little to do with the *Aeneid*. In his poem, Ariosto had poked fun at the conventions of chivalric romance, parodying them, stressing the absurdity of many of the events he portrayed. The Italian poem belonged to the Golden Age of the Italian literary Renaissance, long before the Counter-Reformation brought darker shades to bear against Tasso's pious reworking of the chivalric epic. In comparison with Ariosto, Harington wrote at a time of much greater moral pressure upon the writer, as Sidney's *Defence* demonstrates; therefore, following a long and lively Italian tradition,[6] he appended to each canto (and particularly to those most crammed with unlikely events) an allegory whose aim was to offer a moral explanation of the events. But this was not enough: Ariosto's comic asides and ironic comments could not but disturb the translator, especially when they put the credibility of the narrator or of the events into question – for in the true epic tradition, the narrator had to be omniscient and his voice reliable. Harington erased these comments and asides as often as he reasonably could:

> Ecco a l'orecchie un gran rumor lor viene.
> Disse la Donna: – O gloriosa madre,
> O Re del ciel, che cosa sarà questa? –
> E dove era il rumor si trovò presta.
>
> E vede l'oste, e tutta la famiglia,
> E chi à finestre, e chi fuor ne la via,
> Tener levati al ciel gli occhi e le ciglia,
> Come l'Eclisse o la Cometa sia.
> Vede la Donna un'alta maraviglia,
> Che di leggier creduta non saria;

6 The first critic to attempt a large-scale allegorisation of the poem was Simone Fornari in his *Sposizione sopra l'Orlando Furioso* (1549–50).

Vede passar'un gran destrier alato,
che porta in aria un cavalier armato.
[...] E, come dicea l'oste, e dicea il vero,
Quell'era un Negromante, e facea spesso
Quel varco, or da più lungi, or più da presso. (IV. 3–5)[7]

This is the first appearance of the Hippogryph (apart from Pinabello's description in canto II), and it is made to look remarkably absurd: Ariosto creates, with Bradamante's almost exasperated invocations of the Lord and the Holy Virgin (replicated in the absurd appearance of 'tutta la famiglia' a few lines later), and in the stunned incredulity of the people at their windows and in the street, a comical background for the event, so that the reader can hardly be willing to take it very seriously, and is prepared for something unlikely to happen. Then, after doubting himself the truthfulness of the account ('Che di leggier creduta non saria'), he assures us, with tongue in cheek, that what the innkeeper is saying is true ('e dicea il vero'). To compound the offence, Ariosto makes the innkeeper add superfluous details to his explanation ('e facea spesso | Quel varco, or da più lungi, or da più presso'). It is not difficult to understand how the *Furioso* could baffle commentators who thought Virgil the only acceptable godfather for an epic poem.

Ariosto, of course, did not believe in the Hippogryph; nor, for that matter, did Harington; but Elizabeth's godson had to insist that everything in the poem had an allegorical or moral explanation – a position which would have clashed with such a sceptical stance on the part of the author. Therefore, when he came to this passage, he compressed it, and erased all the ironical hints to be found in the original:

Now while these two did to confer begin,
She to his fingers having still an eye,
The host and other servants of the Inne
Came on the sodaine with a wofull crie,
And some did gaze without and some within
(As when men see a Comet in the skie):
The cause of this their wondring and their crying
Was that they saw an armed horseman flying,

7 A literal translation reads: 'And then they heard a great noise. | The woman said: – O glorious Mother, | O Lord who art in heaven, what will this be? | And she quickly reached the spot where the noise had come from. // And she sees the innkeeper and all his family, | And some at windows and some in the street, | all of them looking up to heaven, | As if it were an eclipse or a comet. | The woman sees a high marvel, | Which will not be easily believed: | She sees a great winged steed | bearing an armed horseman in the air. | [...] And, as the innkeeper said (and he told the truth) | That was a necromancer, and he often passed | Through that opening, sometimes in that spot, sometimes further on.' Harington made use of various editions, but principally of the one Francesco de Franceschi printed in venice in 1584, which has been referred to in the present essay.

And straight by th'host and others they were told
How one that had in Magike art great skill
Not far from thence had made a stately hold
Of shining steele and plast it on a hill
To which he bringeth Ladies young and old
And men and maids according to his will,
And when within that castle they have bene
They never after have bene heard or seene. (IV. 3–4)

Harington's rendering, as is evident, has silenced Ariosto's irony: Bradamante's exasperation has completely disappeared; 'un'alta maraviglia, | Che di leggier creduta non saria' ('a high marvel | which we will not easily believe') has become 'The cause of this their wondring and their crying', nothing more marvellous than a comet; there is no trace left of Ariosto's parenthetic commentary to the innkeeper's words ('E come dicea l'oste, e dicea il vero,') becomes 'And straight by th'host and others they were told'). The innkeeper keeps within the strict limits of essential information as regards the 'Negromante' (who has become 'one that had in Magike art great skill'); and all the absurdity of the people's excitement has disappeared, giving way to a grand but rather stiff scene, the commonplace apparition of the medieval portent.

In order to make the *Furioso* more acceptable, it was not sufficient for Harington to erase many of the most comical passages: he also had to compact Ariosto's continually shifting, elusive, digressive narrative, and this he did by leaving out entire strings of stanzas (altogether, he translated 4096 out of 4842 – 85% of the original), and by telling his readers in advance, by means of notes and of amendments in the translation, when a narrative strand would be picked up again or what would happen to a character whose story was suddenly dropped by Ariosto, thus unveiling the outcome of events which the original author had left incomplete on purpose. Once again, the Elizabethan translator was trying to turn the *Furioso* into an epic, and apologising (in his notes) when the text did not live up to epic standards. But aside from this, we must keep in mind that Elizabethan and Jacobean secular translators saw their art as customer service (or, as in Harington's courtly case, service to lords and, above all, to ladies). Even Philemon Holland, one of very few scholars among the translators of the age, did not hesitate, in his versions of Livy or Suetonius, to alter the revered words of the originals in order to make them clearer; and Harington, by making the *Furioso* more concise, by leaving out many of Ariosto's maddening digressions, by turning Ariosto's deadpan canto endings into promises for more, produced a poem which, if less refined than the original, was quicker and more enjoyable to read as a mere adventure.

Harington also tried to turn the *Furioso*, at least in part, into his own work. In the Renaissance, putting oneself and one's friends into one's writings was, of course, perfectly normal, even as regards translation. Ariosto himself had not refrained from mentioning his own friends and signalling his own presence, to the point of introducing the physical act of writing into the narrative. It was a widely accepted practice; even the greatest Elizabethan courtier, Sir Philip Sidney, had used, in his *Defence*, personal anecdotes to introduce fine theoretical distinctions. However, there must also have been people to whom such authorial intrusions seemed uncalled-for, if Harington felt the need to justify his own and Ariosto's practice by calling upon Plutarch in his preface:[8]

> And wheras I make mention here and there of some of my friends and kin, I did it the rather because *Plutarke* in one place speaking of Homer, partly lamenteth and partly blameth him that writing so much as he did, yet in none of his works there was any mention made or so much as inkling to be gathered of what stocke he was, of what kindred, of what towne, nor save for his language, of what countrey. (15)

Harington's work, of course, is a translation, and not original work, so that the introduction of personal details and anecdotes is more difficult to justify in the English than in the Italian *Furioso*. On the other hand, though a new idea of authorship (of the rights of the author, if not of author's rights) was gaining ground in sixteenth-century England as well as in continental Europe,[9] there is ample evidence that translation was still considered half-way between mechanical reproduction and original work: here and there, in the few Elizabethan and early Jacobean open or covert pronouncements upon translation, we get the sense that a text turned into English belonged to the translator as well as to the original author. Harington, on his part, almost systematically interfered with Ariosto's references to himself and his patrons (as for the latter, sometimes he explained them, sometimes he appropriated them), and very often substituted them with details out of his own life. Usually, this is done in the notes or in the

8 Harington could perhaps also have quoted Castiglione to justify these intrusions: in the first book of the *Cortegiano*, Count Ludovico da Canossa says: 'io ho biasmato il laudare se stesso impudentemente e senza rispetto; e certo, come voi dite, non si dee pigliar mala opinion d'un omo valoroso, che modestamente si laudi; anzi tôr quello per testimonio più certo che se venisse di bocca altrui [I reproved praising oneself shamelessly and without restraint; and certainly, as you say, one must not form a bad opinion of a worthy man who praises himself modestly; quite the contrary: that praise will be more reliable evidence than if it had been uttered by others]' (p. 74). Though what the Count is talking about could seem slightly beside the point, the dialectic between modesty and immodesty, or effacing oneself and putting oneself forward, cannot but bear on the role of the author (and of the translator) in literature.

9 Such epoch-making changes also found parallels in the laws. At the very beginning of the century, 'encouragement to law-abiding printers in both England and Scotland and protection of their commercial rights had also been offered through the adoption of the system of book privileges already in existence on the Continent. This kind of proto-copyright first appears in Britain on 15 September 1507, with James IV of Scotland's grant of leave to Walter Chepman and Andrew Myllar to set up a press in Edinburgh, and prohibition of the import from elsewhere of texts they had printed.' See L. Hellinga and J.B. Trapp, eds., *The Cambridge History of the Book in Britain* (Cambridge: Cambridge University Press, 1999), III. p. 14.

comments appended to each canto; in canto I, for example, Harington glosses Ariosto's dedication to the Cardinal Ippolito by writing in the margin: 'This is by the author intended to Cardinal Hippolito, but by the translator to a Prince far more worthie'. Elsewhere, when the text lends him some excuse, he introduces his dog or his mother. Sometimes he even modifies the original to fit it to his own experiences or ideas, as happens in canto 42, where he slightly modifies a fountain in Ariosto to make it exactly like one he had built in his own country house.

Finally, the English *Furioso* is written in a manner which makes it more akin to English courtly poetry than to the original: in Harington's hands, Ariosto's work became a sixteenth-century English poem. Though not a great poet, Harington was a good connoisseur and a worthy craftsman, and he turned Ariosto's masterpiece into something of which Sidney would not have been ashamed. In his verse, and in its remarkable distance from the original, the cadences and habits of late sixteenth-century English verse can be detected. To begin with, Ariosto's very advanced and experimental syntax, his continued and traumatic enjambements, could not be reproduced in English.[10] Spenser, in those same years, was beginning to open his lines to possibilities which only Milton would exploit to the full: but none of the stanzas of the *Faerie Queene* is comparable to Ariosto's dizzy evolutions:

Lo *I* the man, whose Muse whilome did maske,
As time her taught, in lowly Shepheards weeds,
Am now enforst a far unfitter taske,
For trumpets sterne to change mine Oaten reeds,
And sing of Knights and Ladies gentle deeds. (I. i. 1: emphasis added)

Spenser puts an entire line between subject and verb; but in Ariosto, the line does no longer correspond to the syntactic or semantic unit; the sentences literally dance across the lines, folding upon themselves, and adverbs are made to rhyme with more conclusive words (Agramante | quante | inante):

Per far al Re Marsilio, e al Re Agramante
Battersi ancor del folle ardir la guancia,
D'aver condotto l'un d'Africa quante
Genti erano atte a portar spada, e lancia;
L'altro, d'aver spinta la Spagna inante
A destruttion del bel Regno di Francia. (I. 6)[11]

---

10 Or rather, they could, but at the risk of producing a strange compound creature. This is exactly what was done by Richard Carew, the first translator of Tasso's *Gerusalemme liberata* (a translation of which only the first five cantos are extant). Carew produced a very literal translation which offered an exact reproduction of the rhymes and syntax of the original. As a result, unfortunately, many of his lines can only be understood by English-speaking Italians.

11 A translation which preserves word-order even to the detriment of grammar would be: 'So as to make king Marsilio and king Agramante | Still hit because of their mad

Harington's rendering, though more or less faithful, is decidedly more end-stopped and wooden; sentence and line (or couplet) usually concide, concepts are more evenly divided:

> To make the Kings of Affricke and of Spaine
> Repent their rash attempts and foolish vaunts,
> One having brought from Affricke in his trayne
> All able men to carry sword or launce;
> The other mov'd the Spanyards now agayne
> To overthrow the goodly Realme of France. (I. 6)

Thus it can be said, as a recent commentator has written, that Harington 'blunted' Ariosto.[12] This he did not only by silencing his irony, tightening the plot, and organising the lines in a more ordered, geometrical manner. Harington also brought to the *Furioso* his own vocabulary and diction: he 'blunted' the *Furioso* whenever it contained words which referred too directly to the physical reality of things. This can be observed very well in Canto I, one of the few which Harington translated fully. As we have seen, for 'Battersi ancor del folle ardir la guancia [still hit because of their own mad daring their cheeks]', Harington translates, more vaguely: 'Repent their rash attempts and foolish vaunts'. A little further on, in stanza 10, when Angelica 'le spalle diede [turned her back]', Harington has simply: 'convayd her selfe away'. In the next stanza, 'il freno torse [unloosed the reins]' is rendered with 'did take her flight'; in stanza 14, a detail that makes Ferraù come to life before our eyes ('de l'acqua ingordo e frettoloso [hasty and greedy of the water]) is left out. The battle between Rinaldo and Ferraù, which Ariosto narrates with great relish and attention to detail (not to mention a bit of exaggeration) from stanza 17 onwards, becomes a stylised medieval battle, and one that Malory could have described: 'Between them two a combat fierce began | With strokes that might have pierst the hardest rocks' is all we are given for 'Cominciar quivi una crudel battaglia, | Come a piè si trovar, co i brandi ignudi: | Non che le piastre, e la minuta maglia, | Ma ai colpi lor non reggerian l'incudi [Here they began a cruel battle | As they found themselves on foot, with their naked swords, | So that not only mail and fine plate | But to their strokes an anvil would give way]'.

This might be imputed to the fact that either Harington or the English of his time lacked the necessary elasticity to cope with the thriving physicality of Ariosto's language, but it is an unlikely explanation. Harington himself wrote other works (chiefly *The Metamorphosis of Ajax* in 1596, a prose eulogy of the water closet, a new version of which he claimed he had invented) which displayed a vein not far removed from Nashe or, for that matter, Rabelais.

---

daring their own cheeks, | For having brought, one, out of Africa so many | People as were able to carry sword or lance; | The other, for having pushed Spain forward | In order to destroy the fair reign of France.'

12 See Craig, *Sir John Harington*, p. 39.

Moreover, the chief prose translators of the time, from Hoby (the translator of the *Cortegiano*) onwards, had demonstrated that English, if anything, had difficulties grappling with those philosophical, abstract terms which it kept acquiring laboriously during the course of the century: Florio, North and Holland had all tended to add physical details to the abstract reasonings of Montaigne, Plutarch and Livy; Hoby, the translator of the *Cortegiano*, had problems with the Italian terms 'cortigianeria' and 'sprezzatura', but not with Castiglione's funny anecdotes. Therefore, it is unlikely that Harington lacked the necessary vocabulary to cope with Ariosto's physical details; more probably, Harington automatically turned the *Furioso* into an English courtly poem – and though the stage was beginning to fit heavily physical language to its own needs, such language was generally banned from courtly poetry. There is not much, in Sidney or Spenser, in the way of physical detail, and one ought not to forget that Petrarch was thought infinitely superior to Dante at the time.

When he published the first systematic theory on the subject ever written in England, the *Essay on the Principles of Translation* (1790), A.F. Tytler advocated Pope's methods in domesticating Homer's most offending passages:

> Homer has been judged by the best critics to fall at times beneath himself, and to offend, by introducing low images and puerile allusions. Yet how admirably is this defect veiled over or altogether removed, by his translator Pope.[13]

This kind of strategy, and its defence, could both be ascribed to eighteenth-century decorum, but it is a fact that the domesticating translation had been fashionable for at least two centuries before Tytler's essay. Dryden, though proposing in theory a middle way between metaphrase (rendering word by word) and imitation, had had Virgil speak like a late seventeenth-century man; Denham had adapted book II of the Aeneid to his royalist ideas. Some years earlier, at the beginning of the century, Holland had turned the Latin religious customs described in Livy and Suetonius, whenever he could, into English Christian ones; and Puttenham, in his sixteenth-century *Arte*, had criticised some quite literal renderings of passages in the *Aeneid* by pointing out that they were too undignified for Virgil, thus preceding Tytler by more than two centuries. Harington, who wrote at a time when Puttenham's theories were very influential, and who had to demonstrate that Ariosto's was an epic poem in the tradition of Virgil, created a new work of art, halfway between the refined chivalric tradition linking Boiardo, Ariosto and Tasso (not to mention such maverick figures as Luigi Pulci) and Malory's native adventure romance. He turned Ariosto's ironical, sceptical narrator into a more traditional and moral figure, and he changed the original plot from a rambling mass to a more ordered web. As is

---

13 C.N. Avila, *Studi sulla traduzione nell'Inghilterra del Seicento e del Settecento* (Caltanissetta: Sciascia, 1990), p. 121.

apparent from his preface, he was perfectly aware of what he did, and felt no qualms about doing it:

> For my omitting or abbreviating some things either in matters impertinent to us or in some to tediouse flatteries of persons that we never heard of, if I have done ill, I crave pardon, for sure I did it for the best. [...] But yet I would not have any man except that I should observe his phrase so strictly as an interpreter nor the matter so carefully as if it had bene a storie in which to varie were as great a sinne as it were simplicitie in this to go word for word. (p. 15)

Harington cunningly evokes St. Jerome and Horace[14] in order to justify his alterations, which are obviously far from being mere alterations of word-order: since he is not an 'interpreter' (that is, a faithful translator, or a translator of sacred texts), his interventions are perfectly acceptable. Thus, though it is 'serious' literature in the epic tradition of Virgil, the *Furioso* allows for changes and even corrections. On the other hand, the very fact that Harington needs to defend himself seems to suggest that some might be disturbed by those changes, and points, once again, to the uncertain status of translation.

The sixteenth-century debate between literalism and freedom in translation was not merely a question of sacred *versus* secular translation: different texts might have different cultural importance or 'status', and would have, as a consequence, to be treated with different degrees of faithfulness. Harington might well exercise freedom in his treatment of Ariosto's poem, for after all, the *Furioso* was an imaginative work, and as such, it was perceived as slightly inferior in relation to more theoretical, philosophical books. Translators of other kinds of works would have to behave differently: Hoby, in translating the *Cortegiano* several years earlier, had felt the duty to translate almost word for word, and as a result, his version is sometimes very close to unreadable; but then, *Il libro del Cortegiano* was, all over Europe, as normative a book as any belonging to classical times, therefore there could be nothing 'impertinent to us' in it.

On the other hand, in comparison with the translators of other, less well-known works, Harington could not exercise the same freedom, for quite a few people might have read the *Furioso* – just as they had probably read the *Cortegiano* – in the original. If it is true that Hoby strived to be as faithful as possible to Castiglione's work, for instance, George Pettie, the translator of another important courtesy book, Guazzo's *Civil Conversation* (1581-6), nonchalantly added about two pages consisting of an eulogium of Queen

14 I am alluding, of course, to the popular medieval and Renaissance misreading of Horace's *Ars poetica*, some lines of which were mistakenly thought to contain an indictment against literalism. Cf. G.P. Norton, *The Ideology and Language of Translation in Renaissance France and Their Humanist Antecedents* (Genève: Librairie Droz, 1984), pp. 57–110.

Elizabeth. Harington, on the contrary, could not afford to be so careless in his additions and subtractions: he needed to declare his alterations and justify them in the light of cultural difference and of the needs of his audience; he had to invoke Plutarch's authority so as to defend himself from the accusation of speaking too much in the first person. Thus, for a variety of reasons, we can take Harington's version of Ariosto to be a very good example of the way sixteenth-century translation as a whole was still caught between two worlds, uncertain about which strategy to follow in a cultural practice whose very status was – and has remained – uncertain.

II

Harington produced his translation of the *Furioso* at a time when the English were beginning to be proud of the results achieved by their culture, and to feel a certain confidence in the possibilities of a language which had been branded as barbarous only a few decades earlier. If it is true that towards the end of the century Giordano Bruno, in *La cena de le ceneri* (1584), said that it was perfectly useless for him to learn English in England, 'because all gentlemen of any rank with whom he holds conversations can speak Latin, French, Spanish and Italian' and 'are aware that the English language is used only on this island and they would consider themselves barbarians if they knew no other tongue than their own',[15] on the other hand, the second half of the century had seen a growing number of declarations, on the part of writers and translators, aimed at demonstrating that the vulgar had now nothing to fear in comparison not only with the other European languages, but also with Latin and Greek (indeed, some thought English closer to Greek than to Latin). As a result, freedom in translation was no longer a sign of mere carelessness or incapacity, or a consequence of the inferiority of English as a literary and technical language, but the mark of a culture which had at least equalled its betters, and which could now proceed to conquer them. Military metaphors of this sort, indeed, made their appearance in prefaces around the turn of the century, when Philemon Holland, the 'translator general', uttered his reasonable hope that England would 'triumph now over the Romans in subduing their literature under the dent of the English pen, in requitall of the conquest sometime over this Island, atchieved by the end of their sword'.[16]

The freedom these translators wielded, however, was very different from the one which had been exercised in medieval adaptations of secular texts. In the Middle Ages, also owing to the difficulty of tracing authorship with any

15 Giordano Bruno, *La cena de le ceneri* (1584), cit. and trans. Frances A. Yates, *Renaissance and Reform: The Italian Contribution. Collected Essays* (London: Routledge & Kegan Paul, 1983), II. pp. 165–6.

16 Matthiessen, *Translation*, p. 179.

certainty,[17] the translators had been guided by the idea that literary works were little more than collections of memorable stories to be altered and appropriated at will; but in Renaissance England, that kind of appropriation was no longer practicable. As early as 1513, Gavin Douglas violently attacked Caxton's 'translation' of the *Aeneid* (whose source had been a French book) for being 'intitillit' after a poem to which it bore scarce or no resemblance:

> Haue he na thank tharfor, bot loyss hys pyne,
> So schamefully that story dyd pervert.
> I red his wark with harmys at my hart,
> That syk a buke but sentens or engyne
> Suldbe intitillit eftir the poet dyvyne.[18]

To tell the truth, Caxton, as compared with other fifteenth-century translators and with those of previous centuries, had been unusually honest and eloquent in his exposition of the reasons that had brought him to compile his version and of the manner in which he had chosen to translate – though admittedly, his attention had been mostly confined to a justification of the kind of English he had decided to employ, and to such apparently trivial matters as the distinction between 'eggs' and 'eyren'. Thomas Malory, just to name one famous example, was more typical of his age, in that he did not give his readers any clear clues as to the provenance of his chivalric tales.[19] And yet, less than a quarter of a century later, something had changed in the translator's attitude to his original, which made behaviour such as Caxton's no longer acceptable for the 'serious' translator Gavin Douglas was.

What had happened in the meantime was that new humanistic ideas about authorship and translation had gained ground throughout Europe, and some of them had even managed to land in the relatively benighted England of the sixteenth century. The first important advocate of the new method in translating was Leonardo Bruni, whose treatise *De interpretatione recta* (1424-6) founded the modern idea of translation, or rather, re-founded it, by drawing on the pronouncements of classical authors like Cicero and Quintilian. Bruni's general definition of translation was no novelty: 'In my view, then, the whole essence of translation is to transfer correctly what is written in one language into another

17 In his *Early Theories of Translation* (New York: Columbia University Press, 1920), F.R. Amos notes: 'One wonders also how the source, thus chosen, presented itself to the translator's conception. His references to it are generally vague and confused, often positively misleading. Yet to designate with any definiteness a French or Latin text was no easy matter' (pp. 12–13).

18 Arturo Cattaneo, *Tecniche traduttive nell'Umanesimo inglese: L'Eneide in Gran Bretagna da Lydgate a Surrey* (Brescia: Editrice La Scuola, 1990), p. 22.

19 Amos writes: 'The fifty-six references in Malory's *Morte d'Arthur* to 'the French book' give no particular clue to discovery of his sources. The common formula, "as the French book says", marks the highest degree of definiteness to which most of these romances attain' (*Early Theories*, p. 26).

language'; but the methods he proposed amounted to a hermeneutic revolution. Chastising both free renderings and excessive faithfulness to the letter of the original text, he proposed a kind of translation which reproduced the structures, ornamentation, and, when possible, the music of the original into their target-language equivalents. In particular, Bruni insisted on total identification with the original author, and on the transference of rhetorical features from one language into another. Thus, if on the one hand Bruni set up a new standard of precision in the translation of secular texts, on the other hand he laid a heavy stress on faithfulness to the structures and harmony of the target language, and on the need to 'transform' the original in order to respect its spirit: 'so in translation the best translator will turn his whole mind, heart, and will to his original author, and in a sense transform him, considering how he may express the shape, attitude and stance of his speech, and all his lines and colors' (pp. 58-9).[20] What he advocated was translation *ut orator*, or, 'rhetorical' translation, that is, a translation in which the rhetorical features of the original might remain intact by being reproduced in the target language.

Though this work is less known today than those sixteenth-century treatises which took their bearings from it, Bruni's theories must have been immensely influential in the European Renaissance, even if it is often difficult to distinguish, when similarities appear, between direct influence and independent recovery of classical ideas. However that may be, 'rhetorical' translation begins to make its appearance more and more often during the sixteenth century, and its rules are defined in ways which usually resemble one another, and which never better Bruni's treatise as far as completeness and precision are concerned. Etienne Dolet's *La maniere de bien traduire d'une langue en aultre*, written in 1540, is perhaps the theoretical statement which falls least short of Bruni's; but similar pronouncements are uttered, if fleetingly, by the most important intellectuals of the sixteenth century, among them Erasmus, Juan Luis Vives (who lectured at Oxford for a time), and Joachim Du Bellay (though negatively). As for England, it is difficult to establish how much Bruni's ideas were effectively circulated, though the relationships between the Italian humanist and Humfrey, Duke of Gloucester, are well known. Nonetheless, there are widely-scattered, if scant, elements, which make us suppose that continental ideas about 'rhetorical' translation were widespread in sixteenth-century England as well. In the first place, there are a few statements, made by sixteenth-century translators in their

20 Passages translated by James Hankins, in Douglas Robinson, ed., *Western Translation Theory from Herodotus to Nietzsche* (Manchester: St. Jerome Publishing, 1997), pp. 58–9. The original reads: 'Dico igitur omnem interpretationis vim in eo consistere, ut, quod in altera lingua scriptum sit, id in alteram recte traducantur'; 'sic in traductionibus interpres quidem optimus sese in primum scribendi auctorem tota mente et animo et voluntate convertet et quodammodo transformabit eiusque orationis figuram, statum, ingressum coloremque et lineamenta cuncta exprimere meditabitur.' See Leonardo Bruni, *Opere letterarie e politiche*, ed. by Paolo Viti (Turin: Utet, 1996), pp. 152, 160.

prefaces and dedicatory letters, which point towards something closely resembling translation *ut orator*; the clearest of these is perhaps Nicholas Grimald's, as it appears in his translation of Cicero's *De officiis*, written in 1556, shortly before Elizabeth's accession:

> Howbeit look what rule the Rhetorician gives in precept, to be observed of an Orator in telling of his tale: that it be short, and without idle words: that it be plain, and without dark sense: that it be provable, and without any swerving from the truth: the same rule should be used in examining and judging of translation. For if it be not as brief as the very author's text requireth, what so is added to his perfect style shall appear superfluous, and to serve rather to the making of some paraphrase or commentary. Thereto if it be uttered with inkhorn terms, and not with usual words: or if it be phrased with wrested or far-fetched forms of speech, not fair but harsh, not easy but hard, not natural but violent it shall seem to be.[21]

The exposition is more confused than Bruni's or Dolet's, also because typically English concerns – such as the debate about the use of 'inkhorn terms' – muddle up the matter a bit; yet it is clear that what stands behind Grimald's somewhat polemical stance is the belief in the possibility of reproducing the rhetorical elements of a text, together with the need to respect the integrity of the target language. Again, the fact that such theories show up with such clarity in a translation from Cicero, and with reference to Cicero's precepts, demonstrates that, as has been said, 'rhetorical' translation depended as much on the transmission of continental formulations as on the recovery of classical texts which had a bearing on translation theory; and if we keep in mind that 'throughout the sixteenth century the study of rhetoric in English universities was based on the rhetorical works of Cicero'[22] (upon which Bruni's theories were founded), we may safely take it for granted that such ideas had wide currency in early Renaissance England.

Seeing translation as a transference of rhetorical elements from one language into another entailed an attitude towards the text wich produced two radically different sets of effects: on the one hand, the original began to be viewed with a philological respect which had been formerly granted only to the Bible and its attendant writings; on the other hand, due to the insistence that the integrity of the target language be preserved intact, it was now possible to modify ('transform') the original in a way which, if more unobtrusive than medieval 'licence', was not less strong. The 'libertine' theories of translation which developed in France and England towards the middle of the seventeenth century, in point of fact, are a direct, if extreme, consequence of Bruni's ideas. If transference of meaning is only possible through a re-creation of the original in the target language, it

21 Amos, *Early Theories*, p. 122.

22 Lee A. Sonnino, *A Handbook to Sixteenth-Century Rhetoric* (London: Routledge & Kegan Paul, 1968), p. 4.

follows that the more complete the re-creation, the more precise the translation will be; and if the translator keeps to the letter of the original, only a 'caput mortuum'[23] will remain. Of course, Bruni and Dolet were far removed from such excesses, as were most, if not all, sixteenth-century translators: but the theory of 'rhetorical' translation contributed to shift the accent from the source to the target language, and to turn the translator's role into an active one.

Now, if theories similar to Bruni's were probably fairly widespread in sixteenth-century England – particularly, of course, in humanistic circles – it is also true that in the daily practice of translation 'much of the old freedom in handling material, with the accompanying vagueness as to the limits of the translator's function, persisted throughout the time of Elizabeth'.[24] It was a period of transition: the new ideas made for a new respect for the original text and for the claims of the original author, and made it necessary for even the freest translators to acknowledge their sources and justify the liberties they took with their text. But on the other hand, the philological precision of a Hoby or a Grimald was relatively rare: translators excised or added passages of their own; they Englished their works from languages other than that of the original (particularly, but by no means only, if the original was Greek); they included passages, lines or notes containing allegorical and moral interpretations, and altered or erased terms which might be embarassing for their audience. Harington, though he translated from the Italian, was guilty of all the other omissions, additions and imprecisions.

The reason why the *Orlando Furioso in English Heroical Verse* is so relevant is that it stands mid-way between medieval and Renaissance (or, modern) translation, between the old and the new freedom. Harington exercises many of the liberties of the medieval translator of secular texts: he cuts a fair proportion of the text; he adds details of his own; he adds notes and explanations in the text itself, thus acting much as the medieval translator/exegete did.[25] On the other

---

23 In the preface to *The Destruction of Troy* (1656), Denham writes: 'Poesie is of so subtile a spirit, that in pouring out of one Language into another, it will all evaporate; and if a new spirit be not added in the transfusion, there will remain nothing but a *Caput mortuum*, there being certain Graces and Happinesses peculiar to every language, which gives life and energy to the words' (ed. T.R. Steiner, *English Translation Theory 1650-1800* [Amsterdam: Van Gorcum, 1975], p. 65). As Theo Hermans observes: '"Caput mortuum" is the term used by alchemists for the residue after a process of distillation, and its symbol is a skull.' See his 'Images of Translation. Metaphor and Imagery in the Renaissance Discourse on Translation', in Theo Hermans, ed., *The Manipulation of Literature: Studies in Literary Translation* (London and Sidney: Croom Helm, 1985), p. 122.

24 Amos, *Early Theories*, p. 99.

25 In this context, Rita Copeland's distinction between 'primary' and 'secondary' translation comes in useful: 'Primary translations, such as the work of Notker III of St. Gall, exhibit a close alliance with the aims and methods of exegetical practice, and like exegesis define their purpose in terms of service to a source text. Secondary

hand, unlike the medieval translator, he cannot do so without justifying his practice, at least to a certain extent; and he cannot exceed what have become the limits within which the translator – now clearly distinguished, as Harington himself shows in his preface, from the original author[26] – can move. Furthermore, the *Orlando Furioso in English Heroical Verse* displays certain features which are typical not of medieval, but of Renaissance or modern translation (and of the new freedom connected with it), and which prefigure the age of Cowley, Denham, and d'Ablancourt. For even when Harington remains faithful to the 'spirit' and the events of the original (this happens most often at the beginning of the poem), he takes many liberties with the 'letter': he alters the prosody, the rhythm, the diction, and the metaphors of the *Orlando Furioso*, thus turning an Italian chivalric poem into an English one, Ariosto's refined, ironical language into the stiffer code of English courtliness.

In conclusion, it may be interesting to suggest a comparison among three Elizabethan translations of two Italian chivalric poems (Ariosto's *Furioso* and Tasso's *Liberata*), which, though almost contemporaneous, illustrate an epoch-making change in English attitudes to translation: Richard Carew's *Godfrey of Bulloigne* (1594), Harington's *Furioso*, and Edward Fairfax's version of Tasso's *Liberata* (1600). Carew's work is a very strange and belated fruit of the Middle Ages. He is so respectful towards his source that he seems less a literary translator than a religious 'interpreter': he follows the word-order and the enjambements of the original, and as a consequence, his version is often close to unreadable. Fairfax, on the contrary, is a typical representative of seventeenth-century translation: he is very loose in his rendering of word-order, rhymes, diction, and metaphors, though he does not alter Tasso's original in any showy way, and is very respectful of the main structure of the poem. Finally, Harington, as we have seen, stands mid-way between two worlds, one of the great representatives of late sixteenth-century translation: he combines some of the freedom of the medieval literary translator with the facility of the late Renaissance imitator. That is what makes his *Orlando Furioso* so valuable and interesting a document of sixteenth-century England, while Fairfax's translation is only valuable as a document of literary development, and Carew has been all but forgotten.

---

translations [...] define themselves [...] through rhetorical models of invention, that is, discovery of one's own argument or subject out of available topics or commonplaces.' See her *Rhetoric, Hermeneutics and Translation in the Middle Ages: Academic Traditions and Vernacular Texts* (Cambridge: Cambridge University Press, 1995), p. 6.

26 Harington writes: 'But I had rather men should see and know that I borrow all then that I steale any, and I would wish to be called rather one of the not worst translators then one of the meaner makers. Specially sith the Erle of Surrey and Sir Thomas Wiat, that are yet called the first refiners of the English tong, were both translators out of Italian' (p. 14).

Primary texts quoted

Ariosto, Ludovico, *Orlando Furioso* (Venice: Francesco de Franceschi senese e compagni, 1584).

Bruni, Leonardo, *Opere letterarie e politiche*, ed. Paolo Viti (Turin: Utet, 1996).

Castiglione, Baldassar, *Il libro del Cortegiano*, ed. Giulio Carnazzi (Milan: Rizzoli, 1998).

Harington, Sir John, *Ludovico Ariosto's Orlando Furioso: Translated into English Heroical Verse*, ed. Robert McNulty (Oxford: Clarendon, 1972).

Spenser, Edmund, *The Works of Edmund Spenser*, ed. E. Greenlaw, C.G. Osgood, and F.M. Padelford (Baltimore: The Johns Hopkins Press, 1961).

Chapter 10

Richard the Redeless: representations of Richard II from Boccaccio and Polydore to Holinshed and Shakespeare*

Roy Rosenstein

Soon after Italian-born Polydore Vergil (*c*. 1470–1555) arrived in England for his extended stay (1502–51), he began the vast canvas of the *Anglica Historia*. Authorized in 1505 by Henry VII and published in Basel in 1534, it had been influential in manuscript much earlier. In this work Polydore wrote as an Italian, he said, and certainly as one of the last foreigners to make a successful career in Renaissance England.[1] The naturalized father of English historiography was the first to bring order and coherence to the late medieval chronicles. Their contradictory testimonies he confronted and organized into elegant Ciceronian periods and succinct Tacitus-like moral judgements. His history, in many passages virtually translated by Hall for his *Union of the Two Noble Families of Lancaster and Yorke* (1548), would serve Holinshed in his *Chronicles* (1577, 1587) and thence indirectly Shakespeare as sourcebook for his histories. Today the debate over multiple possible sources in the history plays remains a thorny one only for *Richard III* and *Richard II*. In the former, the role of the *Anglica Historia* is more readily discernible, for Polydore had himself codified the portrait of a murderous, monstrous king. He may have established that pattern by accentuating or exaggerating the monarch's negative features. Polydore's more distant and less apparent part in the long and complicated gestation of Shakespeare's second Richard has not heretofore been noted.

Shakespeare's *Richard II* may be read as a back translation of Hall and Holinshed's versions: a restoration of Polydore's pellucid ethical vision obscured in the shapeless, sensationalist compilation that is Holinshed. Looking beyond

---

* In memory of W.R. Elton (1921–2000) and in honour of Peter Ure (1919–69), editor of the Arden *Richard II* (1961) and Joseph Cowen Professor of English Language and Literature, University of Newcastle upon Tyne.

1 See Denys Hay, *Polydore Vergil: Renaissance Historian and Man of Letters* (Oxford: Clarendon Press, 1952), pp. 153, 174–5.

Shakespeare's superficial debts to Holinshed and Hall, we see how he rejects the massive contradictions and rampant partisanship of his Renaissance intermediaries with the same critical eye that Polydore had earlier trained on medieval sources. Neither the Italian historian nor the English dramatist was pro-Ricardian to the exclusion of pro-Lancastrian sentiments, unlike the generally partisan, largely anti-Ricardian chronicles from which Polydore worked. As if advocating the same scrutiny to which Polydore subjected the chronicles, Shakespeare distances himself both morally and aesthetically from the 1587 edition of Holinshed's *Chronicles*.

Better than contrast the managerial styles of the once and future kings during their interregnum, Polydore and Shakespeare associate Richard's and Bolingbroke's shared errors and common vulnerabilities in keeping with a universal model established previously in Boccaccio's *De casibus virorum illustrium* (*c*. 1358). The common lessons taught by Richard's downfall are immediately echoed in the parallel case of his successor, who is presented as committing the same heinous crimes and will ultimately suffer a similar punishment anticipated in this first play of the second tetralogy. The deliberate assimilation of the two rival kings had been launched in chapter 20 of Polydore's *Anglica Historia*, then lost in the clouded, clumsy chronicles by Hall and successors, only to be staged finally in the architectonics of Shakespeare's *Richard II*. There Boccaccio's *de casibus* warnings as they would apply to Richard's downfall are also taught by extension from the analogous, overlapping case of his successor. Shakespeare never loses sight of Polydore's vision despite the failed translation by Hall and its maladroit transmission by Holinshed. As the present essay undertakes to demonstrate, the *Anglica Historia*, like its Italian humanist author, is also much travelled, from its distant wellsprings in Boccaccio's *De casibus virorum illustrium* and Polydore's native Italy to its compelling authority in his adopted England for Shakespeare's *Richard II*.

Polydore suggests that Richard's mercurial supporters were the very ones who betrayed him: Richard was hailed on ascending the throne, then denounced in favour of Bolingbroke, later revered as a martyr. That same ambivalence or shift toward the king is still more virulent in the propagandizing chroniclers than it had been among his followers. From contemporary accounts in the fourteenth and fifteenth centuries, three schools emerge.[2] For the party-line pro-Lancastrians, mostly English, Richard was a criminal: corrupt, wicked, self-serving. The hagiographic pro-Ricardians, especially the French, read Richard as a saintly victim of the machinations of that scheming politician Bolingbroke who succeeds

2 See Louisa Desaussure Duls, *Richard II in the Early Chronicles* (The Hague: Mouton, 1975); but cf. Richard H. Jones's review of Duls in *Speculum* 52 (1977), pp. 657–8; and John Taylor, 'Richard II in the Chronicles', in Anthony Goodman and James Gillespie, eds, *Richard II: The Art of Kingship* (Oxford: Clarendon Press, 1999), pp. 15–35.

him as Henry IV. Finally, although a third category, Yorkist, has other resonances, it may be the most apt designation for those capricious or hesitating figures who waver in allegiance to Richard, like York himself in Holinshed and Shakespeare. These fence-sitters and turncoats recognize the flaws in the king and in his administration yet convincingly denounce the abuse of law and the misuse of power in his successor also.

Among the chroniclers, the contemporaries were essentially pro-Lancastrian, rarely pro-Ricardian, even when they show a measure of sympathy toward him. Later works are occasionally Yorkist – as defined above – or in one or two cases perhaps genuinely non-partisan. Paul Reyher, Matthew Black and Kenneth Muir reach out to French models as sources to explain Shakespeare's apparent loyalist sympathies in showing Richard as martyr, victim of his own subjects.[3] Peter Ure and Geoffrey Bullough are more reticent in acknowledging possible French sources.[4] Yet Ure and Bullough are also at a loss to find a Tudor chronicle supporting a martyrdom thesis. For a largely unbiased view, just for a generally positive view, we must look to Polydore or wait for Shakespeare. Like Polydore, for whom history was comparative enquiry and not imaginative reconstruction, Shakespeare rejects the often linear and monolithic stances of opposing Ricardian and Lancastrian camps along with any teleological determinism that almost inevitably evolves from historical hindsight. In this way *Richard II* stages not only the enactment of history but also the conflict of its divergent interpretations by dramatizing the opposition between Richard's faith in mythic values and providentialism and Holinshed's valorization of political action and human retribution. Set against this backdrop of historical change and indeterminacy, again as in the *Anglica Historia,* Shakespeare provides an indictment of the fickle nature of all men, including by implication the medieval and Renaissance chroniclers who have deliberately misrepresented the complexity of history in favouring the theses of either a historicist Richard or a revisionist Bolingbroke.

Polydore acknowledges the three camps and attempts to chart a moderate, median path that is less categorical, or at least bi-partisan, compared to extreme Lancastrians and Ricardians. In so doing he might seem to make of himself a Yorkist by the cautious nature of his critical historicism. But rather than swaying in the wind like York, he accuses those in Richard's circle who, like York, had

3 See Duls, *Richard II*, pp. 246–53; Paul Reyher, 'Notes sur les sources de *Richard II*', *Revue de l'enseignement des langues vivantes* 41 (1924), pp. 1–13, 54–64, 106–14, 158–68; Matthew F. Black, 'The Source of Shakespeare's *Richard II*', in James G. McManaway, ed., *Joseph Quincy Adams Memorial Studies* (Washington, DC: Folger, 1948), pp. 199–216; Kenneth Muir, *The Sources of Shakespeare's Plays* (New Haven, CT: Yale University Press, 1978).

4 See Peter Ure, ed., *Shakespeare: King Richard II* (London: Methuen, 1966); and Geoffrey Bullough, ed., *Narrative and Dramatic Sources of Shakespeare* (London; Routledge, 1957–75), III, pp. 353–491.

done just that. He offers instead a largely positive, or at least protective, view of Richard as a man with indefensible weaknesses but with defensible if misplaced virtues. Polydore undertakes to reconcile the inconsistencies of the chronicles and the ambiguities of Richard's nature into a single, harmonious portrait. His overview may not be entirely consistent, but here the fault is his subject's. No doubt there is a measure of truth intact in Richard's characteristic self-pity, in his extreme contradictions. Polydore's portrait is intended to be as historically accurate as its author could make it, based on the chronicles which he time and again takes to task. Shakespeare, whatever his sources, real or imagined, few or many, does not judge his protagonist reductively either. He also presents the problem without any false, foregone conclusions on this perplexing player king, degrading him in the early acts but elevating him in the later ones. Holinshed and Hall, two intermediaries linking Polydore to Shakespeare, are far more emphatic in their judgements than Polydore or Shakespeare, on Richard and on his favourites. The operative link between the two portraits of Richard in Polydore and Shakespeare was more directly spiritual than indirectly genetic. If other historians or dramatists whom Shakespeare may have consulted could account for any link between their history and his drama, Polydore shares with Shakespeare principally a reluctance to label or categorize so readily the complicated historical figure that was Richard II. And so he appears both in Polydore's portrait and in the no less tangled dramatic character that he became in Shakespeare's play. These two writers, unlike their more partisan fellows, understand that character and history are complex and not readily reducible to a unilateral reading.

Boccaccio in the fourth book of *De casibus* had denounced generally the fickleness of Fortune but also its expression through the faithlessness of the common people (pp. 115–16). Following Boccaccio, whose Neapolitan master taught him not to blame the stars when the fallen bring about their own misfortune (p. 68), so Polydore and Shakespeare portray decisive events as the product of human actions among average humans and not of the intervention of Divine Providence. In this they are unlike Holinshed, who differs especially from Polydore in anticipating the due punishment awaiting Henry and his lineal race, scourged afterward by a higher power. Hay characterizes Polydore's history thus: 'The central thread of continuity lies in the succession of kings, where change is the product of royal action, where immutable human nature and mutable fortune play a never-ending game punctuated by rare interventions of divine justice.'[5]

Twinned victims of civil discord, the two cousins, born three months apart (Bolingbroke was the younger), are assimilated because caught up on the same wheel of Fortune, a presiding metaphor in the play overdetermining its taut moral design. Similarly in Polydore: 'The wheel of Fortune, so often invoked by

5 Hay, *Polydore Vergil*, p. 136.

Matthew Paris, is set spinning again.'[6] The *De casibus* pattern inherited from Boccaccio inexorably propels the new king to his triumph and the old king to his downfall on the *fortunae rota,* as Shakespeare's Richard is impatient to recognize (iv. i. 183).[7] By Shakespeare's time, the *De casibus* was a pan-European textbook transcribed and translated for kings and princes, full of negative examples warning these rulers – beginning with the Italian tyrants of Boccaccio's day in the fourteenth century – against the pitfalls awaiting their ambition. *A Mirror for Magistrates* (first edition 1559) was intended as an extension of Boccaccio, but especially of Lydgate's *The Fall of Princes* (1430–38), and it is typically unforgiving in its portrait of Richard.[8] Although Boccaccio was no historian in the full sense of the term, Polydore here generally followed his lead, perhaps also through Lydgate's edited and reconfigured version, where he as an arch-conservative provides positive advice to the nobility that commissioned him while criticizing the common folk as unstable and ungrateful toward their leaders.

In the *Anglica Historia*, Polydore represents neither Richard nor Bolingbroke as so strong or self-righteous that either rival king cares to resist powerful external pressures on his royal person. The Boccaccian wheel creaks on beyond their control or volition, or so Richard particularly might like to believe. Indeed, neither expressly willed nor prepared his kingship, for in Polydore both are pawns of chance occurrence or historical process. Shakespeare concurs in structuring multiple parallels between the careers of two otherwise radically opposite natures: gentle, artistic soul – and hard, calculating politician. At the same time he forefronts a greater degree of individual responsibility in the royal rivals than did Polydore. Yet for Shakespeare as for Polydore, it would be reductive to affirm that the Christian king was lawful *(de jure)* and inefficient and the Machiavellian king lawless (*de facto*) but effective. Both are potentially capable of valour or worthiness but also more conspicuously of unscrupulousness or cruelty.

Before closing, Polydore one last time juxtaposes once and future kings at the end of the interregnum linking their overlapping reigns. He writes that if, as is the nature of mortals, the majority of the leaders of the uprising had thrown Richard headlong into such evil and wanted to grant mercy ('siquidem, ut natura mortalium est, bona jam pars optimatum Ricardo in tanta mala praecipitato misericordiam impartiri', p. 546), so they began to look with malice upon Duke Henry once he was suddenly elevated ('et Henrico duci ita repente in altura sublato invidere coeperat'). That is, on the wheel of Fortune one was cast down

---

6 Ibid., p. 135.

7 See Howard R. Patch, *The Goddess Fortuna in Medieval Literature* (Cambridge, MA: Harvard University Press, 1927), p. 54.

8 See Paul Budra, *A Mirror for Magistrates and the De Casibus Tradition* (Toronto: University of Toronto Press, 2000), *passim*.

('in tanta mala praecipitato') and the other raised up ('in altura sublato'). But now as the respective fortunes of each have advanced in opposite directions, their popular following has moved in contrary fashion. When Richard fell from power the masses increasingly sympathized with him, while for the rising star that was Bolingbroke popular support began to diminish. For Polydore as for Shakespeare, the two cousins are destroyed by their kinship in kingship, since with that shared responsibility over the long term they suffer a collective end. Polydore's impartial association of the two kings in this cyclical paradigm is not echoed in Hall or Holinshed but seems totally in keeping with Shakespeare's exposition of the two kings as linked in destinies. They are in essence no more different from each other than they are from other men, all men. *Richard II* ends with a new king, but burdened like the old one with almost identical crimes and certainly comparable 'guilt of conscience' (v. vi. 41). There are tragic falls awaiting both: one already enacted and the other as yet only anticipated. Despite their apparent initial differences in character, ultimately neither king is favoured. The many dark parallels around which the play is construed represent them both as imprisoned in shared roles and common ambitions.

The last sentences of Polydore's chapter on Richard II are particularly edifying. This is all the more so since Polydore always provides his general observations, including assessment of the king's character and of any *viri clari,* here at the end of each book rather than at its beginning, as Hay noted:[9]

Polydore (1534)		Holinshed (1577)
Fuerunt id temporis	1	
permulti viri amplissimi	2	
in quibus fuit ingenium & literatura	3	
quorum facta mentio supra perapposite	4	
facit, ut non sit, quod repetatur.	5	
In Ricardo autem fuit formae gratia,	6	He was seemelie of shape and fauor
spiritus non vilis,	7	& of nature good inough,
quem consociorum perversitas,	8	if the wickednesse & naughtie demeanor
improbitas, infulsitas extinxit:	9	of such as were about him had not altered it.
fuit item summa infelicitas,	10	His chance verelie was greatlie infortunate,
qui in talem calamitatem incidit,	11	which fell into such calamitie, that

9 Hay, *Polydore Vergil*, p. 97. In this table, quotation for Polydore Vergil is taken from the *princeps* of 1534 (Basel: Bebel), p. 423; and quotation from Holinshed from Black, ed., *Richard II*, p. 435.

ut in maximi beneficii partem acceperit,	12	he took it for the beste waie he could deuise
abdicare se imperio,	13	to renounce his kingdome,
pro quo, mortales solent	14	for the which mortall men are accustomed
caetera omnia projicere.	15	to hazard all they haue to atteine therevnto.
Haec et ejusmodi in eos principes	16	But such misfortune (or the like) oftentimes
saepissime cadunt,	17	falleth vnto those princes, which
qui dum stant nullum sibi	18	when they are aloft, cast no doubt
casum pertimiscendum putant.	19	for perils that maie follow.
	20	He was prodigall, ambitious, and
	21	much given to the pleasure of the bodie … .
	22	Furthermore, there reigned abundantlie the
	23	filthie sinne of lecherie and fornication
	24	with abhominable adulterie,
	25	speciallie in the king.

Here Polydore completes his portrait of Richard after those great men who thrived during his reign and with whom he is linked by association in these concluding remarks. In Richard too, continues Polydore (*autem* is not adversative here), there was a graceful form and a noble spirit which the depravity, wickedness and dullness of his associates quashed.

According to Polydore, this was the supreme misfortune which occurred in the midst of such a great calamity, for it was most to his benefit that he accept to abdicate that rule after which mortals usually throw themselves headlong. That is, fools rush in, while the less than angelic but by no means diabolical Richard did not prostrate himself in the worship of a power which other men (not necessarily Bolingbroke!) would so covet to the last. Such events befall princes: while they stand firm, they think no misfortune need be feared by them. The opposition of *stant* (line 18) and *cadunt* (line 17), preceded by *incidit* (line 11) and followed by *casum* (line 19), confirms that Polydore resumes the *De casibus* vein considerably attenuated in Holinshed. According to Polydore, it was not difficult for Richard to accept his downfall since he wisely recognized his vulnerability and appropriately welcomed his own abdication. By implication, his loss was perhaps more cruelly felt by those who survived the unfortunate ruler (*infelix princeps,* pp. 544 and 546). As so often in this didactic work, Polydore expands and universalizes his judgement to the plural *principes* (line 16) and to the general *mortales* (line 14): Richard and his followers, Richard and other princes, Richard and all men.

Polydore's chapter 20 is even more instructive than it is inaccessible. Some sections from the beginning and end of the *Anglica Historia* were reprinted by Ellis in the nineteenth century, but Polydore's treatment of Richard has not been republished since Anthony Thysius, whose edition was last reprinted in 1651. Similarly Boccaccio's own compendium, *De casibus virorum illustrium*, has not been available since the seventeenth century (except for a 1962 facsimile of the 1520 Paris edition) and has not been translated into any language since Giunta's Florentine editions of 1598 and 1602 (apart from Louis Brewer Hall's abridged English version of 1965 which includes about half the tales).[10] Polydore's world-view and language echo moralizing patterns and verbal structures inherited from the *De casibus,* whose fame through the seventeenth century and subsequent eclipse thereafter his *Historia Anglica* would share. As for Polydore's chapter on Richard II's downfall, it has until now never been translated into any language, aside from certain passages enriched by subsequent compilers, as we will see next in the case of Holinshed. Like most of the chroniclers, and like Boccaccio before them, Holinshed stresses the debauchery and greed of the princes who will be punished for their many sins, hence his censuring by Elizabeth I herself. Although Polydore subscribed to the ethical perspective of his models, he had distanced himself from the provocatively sensational side to those works which deliberately paint the princes of the day in the darkest possible light. For him history remains a guide to virtue or its absence, but Polydore far more than Christian moralists like Boccaccio and vernacular chroniclers like Holinshed targets historical veracity in addition, not just verisimilitude.

Holinshed was Shakespeare's principal source for the histories, as is well known. *Richard II* is no exception. In 1893 it was tempting to affirm simply that 'none of the histories diverges so slightly from Holinshed as *Richard II*',[11] but today that summary judgement requires qualification. Those who would reject the proliferation of proposed sources and analogues since then, more numerous than for any other Shakespeare play, invariably come back to the demonstrable primacy of Holinshed in his 1587 edition, which Shakespeare certainly knew. Only the occasional gainsayers have at various times maintained that Shakespeare need not have known Holinshed at all. Playing the devil's advocate, these would provocatively maintain with J.D. Wilson that the tale of Richard II was so familiar that Shakespeare need not have consulted any book for historical data. As Denys Hay reminds us, in Shakespeare's time an oral historical tradition

---

10 For the diffusion of the *De casibus*, see Claudio Scarpati, 'Note sulla fortuna del Boccaccio. I volgarizzamenti cinquecenteschi delle opere latine', in Gilbert Tournoy, ed. *Boccaccio in Europe* (Louvain: Louvain University Press, 1977), pp. 209–20, at pp. 216–17.

11 See Matthew W. Black, ed., William Shakespeare, *The Life and Death of King Richard the Second* (Philadelphia, PA: Lippincott, 1955), p. 445.

was still quite lively.[12] Others, but again including Wilson, had proposed an unknown play as chief source. This last solution, that of a lost intermediate, conflates the worst of both possible worlds because it presumes a specific model but offers no recoverable text. If there were to be a neglected or forgotten source, for Holinshed as much as for Hall, and ultimately then if indirectly for Shakespeare, one might maintain it is none other than Polydore. A little-considered model, Polydore's *Historia*, looms larger just behind the all too familiar one, Holinshed's *Chronicles*: one source may hide another one.

However, and this point is essential, after Polydore's peroration Holinshed continues his running portrait with a statement not anticipated in Polydore, who concluded his Richard II chapter on the general *De casibus* moral note above. In the passage reproduced above, Holinshed adds that Richard 'was prodigall, ambitious, and much giuen to the pleasure of the bodie' (this passage probably taken from Harding).[13] Both psychologically and stylistically, this additional trait is inappropriate here after Polydore's final judgement. As followed by Holinshed until now, Polydore had provided a majestic and moral conclusion to the question of Richard II's nature, making him a victim of those around him and of his own youth, moving effortlessly among the universal *mortales,* the class of *principes,* and King Richard in person. For Holinshed, Polydore's praise of a king who did not deserve to be overthrown becomes just one more passage among many cribbed and buried in the middle of his discontinuous history where it is immediately undone by a more negative statement that is not in Polydore, indeed is contrary to Polydore's views and intentions. Clearly Shakespeare follows Polydore as he comes to him via Holinshed, whose second edition he must have known, as the passage on the withered old bay trees confirms (*Richard II*, II. iv. 8).[14] But the dramatist implicitly takes issue with and diverges from his intermediate source in dismissing the ruling of Holinshed as appended to Polydore. Holinshed here as elsewhere inserts reports of generalized abuses drawn from Fabyan and Harding (who does not charge Richard personally with lechery).[15] Like other such passages, the charge of lechery was not present in Polydore.

Nor did it suit the purpose of Shakespeare.[16] Here Shakespeare follows the conclusions rather of Polydore, not the derivative middlemen Hall or Holinshed, both of whom represent a Richard II 'with delectacion of worldly and volupteous

12 See Denys Hay, 'Hall and Shakespeare', *Times Literary Supplement*, 17 May 1947, p. 239.

13 See Black, ed., *Richard II*, p. 435.

14 See ibid., p. 419; and W.G. Boswell-Stone, *Shakespeare's Holinshed* (New York: Blom, 1968), pp. 103–4.

15 See Henry Ansgar Kelly, *Divine Providence in the England of Shakespeare's Histories* (Cambridge, MA: Harvard University Press, 1970), p. 140.

16 See Robert Adger Law, 'Deviations from Holisnhed in *Richard II*', *Texas Studies in English* XXIX (1950), pp. 91–101.

appetite' (Hall, p. 12) or 'prodigall, ambitious, and much given to the pleasure of the bodie'. Holinshed pursues: 'Furthermore, there reigned abundantlie the filthie sinne of leacherie and fornication, with abhominable adulterie, speciallie in the king.' No confirmation of this lustfulness is to be found in Polydore's concluding portrait: the accusation of lechery surfaces only in Richard's abdication speech, which Polydore evidently believed authentic but which may have been authored by Bolingbroke's supporters. Polydore, unlike Hall and Holinshed, does not return to this third flaw, confining himself as always to ethical considerations. Nor does Shakespeare take up the matter except perhaps in vestigial, allusive form. Shakespeare alludes only to the prevented marriage of Bolingbroke and at most to a perhaps rocky marriage for Richard, but only in passing. That Shakespeare in pursuing character and motivation sometimes abandons Holinshed has been noted, but it has not been noted how he in effect restores Polydore's reading of Richard.

In recent years critics have also murmured against Richard as adulterer or lecher, presumably based on the scandal-mongering of Hall, Holinshed and *A Mirror for Magistrates*, which has Richard affirm: 'I am a Kyng that ruled all by lust.'[17] To be sure, the sole surviving close-up of Richard, in the *Vita Ricardi* by an unsympathetic monk of Evesham, makes the king an effeminate stutterer, alternately pasty-faced and flushed (as if in his unstable colouring anticipating the War of the Roses): 'Inerant enim ei crines glauci, facies alba, et rotunda et feminina, interdum sanguinis fleumatice viciata, lingua brevis et balbuciens, moribus inconstans' (Stow, p. 10).[18] Except for complexion, none of this physical detail is confirmed in the otherwise purely psychological portrait provided by Polydore and Shakespeare. Nevertheless, today what is ceremonial in Shakespeare may be performed flamboyantly, and Richard's posturing becomes prancing. Why not then homosexual, cross-dresser, transvestite, transsexual? Jean Howard and Phyllis Rackin find Richard represented as stereotypically feminine and emasculated.[19] Writes Paul Gaudet: 'The usual production of the play has them [the three favourites] as effete, homosexual peacocks – their speech honeyed with courtesy, their manners shrewdly obsequious' (p. 147). But as Gaudet accurately observes, this is an interpretation which is not in Shakespeare. Appropriately enough, Deborah Warner's distaff version starring Fiona Shaw is neither effeminate nor otherwise a gender-bender. Ralph Fiennes's Brooklyn stage version of September 2000 perhaps caters momentarily to a

---

17 See Margaret Aston, 'Richard II and the Wars of the Roses', in F.R.H. Du Boulay and Caroline M. Barron, eds, *Essays in Honour of May McKisack* (London: Athlone, 1971), pp. 280–317, at p. 308.

18 But cf. Taylor, 'Richard II', p. 28; and Nigel Saul, *Richard II* (New Haven, CT: Yale University Press, 1997), pp. 451–2.

19 See Jean E. Howard and Phyllis Rackin, *Engendering a Nation: A Feminist Account of Shakespeare's English Histories* (New York: Routledge, 1997).

reading of Richard as high fag, but with scant sexual dynamics or humour between him and the three knights Bushy, Bagot and Green: here there is certainly no YMCA.

Were these caterpillars – the image comes from Holinshed[20] – the king's minions? Are there then closer parallels to Marlowe's *Edward II* beyond the tired *topos* of *Vae tibi, terra, cujus rex puer est* ('Woe to the land which has a boy to its king'), common from Gower to Polydore to *A Mirror for Magistrates*?[21] Were Bushy and Green to Richard what Gaveston was to Edward II, a court favourite who steps between king and consort? Richard's 'flatterers' (II. i. 242, IV. i. 305), were at worst sycophants (Hall uses the term to describe Mowbray at p. 3), as the chronicles generally agree 'time and again'.[22] In any event, their negligible or at worst ambiguous role (like that of the elusive Earl of Wiltshire) is dwarfed by the more numerous presence of his devoted supporters. The three court favourites are given a more sombre role in the chronicles, but Shakespeare does not introduce them fully and nowhere clearly confirms earlier readings of them: they remain shadowy, unindividualized, not pernicious schemers. 'There is a conspicuous lack of any action or speech by the favourites that might depict their guilt and substantiate the charges levelled against them.'[23] Because Hall and Holinshed were sources does not mean we should permit them to colour Shakespeare's less damning or at least equivocal characterization.

Is Richard's development intended to follow the curve of a radical sexual transformation toward manliness? While younger-looking than his years, the historical Richard and probably his stand-in in Shakespeare project a fully grown, manly, impressive six-footer who at most was considered 'slightly epicene' in his beauty and not at all a homosexual playboy.[24] Shakespeare expressly rewrites the queen to make of her a mature woman and model spouse not at all estranged from her husband, indeed trusting Bushy and Bagot enough to confide in them. Shakespeare also rewrites Richard *contra* Holinshed and others into a devoted if absent but not necessarily straying husband. Like the passing reference to Bolingbroke's prevented marriage, any suggestions of Richard's adultery, even of Bushy or Green's dallying, seem to be vestigial or allusive at best (or worst). On the other hand, the chronicles before and after Polydore revel in such indiscretions and accusations, here present only in the mouth of vile Northumberland dedicated to vilifying the favourites. Shakespeare, like

20 See Sarah Dodson, 'Caterpillars, Sponges, Horseleeches, in Shakespeare and Holinshed', *Shakespeare Association Bulletin* XIX (1944), pp. 41–6.

21 See Aston, 'Richard II', pp. 305–9.

22 Duls, *Richard II*, p. 114; but cf. Ure, ed., *Richard II*, p. 91, *contra* Boswell-Stone, *Shakespeare's Holinshed*, p. 129.

23 Paul Gaudet, 'The "Parasitical" Counsellors in Shakespeare's *Richard II*: A Problem in Dramatic Interpretation', *Shakespeare Quarterly* XXXIII (1982), pp. 142–54, at p. 144.

24 See Saul, *Richard II*, p. 452.

Polydore, downplays the three almost to the vanishing point, as a largely silent audience.

Once again, far more important than tracing sources is examining the treatment of such material as Holinshed or others might have offered. Certainly Shakespeare draws upon Holinshed but also diverges significantly from him at every step. His treatment of Richard II is an example in point, not only of the borrowing of events but of the rejection of characterization in Holinshed. Shakespeare subscribes to Holinshed as far as the *Chronicles* follow the *Anglica Historia* but rejects additions to Polydore as out of character, unsuited to Polydore and unworthy of Richard. As this example suggests, Shakespeare might as well have known the strong concluding passage directly from Polydore and unadulterated by Holinshed, given that Shakespeare seems to follow Polydore's portraiture.

From the example of Polydore's conclusion, not at all included in Hall, the degree to which Holinshed draws directly upon Polydore should be evident.[25] Already well known is to what degree Shakespeare himself relies on Holinshed. But Shakespeare perhaps also sees the spectral image of Polydore's Richard through the prism of Holinshed: despite the intrusion of Holinshed between them, the Italian historian and the English dramatist are significantly closer in their portrayal of this king than has been previously noted. Shakespeare does not give place to Holinshed's accusations of lechery and adultery except in atavistic form, perhaps as inherited from some marginal source, *contra* any modern critic who, based on a reading of Holinshed, might inflate this issue beyond its negligible dimensions in *Richard II*. Oscar Wilde reminds us that 'the dramatist alludes to the effeminacy of dress that characterised the reign of Richard II by having Gaunt reproach the king for his foreign apparel' and reads this as another proof of Shakespeare's concern for historical accuracy in the treatment of shields, crests and heraldry.[26] No doubt Wilde also responded to the aesthete and *poseur* in Shakespeare's Richard, a feature not historically documented (even if he did invent the handkerchief). But neither Polydore nor Shakespeare rallies to the reading of Richard as a dissolute, straying sensualist. Rather, instead of lending credence to this accusation by Holinshed, Shakespeare dispatches it by the very fact of placing it in the mouth of Bolingbroke, whose bad faith is in this way further underlined. As Gaudet aptly observes: 'The images of disorder are the immediate result not of Richard's misrule but of Bolingbroke's armed and unlawful return from banishment.'[27]

Thus, here as elsewhere, Shakespeare omits expressly naming any of the sordid vices evoked in Holinshed's deliberately sensationalizing presentation. In

---

25 *Pace* Muir, *Sources*, pp. 52–3.

26 See Josephine A. Roberts, ed., *Richard II: An Annotated Bibliography* (New York: Garland, 1988), p. 1190.

27 Gaudet, 'Counsellors', p. 150.

doing so, he indirectly follows Polydore, not directly Holinshed, whom he explicitly edits, as if restoring Polydore's reading, his ultimate source and Holinshed's immediate source, as in this passage. Just as Alison Hanham has shown that regarding Richard III's usurpation 'Grafton and Hall deserted Vergil in favour of Sir Thomas More',[28] so it appears Shakespeare deserted Holinshed and Hall for Polydore on the subject of Richard II. When Shakespeare draws extensively upon Holinshed, it is always selectively. When Holinshed builds upon Polydore, with or without an intermediary in Hall, he like Hall embellishes and thereby dilutes the force and coherence of Polydore. Through Holinshed, Shakespeare relies upon Polydore, as has been suggested, but how much more faithful he remains to the voice of his distant source has not been remarked. 'I am, however, far from wishing to argue that Shakespeare used Vergil,' affirmed Denys Hay.[29] Yet 'Shakespeare may have consulted Vergil,' or so Josephine A. Roberts glosses Hay.[30] While Shakespeare almost certainly had not read Polydore other than through intermediaries, he nevertheless rejects Holinshed's or Hall's doubtful authority precisely when these immediate informants stray from their own ultimate model in Polydore. Again, the connection between Shakespeare's Richard and Polydore's Richard is not so much a genetic link as a spiritual one: a shared sobriety, a tragic sense of life, above all a great sympathy for human errors.

Primary texts quoted

Boccaccio, Giovanni, *The Fates of Illustrious Men* [*De casibus illustrium virorum*], exc. and trans. Louis Brewer Hall (New York: Ungar, 1965).

Hall, Edward, *Hall's Chronicle; Containing the History of England* (London: Johnson, 1809).

Historia Vitae et Regni Ricardi Secundi, ed. George B. Stow (Philadelphia, PA: University of Pennsylvania, 1977).

Holinshed, Raphael, *Holinshed's Chronicles of England, Scotland, and Ireland* (London: Johnson, 1807–8).

Polydore Vergil, *Historiae anglicae libri XXVII ... Ex nova Editione Antonii Thysii* (Leyden: Jean Maire, 1651), pp. 512–46.

Shakespeare, William, *The Tragedy of King Richard II*, ed. Kenneth Muir (New York: NAL Penguin, 1963).

---

28 Alison Hanham, *Richard III and his Early Historians, 1483–1535* (Oxford: Clarendon Press, 1975), p. 146.

29 Hay, 'Hall and Shakespeare', p. 239.

30 Roberts, *Richard II*, p. 1260.

Afterword

Mike Pincombe

The present volume is a collection of essays written up from papers originally delivered at the second international conference of the Tudor Symposium, which took place at the University of Newcastle upon Tyne in September 2000. The topic – 'Anglo-continental literary relations in the sixteenth century' – was modestly millennial in intention: it was meant to provoke reflection on the new post-communist Europe as well as the United Kingdom's mixed feelings about closer political and economic links with the Continent. It was also designed to be especially inviting to speakers from outside the United Kingdom; and it is a pleasure to record that members of the conference included scholars who live or work in Belgium, France, Germany (indeed, the old *Ostzone*), Greece, Hungary, Italy, Macedonia and Poland. In this respect, this second conference rehearsed a key feature of the first international conference of the Tudor Symposium in 1998, on 'The Tudorness of Tudor literature', the proceedings of which were published, also by Ashgate, as *The anatomy of Tudor literature* (2001). Here I wish merely to testify to the work put in to the conference in 2000 by so many people by offering a synopsis of the papers given on that occasion, but which did not in the end find their way between the covers of the present volume.

These papers were given by the following speakers: Paul Arblaster (KU Leuven): '*The Japonian epistells translated*: A recusant prison manuscript'; Carol Banks (Hertfordshire): 'Framed in France: faith and philosophy, optics and idolatry, love and learning in *Love's Labour's Lost*'; Joyce Boro (Oxford): '"This rude labour': Lord Berners' translation of Diego de San Pedro's *Cárcel de amor*'; Stefanie Brusberg-Kiermeier (Berlin Humboldt): '"Tell me thou lov'st elsewhere": Aemilia Bassano Lanyer revisited'; Emma Clark (Dundee): '"Fill thy own and others songs": Mary Sidney's translation of Robert Garnier's *Marc Antoine*'; Vladimir Cvetkovski (Skopje): 'What is the name of the Macedonian river in Shakespeare's *Henry V*?'; Jonathan Gibson (Nottingham Trent): 'Katherine Parr in French'; Peter Happé (Southampton): 'The management of narrative in the performance of cycle plays: *N Town*, the Cornish *Ordinalia*, and *La passion d'Auvergne*'; Tracey Hill (Bath Spa): '"A faithful affected friend to his country': Anthony Munday and Rome'; Gergély Juhász (KU Leuven): 'Biblical translation in the 1530s' (winner of the Balassi Studentship); Vassiliki Markidou (Athens): *Venus and Adonis*: Greece's authorising/dislocating role in the formation of linguistic and colonialist English authority'; Helen Moore (Oxford): 'The "ancient, famous and honourable history" of *Amadís* in England'; Wolfgang Müller (Jena): 'The rhetorical figure of exemplum in Erasmus's *De copia* and More's *Utopia*'; Mike Pincombe (Newcastle): 'Conjuring emperors in

Doctor Faustus and the German Faust-book'; Duncan Salkeld (Chichester): 'The continental courtesan in English sixteenth-century drama'; Alexander Sansom (St Andrews): 'Textual translations: Castilian books in Tudor England'; Elisabetta Tarantino (Aberystwyth): '*Edward II*'s inferno'; Simon Tibbs (Newcastle): 'Dallam in Turkey'; Keith Whitlock (Open): 'David Rowland's translation of *Lazarillo de Tormes* (1586) and *Love's Labour's Lost*'; Rufus Wood (Liverpool Hope): 'On the margins of Foxe: authority and the anxiety of influence in the marginal gloss of Foxe's *Acts and monuments*'. Other members of the conference included: Teresa Bela (Kraków); Dermot Cavanagh (Northumbria); Kate Chedgzoy (Newcastle); Michael Clark (Oxford); Jenny Richards (Newcastle).

Perhaps, as the convenor of the Tudor Sympoisum, I might be allowed to give a brief indication of its activities to those who have not yet come across its work. The Tudor Symposium was founded in 1997 as a forum for research in sixteenth-century English literature – and related areas. The latter phrase is interpreted generously, and the register of members includes medievalists and Miltonists as well as students and scholars whose work focuses more squarely on the literature of sixteenth-century England. Membership is presently just under two hundred, and includes postgraduates and professors from all parts of the world. If you want to join or simply find out more, you can contact the convenor at mike.pincombe@ncl.ac.uk, or visit the Tudor Symposium website. We hold an international conference every other year, and in addition to the two already mentioned, we met to discuss 'Writing and reform in sixteenth-century England' at Newcastle in 2002, while a fourth conference on 'Courts, courtiers, and courtliness in the Tudor Age' will be held at Kingston University and Hampton Court in 2004, with plans for a further conference in Hungary in 2006. But our more routine activities involve the dissemination of news of publications and events of interest to Tudorists via our electronic mailing list. Membership, of course, is free.

Newcastle upon Tyne
Midsummer's Day 2002

Bibliography of secondary texts

Abbreviation

STC *Short-title catalogue of English books 1475–1640*, ed. W.A. Jackson, F.S. Ferguson and Katherine F. Pantzer (2nd edn 1976–91).

Adair, E.R., 'William Thomas: A forgotten clerk of the Privy Council', in R.W. Seton-Watson, ed., *Tudor Studies* (London: Longman, 1924), pp. 133–60.

Adams, Percy, *Travelers and Travel Liars: 1660–1800* (Berkeley, CA: University of California Press, 1962).

Alyal, Amina, *Changes of Mind: Imitation and Metamorphosis in the Work of Petrarch, Shakespeare, and Their Contemporaries* (doctoral dissertation: University of York, 1997).

Amos, F.R., *Early Theories of Translation* (New York: Columbia University Press, 1920).

Aston, Margaret, 'Richard II and the Wars of the Roses', in F.R.H. Du Boulay and Caroline M. Barron, eds, *Essays in Honour of May McKisack* (London: Athlone, 1971), pp. 280–317.

Augustinos, Olga, *French Odysseys: Greece in French Travel Literature from the Renaissance to the Romantic Era* (Baltimore, MD: Johns Hopkins University Press, 1994).

Austin, J.L., *How To Do Things With Words* (1962; Oxford: Oxford University Press, 1976).

Austin, J.L., 'Performative Utterances', in *Philosophical Papers* (3rd edn, Oxford: Oxford University Press, 1979), pp. 233–52.

Avila, C.N., *Studi sulla traduzione nell'Inghilterra del Seicento e Settecento* (Caltanissetta: Sciascia, 1990).

Ayres, Philip J., ed. Anthony Munday, *The English Roman Life* (Oxford: Clarendon Press/New York: Oxford University Press, 1980).

Basset, Bernard, *The English Jesuits from Campion to Martindale* (London: Burns & Oates, 1967).

Bela, Teresa, 'The Knight and His Queen: Poetry and Politics in the Life of George Gascoigne', in Wojciech Kalaga and Leszek Drog, eds, *PASE Papers in Literature: Proceedings of the Seventh Annual Conference of the Polish Association for the Study of English* (Katowice: PASE, 1999), pp. 19–29.

Berry, Lloyd E., 'Richard Hakluyt and Turberville's Poems on Russia', *Papers of the Bibliographical Society of America* LXI (1967), pp. 350–51.

Black, Matthew W., 'The Source of Shakespeare's *Richard II*', in James G. McManaway, ed., *Joseph Quincy Adams Memorial Studies* (Washington, DC: Folger, 1948), pp. 199–216.

——, *The Life and Death of King Richard the Second* (Philadelphia, PA: Lippincott, 1955).

Bogard, Travis, 'Shakespeare's Second Richard', *Publications of the Modern Language Association* LXX (1955), pp. 192–209.

Bossy, John, 'Rome and the Elizabethan Catholics: A Question of Geography', *Historical Journal* VII (1964), pp. 135–42

Boswell-Stone, W.G., *Shakespeare's Holinshed* (New York: Blom, 1968).

Braudel, Fernand, *The Mediterranean and the Mediterranean World in the Age of Philip II* (1949; New York: Harper, 1976).

Brown, R.E., ed., *The Gospel according to John* (London: Geoffrey Chapman, 1966).

Budra, Paul, *A Mirror for Magistrates and the De Casibus Tradition* (Toronto: University of Toronto Press, 2000).

Bullough, Geoffrey, ed., *Narrative and Dramatic Sources of Shakespeare* (London: Routledge, 1957–75).

Burke, Peter, 'The Renaissance Dialogue', *Renaissance Studies* III (1989), pp. 1–12.

Campbell, Mary B., *The Witness and the Other World: Exotic European Travel Writing 400–1600* (Ithaca, NY and London: Cornell University Press, 1988).

Candido, Joseph, *Richard II, Henry IV, Parts I and II, and Henry V: An Annotated Bibliography of Shakespeare Studies, 1777–1997* (Asheville, NC: Pegasus, 1998).

Cattaneo, Arturo, *Tecniche traduttive nell'Umanesimo inglese: L'Eneide in Gran Bretagna da Lydgate a Surrey* (Brescia: Editrice La Scuola, 1990).

Chew, Samuel C., *The Crescent and the Rose: Islam and England during the Renaissance* (New York: Oxford University Press, 1937).

Colie, Rosalie, *Paradoxia Epidemica: The Renaissance Tradition of Paradox* (Princeton, NJ: Princeton University Press, 1966).

Collinson, Patrick, *The Elizabethan Puritan Movement* (1967; Oxford: Clarendon Press, 1990).

Constantine, David, 'The Question of Authenticity in Some Early Accounts of Greece', in Graeme Clark, ed., *Rediscovering Hellenism: The Hellenic Inheritance and the English Imagination* (Cambridge: Cambridge University Press, 1989).

Copeland, Rita, *Rhetoric, Hermeneutics and Translation in the Middle Ages: Academic Traditions and Vernacular Texts* (Cambridge: Cambridge University Press, 1995).

Copeman, W.S., *Doctors and Disease in Tudor Times* (London: Dawson's, 1960).

Cox, Virginia, *The Renaissance Dialogue: Literary Dialogue in its social and political contexts, Castiglione to Galileo* (Cambridge: Cambridge University Press, 1992).

Craig, D.H., *Sir John Harington* (Boston, MA: Twayne, 1985).

Cressy, David, *Travesties and Transgressions in Tudor and Stuart England: Tales of Discord and Dissension* (Oxford: Oxford University Press, 2000).

Cunliffe, John W., ed., *The Posies of George Gascoigne Esquire* (Cambridge: Cambridge University Press, 1907).

Dasenbrock, Reed Way, *Imitating the Italians: Wyatt, Spenser, Synge, Pound, Joyce* (Baltimore, MD and London: Johns Hopkins Press, 1991).

Davies, Walter R., *Idea and Act in Elizabethan Fiction* (Princeton, NJ: Princeton University Press, 1969).

De Man, Paul, '"Conclusions": Walter Benjamin's "The Task of the Translator"', in *The Resistance to Theory* (Minneapolis, MN: University of Minnesota Press, 1986), pp. 73–105.

——, *Allegories of Reading: Figural Language in Rousseau, Nietzsche, Rilke, and Proust* (New Haven, CT: Yale University Press, 1979).

Derrida, Jacques, 'Des Tours de Babel', trans. Joseph F. Graham, in Graham, ed. *Difference in Translation* (Ithaca, NY and New York: Cornell University Press, 1985), pp. 165–207.

——, 'What Is a "Relevant" Translation?', trans. Lawrence Venuti, *Critical Inquiry* XXVII (2001), pp. 174–200.

——, *Limited Inc.*, ed. Gerald Graff (Evanston, IL: Northwestern University Press, 1988).

Dodson, Sarah, 'Caterpillars, Sponges, Horseleeches, in Shakspeare and Holinshed', *Shakespeare Association Bulletin* XIX (1944), pp. 41–6.

Duls, Louisa Desaussure, *Richard II in the Early Chronicles* (The Hague: Mouton, 1975).

Duncan-Jones, Katherine, *Sir Philip Sidney, Courtier Poet* (London: Hamish Hamilton, 1991).

Dutton, Richard, 'The Second Tetralogy', in Stanley Wells, ed., *Shakespeare: A Bibliographical Guide* (Oxford: Clarendon Press, 1990), pp. 337–80.

Einstein, Lewis, *The Italian Renaissance in England* (New York: Columbia University Press, 1983).

Eisner, Robert, *Travelers to an Antique Land: The History and Literature of Travel to Greece* (Ann Arbor, MI: University of Michigan Press, 1991).

Farnham, Willard, *The Medieval Heritage of Elizabethan Tragedy* (Oxford: Blackwell, 1963).

Fleming, Juliet, 'Dictionary English and the female tongue', in Richard Burt and John Michael Archer, eds, *Enclosure Acts: Sexuality, Property and Culture in Early Modern England* (Ithaca, NY: Cornell University Press, 1994), pp. 290–325.

Foucault, Michel, *The Order of Things*, trans. anonymous (New York: Vintage Books, 1973).

——, *Language, Counter-Memory, Practice*, trans. Donald F. Bouchard and Sherry Simon (Ithaca, NY: Cornell University Press, 1977).

Furnivall, F.J., ed., *Pynson's Contracts* (London: Philological Society, 1868).

Gaudet, Paul, 'The "Parasitical" Counselors in Shakespeare's *Richard II:* A Problem in Dramatic Interpretation', *Shakespeare Quarterly* XXXIII (1982), pp. 142–54.

Gentzler, Edwin, *Contemporary Translation Theories* (London: Routledge, 1993).

Gilman, Ernest B., *Iconoclasm and Poetry in the English Reformation* (Chicago and London: University of Chicago Press, 1986).

Goy-Blanquet, Dominique, *Shakespeare et l'invention de l'histoire* (Bruxelles: Le Cri, 1997).

Grafton, Anthony and Lisa Jardine, '"Studied for action": How Gabriel Harvey read his Livy', *Past and Present* CXXIX (1990), pp. 30–78.

Greenblatt, Stephen, *Marvelous Possessions: The Wonder of the New World* (Chicago, IL: Chicago University Press, 1992).

Grivelet, M., ed. and trans., *Shakespeare: La tragédie du roi Richard II* (Paris: Aubier, 1965).

Hadfield, Andrew, 'The "sacred hunger of ambitious minds": Spenser's savage religion', in Donna B. Hamilton and Richard Strier, eds, *Religion, Literature and Politics in Post-Reformation England, 1540–1688* (Cambridge: Cambridge University Press, 1996), pp. 27–45.

——, *Literature, Politics and National Identity: Reformation to Renaissance* (Cambridge: Cambridge University Press, 1994).

——, *Literature, Travel, and Colonial Writing in the English Renaissance, 1545–1625* (Oxford: Clarendon Press, 1998).

Hamilton, A.C., 'Elizabethan Romance: the Example of Prose Fiction', *English Literary History* XLIX (1982), pp. 287–99.

Hamilton, Donna B. and Richard Strier, eds, *Religion, Literature and Politics in Post-Reformation England, 1540–1688* (Cambridge: Cambridge University Press, 1996).

Hanham, Alison, *Richard III and His Early Historians, 1483–1535* (Oxford: Clarendon Press, 1975).

Hankins, John Erskine, *The Life and Works of George Turbervile* (Lawrence, KA: University of Kansas, 1940).

Hawley, John C., ed., *Postcolonial and Queer Theories: Intersections and Essays* (Westport, CT: Greenwood Press, 2001).

Hay, Denys, 'Hall and Shakespeare', *Times Literary Supplement,* 17 May 1947, p. 239.

——, *Polydore Vergil; Renaissance Historian and Man of Letters* (Oxford: Clarendon Press, 1952).

Hellinga, L. and J.B. Trapp, eds, *The Cambridge History of the Book in Britain* (Cambridge: Cambridge University Press, 1999), III.

Hermans, Theo, 'Images of Translation: Metaphor and Imagery in the Renaissance Discourse on Translation', in Hermans, ed., *The Manipulation of*

Literature: Studies in Literary Translation (London and Sydney: Croom Helm, 1985).

Hill, Tracey E., '"By All Privy Means": History, Power and Representation, the Case of Anthony Munday, 1581–93' (unpublished doctoral dissertation: University of Essex, 1995).

Howard, Jean E. and Phyllis Rackin, *Engendering a Nation: A Feminist Account of Shakespeare's English Histories* (New York: Routledge, 1997).

Javitch, Daniel, *Proclaiming a Classic: The Canonization of Orlando Furioso* (Princeton, NJ: Princeton University Press, 1991).

Johnson, Ronald C., *George Gascoigne* (New York: Twayne Publishers, 1972).

Jones, A. et al., eds, *The Jerusalem Bible* (London: Darton, Longman & Todd, 1966).

Jones, Richard H., review of Duls, *Richard II and the Early Chronicles,* in *Speculum* LII (1977), pp. 657–8.

Jordan, W.K., *Edward VI: The Young King* (London: George Allen & Unwin, 1968).

Kantorowicz, Ernst H., *The King's Two Bodies: A Study in Mediaeval Political Theology* (Princeton, NJ: University Press, 1957).

Kastan, David Scott, '"The noyse of the new Bible": Reform and Reaction in Henrician England', in Claire McEachern and Debora Shuger, eds, *Religion and Culture in Renaissance England* (Cambridge: Cambridge University Press, 1997), pp. 46–68.

Kelly, Henry Ansgar, *Divine Providence in the England of Shakespeare's Histories* (Cambridge, MA: Harvard University Press, 1970).

Kenny, Anthony, 'Antony Munday in Rome', *Recusant History* VI (1961–62), pp. 158–62.

——, 'From Hospice to College 1559–1579', in *The English Hospice in Rome* (Exeter: Catholic Records Press, 1962), pp. 218–73.

——, *Thomas More* (Oxford: Oxford University Press, 1983).

King, John N., *English Reformation Literature: The Tudor Origins of the Protestant Tradition* (Princeton, NJ: Princeton University Press, 1982).

——, *Tudor Royal Iconography* (Princeton, NJ: Princeton University Press, 1989).

Kinney, Arthur F., *Humanist Poetics: Thought, Rhetoric, and Fiction in Sixteenth-Century England* (Amherst, MA: University of Massachusetts Press, 1986).

Krontiris, Tina, *Oppositional Voices: Women as Writers and Translators of Literature in the English Renaissance* (1992; London: Routledge, 1997).

Lamb, Mary Ellen, 'The Cooke sisters: attitudes toward learned women in the Renaissance', in Margaret Patterson Hannay, ed., *Silent but for the Word* (Kent, OH: Kent State University Press, 1985), pp. 107–25.

Lambley, Kathleen, *The Teaching and Cultivation of the French Language in England during Tudor and Stuart Times* (Manchester: Manchester University Press, 1920).

Law, Robert Adger, 'Deviations from Holinshed in *Richard II*', *Texas Studies in English* XXIX (1950), pp. 91–101.

Levine, Laura, *Men in Women's Clothing: Anti-Theatricality and Effeminization, 1579–1642* (Cambridge: Cambridge University Press, 1994).

Lewis, C.S., *English Literature in the Sixteenth Century, Excluding Drama* (Oxford: Clarendon Press, 1954).

Loades, David, *John Dudley, Duke of Northumberland, 1504–1553* (Oxford: Clarendon Press, 1996).

Margolies, David, *Novel and Society in Elizabethan England* (London and Sydney: Croom Helm, 1985).

Marius, Richard, *Thomas More* (London: Weidenfeld, 1993).

Martz, Louis L., *Thomas More: The Search for the Inner Man* (New Haven, CT and London: Yale University Press, 1990).

Maslen, R.W., *Elizabethan Fictions: Espionage, Counter-Espionage, and the Duplicity of Fiction in Early Elizabethan Prose Narratives* (Oxford: Clarendon Press, 1997).

Masten, Jeffrey, *Textual Intercourse: Collaboration, Authorship, and Sexualities in Renaissance Drama* (Cambridge: Cambridge University Press, 1997).

Matthiessen, F.O., *Translation: An Elizabethan Art* (New York: Octagon, 1965).

Mayes, Stanley, *An Organ for the Sultan* (London: Putnam, 1956).

McNulty, Robert, ed. Sir John Harington, *Ludovico Ariosto's Orlando Furioso* (Oxford: Clarendon Press, 1972).

Minois, Georges, *History of Suicide: Voluntary Death in Western Culture*, trans. Lydia G. Cochrane (Baltimore, MD and London: Johns Hopkins University Press, 1999).

Moorman, F.W., 'Shakespeare's History-Plays and Daniel's *Civil Wars*', *Shakespeare Jahrbuch* XL (1904), pp. 69–83.

Morrow, David, '"Reaping eternall glorie of his restless paines": Edmund Spenser and the ideology of *travell*', unpublished paper given at the Cambridge Spenser Conference in July 2001.

Morse, Ruth, 'Telling the Truth with Authority', *Common Knowledge* IV (1995), pp. 111–28.

Muir, Kenneth, *The Sources of Shakespeare's Plays* (New Haven, CT: Yale University Press, 1978).

——, 'Source Problems in the Histories', *Shakespeare Jahrbuch* XCVI (1960), pp. 47–63.

——, ed., *William Shakespeare: The Tragedy of King Richard the Second* (New York: NAL, 1963).

Müller, Wolfgang G., 'The Modernity of the Second Version of George

Gascoigne's Master F.J.', in Wolfgang Görtschacher and Holger Klein, eds, *Narrative Strategies in Early English Fiction* (New York and Salzburg: Edwin Meller Press, 1995), pp. 87–102.

Nelson, William, *Fact or Fiction: The Dilemma of the Renaissance Storyteller* (Cambridge, MA: Harvard University Press, 1973).

Nerlich, Michael, *Ideology of Adventure: Studies in Modern Consciousness, 1100–1750*, trans. Ruth Crowley (Minneapolis, MN: University of Minnesota Press, 1987).

Nevanlinna, Saara, 'The first translation of a young princess', in Ishrat Lindblad and Magnus Ljung, eds, *Proceedings from the Third Nordic Conference for English Studies* (Stockholm: Amqvist & Wiksell International, 1987), I, pp. 243–56.

Nicoll, Josephine and Allardyce, *Holinshed's Chronicle as Used in Shakespeare's Plays* (London: Dent, 1927).

Norton, G.P., *The Ideology and Language of Translation in Renaissance France and Their Humanist Antecedents* (Geneva: Librairie Droz, 1984).

Nutton, Vivian, *Medicine at the Courts of Europe, 1500–1837* (London: Routledge, 1990).

Parker, Patricia. *Literary Fat ladies: Rhetoric, Gender, Property* (London: Methuen, 1987).

Parks, George Bruner, *Richard Hakluyt and the English Voyages*, ed. James A. Williamson (New York: American Geographical Society, 1928).

Patch, Howard R., *The Goddess Fortuna in Medieval Literature* (Cambridge, MA: Harvard University Press, 1927).

Patrides, C.A., '"The Bloody and Cruell Turke": The Background of a Renaissance Commonplace', *Studies in the Renaissance* XIX (1963), pp. 126–35.

Perlette, John M., 'Of Sites and Parasites: The Centrality of the Marginal Anecdote in Book 1 of More's *Utopia*', *English Literary History* LIV (1969), pp. 231–52.

Perry, Maria, *Elizabeth I: The Word of a Prince* (London: The Folio Society, 1990).

Pigman, George W. III, ed. George Gascoigne, *A Hundreth Sundrie Flowres* (Oxford: Clarendon Press, 2000).

Poole, Kristen, *Radical Religion from Shakespeare to Milton: Figures of Nonconformity in Early Modern England* (Cambridge: Cambridge University Press, 2000).

Prescott, Anne Lake, 'The Pearl of the Valois and Elizabeth I: Marguerite of Navarre's *Miroir* and Tudor England', in Margaret Patterson Hannay, ed., *Silent but for the Word* (Kent, OH: Kent State University Press, 1985), pp. 61–76.

Prouty, C.T., *George Gascoigne: Elizabethan Courtier Soldier, and Poet* (New York: Columbia University Press, 1942).

Quinn, D.B., ed.,*The Voyages and Colonising Enterprises of Sir Humphrey Gilbert* (London: The Hakluyt Society, 1940).

Raab, Felix, *The English Face of Machiavelli: A Changing Interpretation, 1500–1700* (Toronto: Toronto University Press, 1964).

Rabb, Theodore K., *Enterprise and Empire: Merchant and Gentry Investment in the Expansion of England, 1575–1630* (Cambridge, MA: Harvard University Press, 1967).

Redmond, Michael J., '"I have read them all": Jonson's *Volpone* and the Discourse of the Italianate Englishman', in Michele Marrapodi, ed., *The Italian World of English Renaissance Drama: Cultural Exchange and Intertextuality* (London: Associated University Presses, 1998), pp. 122–40.

Relihan, Constance C., *Fashioning Authority: The Development of Elizabethan Novelistic Discourse* (Kent, OH and London: Kent State University Press, 1994).

Reyher, Paul, 'Notes sur les sources de *Richard II*', *Revue de l'enseignement des langues vivantes* XLI (1924), pp. 1–13, 54–64, 106–14, 158–68.

Rice, Warner G., 'Early English Travelers to Greece and the Levant', in *Essays and Studies in English and Comparative Literature* (Ann Arbor, MI: University of Michigan Press, 1933), pp. 205–60.

Ridley, Jasper, *The Statesman and the Fanatic: Thomas Wolsey & Thomas More* (London: Constable, 1982).

Roberts, Josephine A., ed., *Richard II: An Annotated Bibliography* (New York: Garland, 1988).

Robinson, Douglas, ed., *Western Translation Theory from Herodotus to Nietzsche* (Manchester: St Jerome Publishing, 1997).

Robson, Mark, 'Swansongs: Reading voice in the poetry of Lady Hester Pulter', *English Manuscript Studies, 1100–1700* IX (2000), pp. 238–56.

——, 'Writing limits in William Roper's *Life of Thomas More*', in Warwick Gould and Thomas F. Staley, eds, *Writing the Lives of Writers* (Basingstoke and New York: Macmillan/St Martin's Press, 1998), pp. 79–89.

Rowe, George E., 'Interpretation, Sixteenth-Century Readers, and George Gascoigne's "The Adventures of Master F. J."', *English Literary History* XLVIII (1981), pp. 271–89.

Ruggeri, Romano, *Polidoro Virgili, Un umanista europeo* (Bergamo: Moretti and Vitale, 2000).

Rupp, Gordon, *Thomas More: The King's Good Servant* (London: Collins, 1978).

Ryan, Lawrence V., *Roger Ascham* (Stanford, CA: Stanford University Press, 1963).

Said, Edward, *Orientalism* (Harmondsworth: Penguin, 1978).

Salminen, Renja, ed., Marguerite de Navarre, *Le miroir de l'âme pécheresse* (Helsinki: Suomalainen Tiedeakatemia, 1979).

Salzman, Paul, *English Prose Fiction, 1558–1700: A Critical History* (Oxford: Clarendon Press, 1985).

Satin, Joseph, *Shakespeare and His Sources* (Boston, MA: Houghton Mifflin, 1966).

Saul, Nigel, *Richard II* (New Haven, CT: Yale University Press, 1997).

Scarpati, Claudio, 'Note sulla fortuna editoriale del Boccaccio. I volgarizzamenti cinquecenteschi delle opere latine', in Gilbert Tournoy, ed., *Boccaccio in Europe* (Louvain: University Press, 1977), pp. 209–20.

Seidman, Steven, ed., *Queer Theory/Sociology* (Oxford: Basil Blackwell, 1996).

Simopoulos, Kyriakos, *Foreign Travellers to Greece* [Oi xenoi taxidiotes stin Ellada] (Athens: Ekdotiki Athinon, 1981).

Simpson, Richard, *Edmund Campion: A Biography* (London: John Hodges, 1896).

Sonnino, Lee A., *A Handbook to Sixteenth-Century Rhetoric* (London: Routledge & Kegan Paul, 1968).

Spencer, Terence, *Fair Greece, Sad Relic: Literary Philhellenism from Shakespeare to Byron* (London: Weidenfeld & Nicolson, 1954).

Spufford, Margaret, *Small Books and Pleasant Histories: Popular Fiction and its Readership in Seventeenth-Century England* (London: Methuen, 1981).

Staub, Susan C., '"According to My Source": Fictionality in *The Adventures of Master F.J.*', *Studies in Philology* LXXXVII (1990), pp. 111–19.

Steel, Anthony, *Richard II* (Cambridge: Cambridge University Press, 1941).

Steiner, T.R., ed., *English Translation Theory 1650–1800* (Amsterdam: Van Gorcum, 1975).

Stone, Lawrence, *The Family, Sex and Marriage in England 1500–1800* (1977; rev. edn Harmondsworth: Penguin, 1979).

Stoneman, Richard, *Land of the Lost Gods: The Search for Classical Greece* (London: Hutchinson, 1987).

Stow, George B., ed., *Historia Vitae et Regni Ricardi Secundi* (Philadelphia, PA: University of Pennsylvania, 1977).

Stoye, John, *English Travellers Abroad 1604–67* (New Haven, CT: Yale University Press, 1989).

Taylor, Anthony Brian, '"The Adventures of Master F.J." and *Twelfth Night*', *Notes and Queries* n.s. XLV (1987), pp. 331–3.

Taylor, John, 'Richard II in the Chronicles', in Anthony Goodman and James Gillespie, eds, *Richard II: The Art of Kingship* (Oxford: Clarendon Press, 1999), pp. 15–35.

Tillyard, E.M.W., *Shakespeare's History Plays* (New York: Barnes and Noble, 1964).

Turner, Celeste, *Anthony Mundy, An Elizabethan Man of Letters* (Berkeley, CA: University of California Press; London: Cambridge University Press, 1928).

Turner Wright, Celeste, 'Young Anthony Mundy Again', *Studies in Philology* LVI (1959), pp. 150–68.

Ure, Peter, ed., *Shakespeare: King Richard II* (London: Methuen, 1966).

Vigopoulou, Iole, 'The First Approaches' [Oi protes prosegiseis] in 'Travellers: Images of Greece', *Kathimerini* (2000), pp. 14–15.

Warner, Michael, ed., *Fear of a Queer Planet: Queer Politics and Social Theory* (Minneapolis, MN: University of Minnesota Press, 1993)

Weber, Shirley Howard, *Voyages and Travels in Greece, the Near East and Adjacent Regions Made Previous to the Year 1801*, Catalogue of Works in Gennadius Library in Athens (Princeton, NJ: The American School of Classical Studies at Athens, 1953).

Weiss, Beno, and Louis C. Pérez, trans. and eds, *Beginnings and Discoveries: Polydore Vergil's De Inventoribus Rerum* (Nieuwkoop: De Graaf, 1997).

White, R.S., 'Functions of Poems and Songs in Elizabethan Romance and Romantic Comedy', *English Studies* LXVIII (1987), pp. 392–405.

Wilson, John Dover, ed., Shakespeare, *King Richard II* (Cambridge: Cambridge University Press, 1951).

Winny, James, *The Player King: A Theme of Shakespeare's Histories* (London: Chatto, 1968).

Wright, Herbert G., *Boccaccio in England from Chaucer to Tennyson* (London: Athlone Press, 1957).

Yates, Frances A., *Renaissance and Reform: The Italian Contribution*, *Collected Essays* II (London: Routledge & Kegan Paul, 1983).

Yegenoglou, Meyda, *Colonial Fantasies: Towards a Feminist Reading of Orientalism* (Cambridge: Cambridge University Press, 1998).

Zeeveld, W. Gordon, 'The Influence of Hall on Shakespeare's English Historical Plays', *English Literary History* III (1936), pp. 317–53.

Index

For Product Safety Concerns and Information please contact our EU representative GPSR@taylorandfrancis.com
Taylor & Francis Verlag GmbH, Kaufingerstraße 24, 80331 München, Germany

www.ingramcontent.com/pod-product-compliance
Lightning Source LLC
Chambersburg PA
CBHW071528120726
47907CB00013B/1257

* 9 7 8 1 1 3 8 2 6 3 6 4 2 *